Pathways to Red

Barry Emslie was born in Yorkshire and moved to New Zealand with his family when he was five. After school he went to university but left after a year to write. He did many jobs, chief among them an actor for TV ONE and a dustman for the Wellington City Council. In 1979 he returned to Britain. He was awarded a first class degree in Cultural Studies from what is now the University of East London. He then wrote his doctorate: Bertolt Brecht and the Problem of a Marxist Dramaturgy (1989).

Reflecting his cultural studies background, his published articles and essays cover a broad field. His previous books are: *Richard Wagner and the Centrality of Love* (Boydell & Brewer 2010) *Narrative and Truth* (Palgrave 2012), *Speculations on German History* (Camden House 2015). He now lives in Berlin where he has worked as a music critic and freelance journalist. He teaches English in a community college.

Pathways to Redemption
Richard Wagner and Benjamin Britten

Barry Emslie

Methuen

First published in Great Britain in 2020 by Methuen & Co. Ltd.

1

Methuen
Orchard House
Railway Street
Slingsby, York, YO62 4AN
www.methuen.co.uk

Methuen & Co Ltd Reg. No. 05278590

The author and publisher would like to thank the following for permission to include brief extracts from *Letters from a Life: Selected Letters and Diaries of Benjamin Britten Volumes One to Three* (Faber & Faber) and *Volumes Four to Six* (The Boydell Press) (edited by D. Mitchell et al. Courtesy of and copyright © The Britten-Pears Foundation); *Cosima Wagner's Diaries Volumes One and Two* ed. and annotated by M. Gregor-Dellin and D. Mack (trans. © by G. Skelton; William Collins & Sons); *Selected Letters of Richard Wagner* (ed. and trans. © B. Millington and the Estate of S. Spencer; J. M. Dent & Sons. Courtesy of and copyright © the translators); Schopenhauer, Arnold, *The World as Will and Representation* by A. Schopenhauer (trans. © The Estate of E. F. J. Payne; Dover Publications). Every reasonable effort to locate current copyright holders has been made. The author and publisher apologise for any omissions. Future editions will be updated with any amendments notified to them.

ISBN 978-0-413-77829-1

A CIP catalogue record for this title is available from the British Library

Typeset by SX Composing DTP, Rayleigh, Essex, SS6 7EF
Printed and bound in Great Britain by CPI Group (UK) Ltd, Croydon, CR0 4YY

Contents

A Note on the Text

The six volume collection *Letters from a Life: Selected Letters and Diaries of Benjamin Britten* edited by Donald Mitchell et al and published by Faber & Faber and The Boydell Press (1991–2012) is referenced in the endnotes according to volume and page number (i.e. LfL 2: 1338–9).

The standard English edition of Wagner's writings is *Richard Wagner's Prose Works* translated and edited by William Ashton Ellis, eight vols. London (1892–9). They are also referenced in the endnotes according to the volume and page number. The date of Wagner's original, as far as one can be clear on the matter, plus the English title is also given as in the following example: *The Art-Work of the Future* (1849) PW I: 113. The translations, however, are far from unproblematic and I have on occasions altered them. When this has been done it is indicated either in the text or in the endnote. Most of the Ellis translations can be found on the web at: http://users.belgacom.net/wagnerlibrary/prose/wlpr0063.htm

Quotations from *Cosima Wagner's Diaries* edited and annotated by Martin Gregor-Dellin and Dietrich Mack, translated with an introduction by Geoffrey Skelton, two volumes, London: William Collins & Sons (1978–80) are identified in the endnotes by the date of the entry (for example CD: 26 April 1870).

The standard English collection of Wagner's letters is *Selected Letters of Richard Wagner* translated and edited by Stewart Spencer and Barry Millington, J. M. Dent & Sons, London (1987). The entries are identified in the endnotes by date (for example Letters: 23 October 1877).

Sometimes I have kept the titles of Wagner's operas in German, sometimes not. My reasons are, for the most part, entirely arbitrary. *Tristan und*

Isolde, however, refers to the opera and Tristan and Isolde to the two title characters. Titles are put into italics.

I have used on occasions the German noun *Weltanschauung*, roughly speaking a worldview. This is a personal preference. I think the German carries the better (philosophical) connotations. In general, when using a German noun I have stuck to the convention of leaving the first letter in higher case.

As I have made use of web links for the classical Greek texts, I have also given the titles along with the dates in the endnotes. This should avoid any confusion.

Preface

Redemption, however nebulous a concept, suggests salvation. In order to realise fully its lofty connotations it needs spiritual values or even an assumed realm that amounts to more than just the everyday reality we experience empirically through the physical senses. Moreover, no matter how credible or otherwise we find the idea of such a realm, and no matter how much we may give it a conventional religious form or define it according to our own wilful agenda, it is likely to exist as an unblemished ideal. It is a higher state. In that sense it has an antagonistic relationship to everyday reality. Quotidian life, whatever its virtues, will always be characterised as to some extent flawed and contaminated. Sin and evil are in the world.

Both Wagner and Britten tackle the notion of redemption in the context of these tensions. Wagner, for instance, in both his operas and his essays repeatedly and explicitly draws our attention to redemption, or *Erlösung*. It is arguably the critical thematic element of all the operas following *Rienzi*. In Britten's case redemption is often explicit and when not, invariably implicit.

Wagner and Britten do not, however, have the same exact notion of redemption, although salvation and spiritual values are common to both. To be redeemed implies that one is saved from one's sins, one's sufferings, and from the corruptions of the everyday world. One might well become, in a wholly positive sense, resigned. This assumption is pretty much applicable to Britten across the board. But Wagner, although he deals deeply and powerfully with suffering, also dramatizes heroic and, allegedly, near impeccable characters whose redemption is pre-programmed. A Wagner redemption drama customarily reaches a climax framed in terms of a death-dependant transfiguration that takes the chosen ones out of the phenomenal world and into an alternative higher realm. Nothing is as straightforward as this in Britten.

The arbitrary and wholly subjective claim of this book is that an examination of these similarities and differences will, at the very least, prove instructive and revealing for anyone interested in the music dramas of Wagner and Britten's compositions, operas or otherwise. I hope it might also prove stimulating and a pleasure. Naturally, if the assumptions in play are not shared by the reader, none of this is likely to turn out to be the case.

The book has been structured as an extended, ideas driven, essay. That is, it is not a chronological march through the careers and compositions of both men, but rather a set of speculations organised around specific notions. The bulk of its argument is to be found in the three large central chapters, each of which deals with a binary pair of concepts. It is to be admitted, however, that the last operas of both men (*Parsifal* and *Death in Venice*) are taken to be exceptionally important. They may not have been intended as final operatic statements, but they can be seen legitimately as enjoying a special and culminating status in the oeuvre of both men.

Because redemption is the defining ingredient, Wagner's stage works preceding *The Flying Dutchman* do not enter the discussion.

While the book is not biographically based, it is very much interested in the lives of both composers. The non-musical statements, beliefs, and actions of the two men, and those around them, are not only of interest but also of relevance. They elucidate further the differing pathways to redemption. This extended essay is not, therefore, simply concerned with texts. Such an author (or composer) free approach was once fashionable in radical literary theory – particularly post-structuralism – but it is not followed here. Nonetheless, there are aspects of post-structuralism that I find helpful and have, consequently, employed. This is a matter addressed in a more upfront fashion in the final chapter.

Even so, there are speculative biographical matters that I have not spent a great deal of time on. Wagner's cross-dressing or suppressed homosexual tendencies, or the recent theory that Britten (and Peter Pears) suffered from syphilis which, allegedly, made Britten's heart operation a forlorn step from the beginning, or the claim that Britten's father was a paedophile and was using his son as an ersatz pimp, or the story that Britten as a boy was raped by a schoolmaster, are all mentioned in the text and referenced. The reader can pursue them if he wants. I have not found them substantive, or indeed fruitful enough to make much of.

Despite being an essay, I have put the text in the academic apparatus but in the least invasive manner possible. With the exception of endnote 94, which deals solely with a translation problem, nothing is discussed in the endnotes. If anything was thought important enough to be mentioned, it is in the text proper. The endnotes give only the references for the relevant books, all of which are listed in the bibliography. No publication not endnoted or mentioned in the text is to be found in the bibliography. Many of the relevant texts are also on the web. When I have taken advantage of this, the web link is given.

The book has been written for the general reader interested in these two composers. No expert knowledge of the works of Wagner and Britten is, therefore, assumed. Consequently, I have given plot information for the operas when I thought it essential, although summaries are readily available on the internet.

Because this is a book of ideas the text tends to spread. The material is conjectural and I have not been able to – nor have I wanted to – shoehorn it into a rigid structure. The discussion does not proceed progressively on a stringent step by step basis. For instance, it has not been possible to keep any of the important ideas within a single chapter, let alone within a discrete section of a chapter. Themes are put aside only to be taken up later. As a result I often flag what is to come and remind the reader of what has already been dealt with. I hope this is not irritating. It was designed to be helpful; to keep us both on track.

This may be a book of ideas, but it is not a book of musical ideas. I am not equipped to engage in a technical exegesis of musical scores and I have not, but for a couple of essential passing references, taken advantage of the publications of those who are. However, I am neither wise nor disciplined enough to avoid recording on occasions my own responses to the music qua music. The relevant remarks will strike the expert reader as vapid and gratuitous. Nonetheless, my own subjective reactions are important if my ideas and arguments are to be explained.

The question of Wagner's anti-Semitism remains controversial for a variety of reasons and it will be addressed head on in the following pages. However, as the terminology itself is also controversial I ought to make plain now that I treat anti-Semitism as a form of racism.

I am, in particular, indebted to the trenchant criticisms and generous encouragement of a Berlin friend: Christian Koehler. Naturally he is protected by the usual caveat. The shortcomings of this book are all my own work.

Let me finish then on a personal note. Wagner and Britten are two composers who have always had an unequalled power to move me. This is something that should not be forgotten if the reader discovers, to his surprise, that what follows is not a hagiography of either man. This is not a book of propaganda nor, I hope, of special pleading, but it is one that couldn't have been written if I were not compelled to return again and again to the works of these two creative giants in order to discover how deeply engaging, sometimes profoundly upsetting, and always indispensable their compositions are.

One

An Overview

It is probably wise to begin an extended essay designed to take us to the point where we can best appreciate the exceptional role redemption plays in the work of Richard Wagner and Benjamin Britten with what I take to be their most fundamental structural and intellectual difference. Wagner is integrated, focused; Britten is heterogeneous, eclectic.

Wagner is a man who thought deeply about his operatic project, which for him was a great deal more than a purely musical and theatrical undertaking. Consequently, he found it necessary throughout his life to produce a wide body of theoretical work explaining, in sometimes turbid prose, his aims and the greater sociological agenda that underpinned them. Between 1849 and 1852 during his exile in Zurich as a political refugee, he went so far as to largely put aside composition in order to produce what he took to be major explanatory texts on art, culture, race, and nation. He was a self-appointed teacher and a polemicist. And being a genius and a revolutionary he was not disposed to self-doubt. He had the revolutionary's conscious conviction of not only his own righteousness and wisdom, but, more significantly, the folly of the existing state of affairs and the stupidity and baseness of all those, without exception, who either didn't agree with him or stood in his way. He was driven by an unshakeable *Weltanschauung*, or worldview, and consequently was inclined to assume that he had the answer to everything. His broad and erudite reading, his attempts at self-study (he never quite managed to teach himself classical Greek and admitted, like the rest of us, to being bamboozled by Hegel), his general intellectual fecundity, were all dragged into service. They were to vindicate his singular view of the world, of what was wrong with it, and thus of what was to be done to redeem it. His, perhaps justifiable, reward was to find himself in his last grand years in a position where all his pronouncements and pontificating, no matter the subject or how prejudiced the utterance, were diligently and devotedly recorded by his most committed disciple: his second wife Cosima.

One sees immediately that this mighty project axiomatically sprang the boundaries of art. His art was not practised for its own sake, nor even for the sole purpose of lighting the path of redemption for the privileged heroes and heroines of his operas and those who might have felt themselves their blood-brothers and blood-sisters. It would also have to educate the Volk and to save and renew German culture and the German nation. Thus, it was a project that had to be of necessity pursued both within and without the opera house. His life's work should, therefore, be seen as all of a piece. Whether we have before us the man who thought himself one of the leading intellectuals of the age, or the fairly young revolutionary (he was in his mid-thirties) who took to the barricades in Dresden in 1849, or the royal favourite who in his last decades attempted to interfere in Bavarian state politics and the appointment of ministers, he remains true to his steadfast self-image. Of course, being human, he was contradictory and temperamental, and naturally he changed and developed. In his last years he shifted in his attitude to Christianity and thereby altered the parameters of his notion of redemption (see particularly chapter four). But such developments were the product of the one unwavering, focused, goal-orientated life struggle, the clear waters of which were never muddied . . . at least not in his opinion.

Britten had no such grand agenda and never assumed a public mantle other than that of the composer, albeit one that played the piano and viola, and conducted. We know, of course, that privately he was intellectually stimulating and inquisitive. We know also that in his youth he was surrounded by brilliant people, invariably at least slightly older than him. The most notable and, initially, influential was undoubtedly W. H. Auden, who opened Britten's mind to many things, not the least being his sexuality. In fact, according to the poet Stephen Spender, Christopher Isherwood claimed that he and Auden 'can do anything with him [Britten].'[1] However, unlike Wagner, Britten was a musician through and through. It was the destiny that his mother had marked out for him (Wagner came from a family more involved with the theatre) and from the beginning he fulfilled it to the hilt.

Whereas Wagner had long years of struggle and rejection, Britten was hit by setbacks only rarely. He dazzled and succeeded immediately. Furthermore, music was not usually for Britten – at least not for the young Britten – a struggle. Unlike Wagner, who had to labour hard and developed relatively late, Britten was a prodigy. Hans Keller has compared him to Mozart, though Britten himself didn't,[2] and many professional musicians who came to work with him thought him the most complete musical personality they had encountered. His fellow composer Michael Tippett said that he was 'the most purely musical person that I have ever met.'[3] In 1930 at the age of seventeen he sat the exam for the Royal College of Music and the supervisor refused to believe that he could have successfully completed the theory paper in twenty-five minutes and duly sent him back to check his answers.[4] Yet well before this he had produced reams of compositions; no matter that he did not think they were worthy of opus numbers.

It is true, however, that at one time Britten felt himself a semi-revolutionary in the political sense. He was a lifelong pacifist, something which, along with his homosexuality, made him, like several of his operatic heroes, a natural outsider. Moreover, influenced by his left-wing friends, he came to support, among other things, the Republican cause in Spain for which he composed the *Ballad of Heroes*. But whereas Auden announced that he was going to fight – in fact he was even more circumspect than Wagner in Dresden, and although planning to drive an ambulance he ended up playing a lot of table tennis, chess, and making a few rather pointless radio broadcasts – there was never any suggestion of Britten doing anything other than practise the life of a professional composer; a composer who also performed and conducted, chiefly, but by no means exclusively, his own compositions.

Nonetheless, there is a contradiction at work. Although, due to his pacifism, he was awkwardly placed socially – and because of his sexuality he was a criminal until late middle age – Britten became a major establishment figure. In passing we might note that Wagner, for most of his life, found anything that smacked of pacifism uncongenial (his most archetypal hero is all action, indeed a dragon slayer), although his last statements in *Religion and Art*, and in the 'sacred festival drama' *Parsifal*, display a new anti-militaristic attitude. And while his opinion of homosexuality might seem conventional and of the time, it is, as is customary with Wagner, explicitly Teutonic. Cosima records him saying that the 'Greek attitude to love is foreign to Germans.'[5] Nonetheless his only son was homosexual and, it seems, had to be forced into marriage. Furthermore, several commentators have remarked upon the feminine side of Wagner's character. There has even been speculation as to a taste for cross-dressing,[6] and certainly there can be no doubt that he knowingly exploited gay King Ludwig's infatuation with him, as Cosima's *Diaries* heavily imply.[7] But he was not comfortable with homosexuality. He associated it with masturbation, a pastime that, going by his indiscreet letter to Nieztsche's doctor, Otto Eiser, he regarded with a mixture of distaste and fear.[8]

Clearly, Britten's assumption of a public, and highly respectable, persona is an interesting phenomenon. One could see it as either an act of overcompensation for his intrinsic status as an outsider or even an adept strategy to dissuade investigation and prosecution. After all, he was interviewed by the police in late 1953 during a period when prominent gays were being pursued. John Gielgud had been arrested in October of that year.[9] I suspect, however, that there is a deeper reason. Auden is, perversely, aware of it. In a letter from 31 January 1942 he warns Britten that he is overly susceptible to 'Bourgeois Convention.' Clearly bourgeois convention is, for Auden and his set, a bad thing and he infers that Britten has succumbed because he has no taste for 'Bohemianism.'[10] This may, however, be the wrong inference.

Certainly Britten's public role – the founder of a much admired festival at Aldeburgh (where he was no less in charge and surrounded by acolytes than Wagner at Bayreuth), friend for a long time of the Earl of Harewood (the Queen's first cousin), writing the opera *Gloriana* for the 1953 coronation, making his own extremely effective and thoughtful version of the national anthem, lots of visits to the Queen Mother, taking a peerage – engendered a lot of criticism, gossip, and bitchery. Yet those who suggest base motives or a lack of courage (a striking example of this can be found in Tom Sutcliffe's television documentary *Benjamin Britten 'A Failure'*[11]) forget that Britten was himself clear that he needed to be a composer in the community. He wanted to write for people he knew, to be 'a useful part of the Borough' which was 'the highest possible compliment for an artist.'[12] He was, like Peter Grimes, the eponymous hero of his first opera, 'native rooted' in East Suffolk and he left America and returned to Britain in wartime (even though as a pacifist he might well have been, like his fellow composer and friend Michael

Tippett, imprisoned) precisely because he saw that he could no longer gainsay this. Moreover he could not have been more explicit about it. Most obviously, it is the key point of his speech when admitted as an Honorary Freeman of the Borough of Aldeburgh in 1962. And although he had strong universal beliefs, expressed in his pacifism and quite possibly born of his sexuality – both of which no doubt drove him into a form of isolationism where the company of carefully selected friends was critical, not least because they gave him the reassurance that he, somewhat surprisingly, continually needed – he sought a place, and a particular given place at that. If this is bourgeois convention, so be it. But it is a stretch to say that it was born of fear. Not liking 'bohemianism' is not in itself a sign either of moral failure or lack of courage. Whatever the case, the profound community-based character of Britten's sense of belonging did mean he was never to assume the grand identity of the national guide and mentor that came naturally to Wagner.

While this is a difference that we will return to with respect to nationalism and the folk in chapter three and, with respect to Wagner's own alleged contempt for bourgeois convention, in the next, it needs to be underlined now that Britten's eclecticism was all in the music. In this he differs sharply from Wagner whose music dramas are, despite their vast proportions, exceptionally homogeneous, as well as being contingent with his non-musical intellectual labours.

But in basing this essay on the homogeneity of the one composer vis-à-vis the eclecticism of the other, one is not merely, or indeed chiefly, drawing attention to the fact that Wagner was almost exclusively a composer of operas and Britten, while being a major opera composer (after the success of *Peter Grimes* he called it his 'real métier'), was much else besides, producing a large opus in an exceptional variety of forms. Indeed it is notable that Britten avoided using classical terms (symphony, concerto, sonata etc) in the customary way, as though to underline that his works do not fall neatly within the parameters of the traditional musical genres. Despite his brilliance as a pianist, there is no collection of piano sonatas, and although producing a considerable body of orchestral works he has not left us with a series of numbered symphonies or piano concertos etc. Instead the 'symphonies' are titled *Simple*, *Spring*, or *da Requiem*, there is only one standard piano concerto (the others are for two players or for the left hand alone) and the large cello concerto for Rostropovich became the *Cello Symphony*. Beyond the three string quartets and the three cello suites, there is little orchestral or instrumental music that fits neatly into the musical genres used in standard cataloguing. No doubt his commitment to composing for given forces and his desire to work within the community underpins the tendency to employ a plurality of forms, inventing new ones (the *Church Parables*, *Canticles* turned into dramatic cantatas, and the innumerable works for children, sometimes with parts for the audience), just as he discovers new forms of music-making; perhaps most perfectly illustrated by the Slung Mugs that produce the raindrop sounds in *Noye's Fludde*; incidentally, mentioned in just this context by Britten when accepting the 1964 Aspen Award in Colorado. And whereas Wagner is committed to a compositional style and a sonic world that he insists is, and at length explains as, quintessentially German, Britten casts his net wide with respect to 'foreign' influences, drawing on everything from twentieth century 12 tone European innovations (he wanted to study with Alban Berg) to the music of Japanese Nō theatre and traditional Balinese gamelan. The latter, in particular, turned out to be a long term interest. It began when he met Colin McPhee in wartime America and was further developed on visiting Bali in 1956. Balinese influence is, for instance, marked in Britten's last opera. Furthermore, while Wagner proselytises that the German tongue is uniquely profound and productive with regard to song, for major works Britten will, alongside his mother tongue, turn to French, Latin, Italian, German and Russian texts.

Therefore, whereas Wagner is seen as producing a profoundly integrated and intoxicating sound world based on a given compositional technique (the so-called Leitmotif System), Britten is brilliantly, or, as his critics would say, superficially showing off his seemingly inexhaustible box of tricks. But Britten's eclecticism is also remarkable because it is written to be readily understood. It is not merely in his compositions for children that he is eminently approachable. For, despite being universally acknowledged as utterly musical in nature, he does not retreat into a private or obscure aesthetic language, one for which the listener finds no inviting point of entry; a judgement that is just as valid for his austere later works as for his exuberant youthful ones. It should be noted that in 1946 he maintained that it was the task of the young composer to 'be able to write every kind of music – except bad music. That has nothing to do with high-brow or low-brow, serious or light music.'[13] Prolific young Britten, of course, had already fulfilled this obligation in spades, having succeeded with film music, incidental music for plays, soundtracks for radio pieces, folk song arrangements, the *Cabaret Songs*, and so forth.

Nonetheless, the fundamental clarity and immediacy of Britten's musical writing is such that its eclecticism might seem banal; an unfortunate misapprehension to which his critics are enthusiastically prone. The boldness and range of what is in fact attempted is hidden – or avoided – by the easy option of critical derision of what is, superficially at least, so easily understood. Its stylistic strangeness then makes it ridiculous to the professional observer who can readily dismiss it as 'too clever by half' or, in the words of the critic Tom Sutcliffe, in his television documentary, as 'superficial smartness.'[14] This becomes, or, better said always was, the standard anti-Britten line. Examples proliferate. For instance in an astonishingly inept report on *Peter Grimes* soon after the première in 1945, the BBC's Julian Herbage dismisses the composer's 'facility' and claims that he gives his 'first musical thought . . . a technical twist which produces a superficial illusion of originality' and that he lacks 'heart,' which he has sacrificed to 'intellect.'[15] Britten himself often recorded how in the early days his music was sniggered at,[16] and one is not wholly surprised to read of the way the players of the London Philharmonic Orchestra, with Britten conducting, took the piss when rehearsing for the première of *Our Hunting Fathers*; their derision during 'Rats' reaching farcical schoolboy proportions. It 'brought shreaks (*sic*) of laughter,' Britten recorded unhappily in his diary for 9 September 1936.[17] It was understandable perhaps; but pig ignorant nonetheless. Even so, one should record that after the first performance the *Observer*'s reviewer found the piece 'dire nonsense'[18] and his colleague in the Musical Times thought it 'clever almost to a fault.'[19] Nonetheless, in the service of full disclosure one should also record that Britten admits that he and his party at first 'giggled' when watching what was to prove a seminal experience: the Japanese Nō play *Sumidagawa* in 1956. By the end, however, he was won over and he saw the piece twice.[20] After a gestation period of eight years the result was the extraordinary *Curlew River.*

With Wagner the opposite tendency is at work. Even though he is no doubt a great deal more complex and multifarious than some of his devotees allow, one is struck by how homogeneous Wagner's mature operas are. In this context one is also struck by how many Wagnerites are seduced by the leitmotif system. Although Wagner never practised it in a consistent manner, any more than he practised his privileged notion of operatic verse (the non-rhyming assonance and alliteration heavy *Stabreim*) consistently, it is often assumed that we can unlock the master's genius by revealing how comprehensive and interwoven the musical language is. It is a code which the gifted musicologist can break and then . . . Eureka! . . . everything about the *Gesamtkunstwerk*, Wagner's complete and integrated work of art, is clear. This process, which paradoxically is more likely to obscure rather than unfold the composer's genius, might drive the analyst to claim that the whole of the four opera *Ring des Nibelungen* can be rewound back to the initial E flat arpeggio with which the first opera, *Das Rheingold*, opens. The secret of Wagner's genius is then seen in the riches the system produces. Moreover, this is often treated as a synonym for its fecundity. The developments of the various motifs are taken to be successful simply because they proliferate, and consequently we have arguments that privilege quantity over quality of musical invention. One commentator praises *Götterdämmerung* because, being the last opera of the tetralogy, it has, inevitably, the greatest accumulation of themes: to wit '1,003 . . . separate occurrences,' which is, we are told, twice the number to be found in *Die Walküre*, the second opera of the cycle.[21] That someone has counted them, though surely the numbers are arbitrary and subjective, is remarkable enough. But what is perhaps more disturbing is that it seems we are being invited to regard the former as twice as good as the latter. Frankly, with respect to both the treatment of the cycle's ideological programme as well as the aesthetic pleasure to be got from the drama and the music, I hold the reverse opinion.

This is not to deny that the overwhelming effect of Wagner's huge music dramas depends to a great degree upon the interwoven nature of the musical language when it is encountered at its seamless best. Of considerable importance here is the goal-orientated and teleological character of the operas. Wagner is forever narrowing to the single point of final transcendence, not least because that point is often inscribed in the opera from the beginning. *Tristan und Isolde* essentially takes us on a huge sonic journey, which is utterly repetitive and tautological, and leaves us at the end drained and quite possibly, in the metaphorical language of its final vocal utterance (Isolde's so-called Liebestod), emotionally drowned. It is a journey 'from that eternally incomplete . . . [initial] . . . "*Tristan* chord" to something definitively closural.'[22] So whereas Britten is manifold and generous in his musical aesthetic, Wagner is grand but unwaveringly true to an authoritative, but flexible, mode of utterance. And this allows him to declare implicitly, and his devotees to pronounce explicitly, that a particular crowning perfection is reached. For instance, Richard Strauss was underlining exactly this homogeneity and synthesis when he pointed out to Georg Solti that in the final bar of *Tristan und Isolde* the telos – which has been longed for, worshipped even, since the work's opening bar – can be best understood if it is brought to our attention that the cor anglais (which supposedly expresses the poison that has corrupted the lovers' relationship) has been removed from the sound world.[23] Thus we know that the higher Idealist or non-phenomenal world – what Schopenhauer called the noumenal realm – has been attained and everything is now perfect.

Schopenhauer was the enlightened thinker whose master-work *The World as Will and Representation* Wagner regarded as the perfect vindication of his own *Weltanschauung* (see particularly chapter four). He first read it in December 1854 and then re-read it for the rest of his life. That initial encounter was, not surprisingly, especially striking. In fact Wagner immediately saw that the three 'mature' operas (what his devotees prefer to call music dramas) that he had up to then composed (*The Flying Dutchman*, *Tannhäuser*, and *Lohengrin*) could be best explained according to Schopenhauer's philosophical scheme. Above all, he realised, or convinced himself, that his privileged notion of redemption would gel unproblematically with Schopenhauer's equally privileged notion of renunciation and he explained as much to August Röckel in a letter from 23 August 1856. Nonetheless, as will become clear in later chapters, there is a tension in the composer's devotion. For while Wagner will never desert Schopenhauer, he knows there are points at which their meeting of minds is abrasive and unconvincing. This is clearest in respect of sex. For Schopenhauer it is an easily accounted for, wholly genital and sensory phenomenon. It is instinctual and bound to the earthy, phenomenal world. For Wagner it is the royal road to salvation. Ironically, it is the means by which his privileged higher characters gain entry into Schopenhauer's ethereal, noumenal world.

Placed alongside Wagner's focused, goal-orientated, and homogeneous oeuvre, the multiplicity of forms used by Britten seems flagrant, indecent even. It is not merely the considerable corpus of occasional music and stage, film, and radio scores that is striking. Of more significance is his customary rejection of sonata form in favour of suites, variations, passacaglias. Often the movements of these pieces are brief, brilliant, and highly characterized. From the alliterative titles (Boisterous Bourée, Playful Pizzacato, Sentimental Saraband, Frolicsome Finale) of the youthful *Simple Symphony Op 4* onward, they flaunt their discrete, self-contained character. Among the most dazzling examples is his first major international success, the *Variations on a Theme of Frank Bridge for String Orchestra. Op.10.* The eleven movements (including a Bourrée classique, a Wiener Waltzer, a Funeral March) were sketched in ten days.[24]

Put this skill in the operatic context and one sees a clear difference with Wagner. Firstly one might note the composer Aaron Copland's surprise when Britten answered his question as to 'the most important requisite in composing opera.' The answer had nothing to do with the relationship between drama and music, as Copland had expected and Wagner had already explained, albeit confusingly, in *Opera and Drama*, but instead 'the ability to write many kinds of music – chorus alone, chorus with orchestra, soloists separately, soloists in ensemble, and so on.'[25] And it is just this facility, which impressed Copland as it did almost everyone else, that is manifest in Britten's ability to character sketch in music. It is not then surprising that his operas are teeming with sharply delineated stage figures. Unlike Wagner, he is not constricted by a singular dogma (albeit one that the master on occasions violated) that outlaws recitative, ditties, songs, and any number of orchestral and vocal games. This in itself is hardly a criticism of Wagner whose long scores rest on an accumulative effect and whose leading stage personalities thereby acquire a weight and depth that is formidable. They take us via what Wagner called 'swelling, sinking waves of melody' – which rather undercuts the discrete world of signposted leitmotifs – to extremes of suffering and ecstasy that, for the receptive punter, are unequalled in the theatre.[26] Furthermore, it is clear in the short but plot rich *Das Rheingold* (the Prologue to the three major evenings of *The Ring*) as well as in the only mature comic opera, *Die Meistersinger von Nürnberg*, that the leitmotif system can etch immediately a character on to our imagination. Even after repeated hearings, who does not smile as the Giants come lumbering on? But neither of these operas are stylistically typical. It is a very relevant irony that the aesthetic function and effect of the seemingly innumerable, and one might have thought discrete, musical motifs (there are occasional claims that a new one has been found or arguments over the identity – naming – of the ones already in the canon) is in fact the creation of seamless melodic stretches that build to overwhelming climaxes. In many of Wagner's later operas an act of perhaps ninety minutes also comes all of a piece.

Britten's eclecticism produces a different kind of fecundity. His characters are immediately manifest as a result of boundless tuneful invention, often expressed in brief and quite simple songs or refrains. Consider the musical/stage identities of the village people in *Peter Grimes* (largely serious) and *Albert Herring* (largely comic), or the cosmopolitan cast of the last opera, *Death in Venice*. Of course all these various elements are not likely to evolve into extended, organic and overwhelming melody as in Wagner. Rather they produce a controlled and manipulated heterogeneity; a complex and disciplined musical and aesthetic structure that tends to proceed on disparate, even contradictory, fronts. This is underpinned by Britten's many-sided use of discursive means, such as various forms of recitative, employed, for instance, in an exceptionally free manner in *Death in Venice*. This is a practice that for the true Wagnerian must sound like a denial of adult and meaningful 'through-composed' music-making.

This difference is also the product of a deeper divergence that we have already touched on. Wagner's teleological agenda is always driving the operatic narrative and its attendant ideology on to the cataclysmic and exhausted endpoint. Certainly it is possible to believe that life goes on after the telos has been attained (in fact Wagner's notion of transfiguration and entry into the noumenal world needs such an assumption), but this lies outside the parameters of the drama which we have just experienced. It is theoretically potent, but experientially or empirically vacuous. No doubt it's nice to feel after the conflagration that ends *Götterdämmerung* that the Volk, once the Rhine has cleaned everything up, are still around. And this would seem to be Wagner's intention in all the various versions that he sketched. But it makes of the Volk meagre stuff. Likewise Senta and the Dutchman may well be seen, as Wagner instructed, on a projection at the end of *The Flying Dutchman* so that we know that they are united in the post-death noumenal world, but such knowledge is only a sop to the tragedy we have just witnessed. It can have, by definition, no effective purchase on our own quotidian lives. And what post-opera consolation is there at the end of *Tristan und Isolde*? The world the two transcended lovers have left behind is bereft, as well as spiritually and sexually downgraded, precisely because of their absence. The most they have bequeathed us – although it is no small thing – is a sense of the bliss and agony that human love might generate. These are all mighty things but they are utterly contained in the realm of an artwork that celebrates its own denouement. How different it is with Britten.

Britten is not in hock to a ruthless telos – an aesthetic guillotine as it were – so that there is nothing more to be said once the final chord has died. In *Death in Venice* Aschenbach tells Tadzio (who cannot hear him) to go on; there is something eternal about the boy. But the fact that Aschenbach then expires does not mean that we have to, or that we should want to. *Tristan und Isolde*, however, has an entirely different effect and any acolyte would be lacking in spirit if he or she did not consider ceasing on the midnight with no pain while those two were pouring out their souls in such a post-Keatsian ecstasy. And while Grimes's tragedy in the first opera is certainly a tremendous event for us in the theatre, life in the stage Borough demonstrably goes on in the old manner after he is drowned. The villagers remain fixed in their narrow yet diverse roles. They will no doubt integrate the fisherman's suicide into local history and devise their own individual, dishonest rationalisations to assuage any guilt they might feel. True, in *Albert Herring* there has been a momentary change with social losers and winners (those who remain inhibited, and those who have smelt freedom and might even, one day, escape suffocating convention), but there has been no reduction, whether spiritual or social, in the rich human landscape. And with respect to the last opera we can confidently assume that next season the guests in all their heterogeneity will return to the polyglot Grand Hotel in a cholera-free Venice. Last season's pre-ordained death of 'the writing gentleman' will be almost forgotten – although those who conspired to bring him down to the point where he grasped knowledge at its most mysterious, ethereal and dangerous will no doubt remember their handiwork with justifiable satisfaction. So while Tadzio, and all the coming Ganymedes, must – bless them – go forth, just as Aschenbach instructed, they will do so only in as much as they or their successors return to save and liquidate the chosen. We might at least entertain the proposition that this is, in its own very different way, at least as significant a business as anything that goes on in Wagner's last opera, *Parsifal.*

Now all this might be reduced to the simple observation that Britten's *Weltanschauung* profits richly from the banal fact that he is, in every sense, aware of the seasons and the ever-turning world. Consequently his grasp of reality is profound; though in immediate common sense terms it is no more revelatory than that of a farmer or a fisherman. What, one wonders, did he think – if he ever did – of Janáček's *The Cunning Little Vixen*, especially the final scene? This speculation is partly induced by the *Spring Symphony* which was on Britten's mind for two years and at whose heart lay, as he explained it, a sense of renewal, of 're-awakening' as the northern world moves out of winter.[27] Now Wagner certainly resorts constantly to nature – one thinks of the climax to act one of *Die Walküre* when Spring bursts across the stage, or the deep manner in which Young Siegfried is, on the next evening, embedded into the natural world. But he is only aware of linear time, and this ends on earth when the elect among his characters escape the tangible world and ascend into a posited, but fanciful, other world. True, this is transcendence and redemption in the classic (quasi) religious sense; but that is simply another way of saying that it is longed for and self-deluded propaganda. It is, however, hugely seductive, and it certainly packs a punch.

Yet when Britten's Aschenbach cries out 'What if all were dead and only we two left alive' he is utterly sincere and fully – painfully – conscious of how uncoupled from reality his cry is. But it is the sort of cry that in its arrogance, megalomania even, lovers in Wagner make with absolute sincerity . . . and as a matter of righteous principle. In fact, despite seemingly upturning the terms of Aschenbach's longing, the heroic Wagnerian couples will realise exactly this absurd fantasy. It hardly matters that in their case the others are to live out their wretched lives, while they give themselves over ecstatically to liberatory death. Nonetheless, this is a fantasy born of forbidden, allegedly asocial and even incestuous, sexuality. And in the music dramas exactly this pungent, and paradoxically earthy, business is both the manifest or ideologically implied (stage) reality. Which is to say that while prima facie the elect will indeed die and more or less everyone else will be left alive, whether standing like stupefied spear carriers around the corpses or seated as spent spectators in the darkened auditorium, the peculiar Wagnerian redemption card will trump everything. Consequently this death is not death, rather it is life, albeit an afterlife. At the final curtain Wagner manages – as so often – to be brilliantly exploitative. His most typical denouements are facilitated by the best of both worlds in that his polytheistic pagan model (whether Greek or Nordic) and the monotheistic Christian paradigm are each employed coterminously, allowing him to move the goalposts as he pleases and to cash-in across the board, even though the ambivalent pay-off can never be made explicit. Nonetheless, it is heavily implicit that while his gods are immortal and utterly corporeal creatures driven by (all too) human sensibilities, the heroes of both sexes who enter their realm do so draped in splendour. They are to receive the conventionally promised 'spiritual' reward enshrined in the notion of a Christian Heaven. But it is a carnal heaven. With respect to this contradictory ideological nexus we might recall that in the 1848 essay *The Wibelungen*, Siegfried – profoundly embedded in, and productive of, the coming early middle German and Norse based tetralogy, *The Ring* – is initially described as not only an ersatz sun God, and as an ersatz Apollo, but also as an ersatz Christ.[28] These matters, however, can now be best left until chapter four when it will be necessary to look more closely at death and religion. Of more immediate interest is sex, and here the basic distinction with which this chapter began remains in force. Wagner is – or struggles to be – focused; Britten is all over the place. Sex, however, is in aesthetic terms a surprisingly nebulous and slippery commodity. It would be nice and easy if it could be reduced to a straightforward, corporeal, hands-on business. But it is seldom that – or seldom only that – and comes with so much psychological and, in this context, aesthetic baggage, that dealing with it means digging promiscuously around in a minefield. Above all, it raises the question of love. And while it is often the goal of art as kitsch to make love and (then) sex indissoluble, as though the latter were the reward for, or the climactic fulfilment of, the former, in any serious discourse (aesthetic or otherwise) the one is never wholly the other.

Wagner is clearly much bothered by this dichotomy and labours to overcome it. He is determined that, for his higher characters, sex should be unproblematically shackled to love. The complete sexual experience must be, synonymously, the full expression of love. Consequently the Wagnerian ideal – an ideal that is to be sought for, fought for, precisely because it is attainable – can be said to blend completely the libidinous and affective qualities of everything that we usually reduce to the banal term 'true love.' As such the sex/love pairing is redolent with oceanic meaning. For instance, the emblematic confrontation on the stage between an often inexperienced young man (Siegfried being the classic example) and a wiser 'knowing' woman (in this case Brünnhilde) is not solely about an ersatz earth-moving instance of successful sexual congress in, let us say, the best Hemingway-esque fashion. Rather, the true personalities of both partners are revealed and completed by just this encounter. Which is to say that there is an attendant entry into knowledge of a privileged, even a magical or religious, sort. Sex is nothing less than the exclusive route to Wagnerian redemption.

This is such an important matter that Wagner attempts in his largest prose work, *Opera and Drama*, to provide a wider theoretical underpinning for it; an underpinning that, supposedly, pays due respect to both individual psychology and human anthropology, wrapping them up nicely in a good deal of philosophical mumbo jumbo and placing them under the rubric of text and music (see chapter two below). These latter two are then defined as the aesthetic expressions of the opposed, but potentially inter-dissolved, male and female souls. By this means a great truth is explicated and the operatic agenda given its most potent dynamic impetus; an impetus that not only drives on the stage narratives but also reveals the human and spiritual fundamentals as Wagner imagines them.

Of course, should the privileged pairings (love/sex, female/male, music/text, spiritual redemption/corporeal pleasure) that this presupposes become detached or be thrown off balance, the edifice on all levels will start to wobble. So when the eponymous hero of *Tannhäuser* allows himself to be trapped in the exclusively erotic realm of the pagan goddess Venus he has got everything out of kilter. Sex in her grotto is cloying and imprisoning. In this, ideologically regarded, rather crude early venture that plays with the discrete polarities of love and sex in a wholly simplistic manner, Wagner has undermined his own agenda. Hence he cannot manage the synthesis he is seeking and which he will later engender triumphantly. Poor Tannhäuser's only logical option is a flight into fresh air and the never to be consummated love of a virgin who is more devoted to God than interested in the revelatory power of human sensuality. As a result the redemptive climax is framed according to near exclusive Christian piety and chastity, and when salvation is attained sexual bliss is not merely irrelevant, it is inimical. This is no doubt very nice for the respectable punter, but it is to short-change what the privileged programme is designed to produce and what in fact it will, above all in *Parsifal*, sensationally accomplish. We will return to *Tannhäuser*, above all in the final chapter.

I remember hearing Peter Pears in a television documentary – I can't remember which – saying that Britten was not so much interested in sex as sexuality. This might be seen as a necessary strategy born of the difficulty of talking about, or admitting to, homosexuality, although the programme post-dated legalisation and, I think, also post-dated Britten's death. But the remark should be taken seriously. Sex is not for Britten the unproblematic and radiant fount of knowledge that it is for Wagner, therefore he is neither interested in constructing an explanatory edifice on the basis of sex, nor is he going to write more popular Puccini-esque operatic music, flush with love duets and heady arias. Certainly there is love music in his and Pears's adaptation of Shakespeare's *A Midsummer Night's Dream*, and in *Albert Herring*, where there is a nice ironic quote of Wagner's philtre motif from *Tristan und Isolde*, but Britten's world is too difficult to be satisfied with such strategies. Unlike Wagner he is not interested in dogma. When sex is explicit and potent in Britten it tends to be destructive. It is the agency of disorder, and is everything but redemptive. Explicit heterosexual desire drives *Phaedra* mad and then to suicide in the late cantata, it turns Tarquinius into a wild animal in *The Rape of Lucretia*, and one wonders what role it is playing in the ferocious passion of proud Kate Julian in *Owen Wingrave*. She subdues the charity (love) and understanding of her better nature all too readily, whereupon her sexual passion turns to sardonic derision. Her belligerent (Brünnhilde-like) accusations finally push the pacifist Owen to the point when he takes the step that will kill him.

It is an interesting irony that while Britten does not produce sexually expressive heterosexual love scenes in the grand operatic tradition, he certainly comes up with stunning mad scenes. Think of *Grimes* and *Curlew River.* But the madness is not the unambiguous result of losing the love object. Rather its roots lie deep in social malaise and the moral wickedness that is 'in' the world. In this, as in so many things, Britten's own sexual identity forces him into both a variety of aesthetic strategies in order to circumvent conventional expectations, and into a profound awareness of moral and spiritual questions that simply cannot be reduced to either a happy or a tragic end expressed wholly in terms of whether the lovers finally get to pair off successfully or, instead, die. (Wagner's lovers do both.) Implicit homosexual desire, being repressed, is inevitably complex and messy, and thus often more useful aesthetically. It enables Britten to sublimate sexuality so that it covers a great deal of territory. It flows naturally not only into love but more importantly into the notion of innocence.

At this point it must be stressed that Britten raises the ideal of innocence to the highest ethical level possible. It could be seen as his morally equivalent notion to Wagner's ideal of redemptive sex. Like pacifism, to which it is related, innocence stands in opposition to the evils of the world. It does not, however, stand in opposition to the animal world, as Auden's Epilogue set in Britten's *Our Hunting Fathers* makes clear. The natural world, it seems, is free of the deliberate and calculated malevolence that must to some degree or other contaminate human society. Above all, innocence is embodied in children. Here boys take pride of place and therefore innocence is expressed innately in boys' voices. Thus sex, or sublimated homosexual desire, is fruitful for Britten because it is not contained within a singular discourse or allowed a singular overt outlet. Of course with respect to innocence and boys (it has been argued by John Bridcut that 'thirteen was the age for Britten,' partly because, as Britten told Imogen Holst, 'I'm still thirteen',[29] and we might note that Tadzio is about fourteen in Thomas Mann's novella[30]) it is not allowed direct expression at all. For any explicit acknowledgement of paedophilia would explode both the moral and the aesthetic undertaking, even if its sublimated presence can be readily decoded. Instead the sexual drive is so lacking in specificity that it irrigates a whole geography of works, enriching their pleas for tolerance and for pity. Which is also to say that it enriches their plea for love in all its benign, whether spiritual or corporeal, varieties.

Furthermore, Britten regularly employs Christian and liturgical forms to realise this. In fact it has even been argued that in this he is implicitly contradicting his denials of church allegiance, or that he was, as Pears said, 'an agnostic with a great love for Jesus Christ.'[31] For it might well have been love, but Britten did not, as he made clear to the tribunal considering his first application as a conscientious objector in 1942, believe in Christ's divinity.[32] However, trying to fold Britten within the Anglican church – in his last days he took Holy Communion from Bishop Leslie Brown – diminishes the nature of his non-doctrinaire faith and the role it played throughout his life. Till the end he had doubts as to the afterlife.[33] He was, like Wagner, an unconventional Christian. Above all, there is a tension in his work between church dogma and what we might think of as true universal Christian charity; indeed so universal that, unlike Wagner, it is not to be placed within either the faith parameters of a single church or the race parameters of a single nation. Even Graham Elliott, when discussing the operas, remarks that, while they are best seen as 'moral parables . . . it would be wrong to suggest that the message is always Christian, except in so far as the Christian tradition does encompass many of the moral concerns which are manifest' in the operas.[34] Furthermore, in resorting on occasions to Latin, Britten serves to underline the universal element fundamental to his *Weltanschauung*. This is particularly notable, for instance, in an ostensibly religious work that is not intended for exclusive church performance: the *Cantata Misericordium* composed for the International Red Cross's centenary in 1968. As a result, the loss of innocence has, in Britten's *Weltanschauung*, not only a non-sectarian form but also an immediate potency. It is the catastrophe that sets us on the way to death *in* the world. For instance, the new apprentice (John) in the first opera *Peter Grimes* is certainly well on the way to an understanding of how wretched the world can be. The school teacher Ellen Orford sings to him 'Child you're not too young to know/ Where the roots of sorrow are/ Innocent, you've learnt how near/ Life is to torture.' And when the tormented, ten-year-old Miles dies in *The Turn of the Screw* we know that the 'the ceremony of innocence is drowned.' What the nature of redemption can be beyond that is always mysterious: desired, imagined . . . and doubted.

Now, because this nexus of ideas (innocence and boys and implied homosexuality and pacifism and redemption) is so central to all the sections on Britten in this book, it had better be acknowledged now that at one point he explicitly rejected it; or rather, he rejected one – albeit, arguably the most privileged – aspect of it. A sceptical Colin Matthews recalled that 'around the *Death in Venice* time Britten read out to me an article in *Opera* Magazine which said, "All Britten's operas are concerned with the loss of innocence." And he said "This is absolute *rubbish*!" and picked up the thing and threw it to the other side of the room.' True, this is a rejection of something more specific than the confluence of ideas I have just laid out, but it is clearly significant that Britten should react so strongly. Furthermore, in a prima facie sense he has a case in that his operas deal with a wide variety of themes and portray an equally wide variety of human types. Perhaps he was angry to see all this heterogeneity, born of decades of hard creative labour, reduced to a single, explanatory trope. However, that does not mean that there are not deep underlying values that invest, in an equally multifarious way, Britten's creative output with a shared moral disposition that binds innocence, sexuality, and redemption, So my sympathies are wholly with Matthews when he goes on to remark: 'And I have regretted ever since that I didn't have the courage to say, "Well what are they about then?"'[35]

Staying with sex, one should note that it is only in Britten's last opera that there is any upfront engagement with homosexuality, although he comes close to it in *Canticle V*, a setting of T. S. Eliot's (later suppressed) poem *The Death of Saint Narcissus*. And this is, of course, to put aside the sexual decoding that, to take the most obvious examples, *Peter Grimes*, *Billy Budd* and *The Turn of the Screw* invite. But it is in *Death in Venice* that explicit sexuality is tackled in the deepest, most troubling, and certainly most revealing manner. The famous German writer Gustav von Aschenbach, dying and diseased, is led by his love and lust for the beautiful boy Tadzio to his doom, but that doom is dependent on attaining an exceptional degree of understanding of the world. More importantly, he also attains an understanding of the highest things as explained or intimated in large part in the Socratic dialogue *Phaedrus*. But this is engineered precisely because Aschenbach descends into the abyss. It is a remarkable and disturbing accomplishment and it would be a much lesser thing if it were treated as merely a piece of 'coming out' propaganda. Moreover, with regard to innocence, it does not lie easily alongside the earlier works. In them, if there is to be death it is often associated with sleep and packaged as a release from suffering and from evil. Innocence is thereby allowed a final triumphant benediction. But with Aschenbach, Britten, in confronting more frankly than before his own sexual nature and quite possibly sexuality in general, has muddied the waters in a profound manner: sin and goodness have become not only entangled but interdependent. Certainly we may choose, and with justice, to imagine that Wagner's redeemed heroes and heroines are destined to end up gambolling on heavenly sunny uplands in the fresh air, all their sins having been washed away by the clean waters of old father Rhine. But Britten's final statement, in contradistinction, is much more problematic and dark, not least because it, too, is about salvation, love, redemption . . . and sex.

Even so, one should be chary of inferring too negative a view of Wagner's aesthetic use of sex and all its connotations on the basis of Britten's good fortune in never being able to be unambiguous and proselytising in the matter. While this is once again to underline the lack of dogma in Britten, it does not mean that Wagner is merely dogmatic and preachy. As we will see, he will manipulate his ideology until it covers all of his conscious, and probably unconscious, desires. In other words he, at the end, is not debilitated by his homogeneous belief system, but liberated. Indeed liberated in ideological terms to a degree unequalled by any other artist.

Before developing this last point a little, one should acknowledge that all this amounts to saying nothing more than repression is productive for artists in that it is in itself a type of sublimation, and sublimation is essential for the creative activity; for the making of works of art. This is no less valid for Wagner than for Britten. It is not, for instance, the case that Wagnerian dogma is unambivalent. Behind the propaganda – whether for sexual freedom or for social revolution or for national revival – there stands a deeper and unspoken agenda. It is not merely that Wagner will violate the social norms, notably the most fundamental and debilitating of all: the incest taboo. He will, in addition, invest dominant Christianity in order to remake it to his own purposes. He will turn the breaking of the incest taboo into a sacrament and thereby, in the figure of his last operatic hero, Parsifal, gain for himself a limitless field of action while draping himself in the religious authority of the dominant ideological system of his time. He has, in fact, obtained the megalomaniac's blank cheque. How conscious of all this he is I cannot say, but he is conscious of enough of it, clear above all in his last essays – notably in *Religion and Art* – as to make one suspect that he had some inkling of how far he had gone.

Therefore, both Parsifal and Aschenbach are the final statements of two composers who approach redemption in a complex and highly ambitious manner. They are not, whether focused or eclectic, simple. Nor are they shallow. Rather, as should be the case with great artists, they are redolent with deep problems, with what is unspoken, with what is desired, and with what is for the best. They are, also, despite their deeper thematic similarities and the common (possibly unconscious) attempt to make of sin something sacred, very different in both aesthetic language and intellectual disposition. A fuller elucidation of these considerations is the ultimate goal of this essay.

Finally, if only for illustrative purposes we might, with respect to the defining distinction employed in this chapter, think of the two festivals established by both men. At Bayreuth the homogeneous character of the Wagnerian project is unmistakable. It is not simply that only the master's works are performed, it is that only those operas (post *Rienzi*) that are characterized as 'redemption music dramas' are given. Furthermore, family members have themselves staged many of the productions. It is not surprising then that the festival has, famously or notoriously, become a place of pilgrimage, the sacred site of a Wagner cult. Aldeburgh, however, is many-sided. The repertory is open, works were/are given by many important composers, even some whose music Britten did not find congenial, New works by contemporary composers are programmed. There are lectures, talks, literary events, recitals of every sort, master-classes, films; in short, a general sense of discovery and intellectual heterogeneity.

But now we will return to sex and all its connotations in order to begin putting some flesh on the bare bones of this brief outline.

Two

Love and Sex

In December 1950 Britten received a letter from E. M. Forster that he found upsetting. Forster, with Eric Crozier, was writing the libretto for Britten's opera *Billy Budd*, based on the novella by Herman Melville. Billy, a seaman during the Napoleonic Wars, is a symbol of innocence and goodness and seen (instinctively) as such by his shipmates. This is painfully clear to the master-at-arms, John Claggart, who is as intrinsically evil as Billy is good. Pretending admiration, he sets out to destroy him. Placed between the two is Captain 'Starry' Vere, universally admired by the crew (but for Claggart), a man of sensibility and erudition. Billy, meanwhile, despite his virtuous, albeit simple, character, has a fatal flaw: he stammers. And when falsely accused by Claggart of mutiny his inability to speak at a moment of crisis (he is, by the way, a natural born singer) leads him to hit out. Claggart is killed by a single blow and Vere is duty-bound to have Billy hung from the yardarm.

Forster's letter concerned the musical setting of Claggart's long monologue 'O Beauty, O handsomeness, goodness.' He didn't like it. He wrote 'I want *passion* – love constricted, perverted, poisoned, but nevertheless *flowing* down its agonizing channel; a sexual discharge gone evil.'[1] I have some sympathy for Forster and it should be said that Britten, always hypersensitive to criticism, was sufficiently shaken as to consult Eric Crozier, Peter Pears, and Erwin Stein, who worked for his then publishers Boosey & Hawkes, on the matter.[2] He later made some revisions. Nonetheless, the solo remains essentially an expression of pure wickedness. Certainly it is full of implied sexuality, in accordance with Forster's wishes, but even here there is a problem. Clearly with an all-male cast well-nigh incarcerated on a warship, to say nothing of Claggart's (and others') repeated references to Budd's physical power and attractiveness, the context is, by implication, heavily homosexual. But the erotic subtext had to be kept very much under wraps. After all, bitchy gossip in London's musical circles at the time of the first production at Covent Garden was all about the 'buggers' opera.' Forster like Britten and Pears, for whom the part of Vere was written, was gay. Accordingly the dilemma at the centre of the drama was raised to the level of unbodily abstract values. In this it was, superficially, true to Melville. And it was also true to Britten. Such an elevation and the attendant transformation of physical sexuality into abstractions was, after all, his customary strategy and the source of much aesthetic richness. As a result Claggart's monologue (it was at the time compared to Iago's Credo in Verdi's *Otello*) is limited because the (homo)sexual subtext is never allowed to break through. But if sex is there by implication something else, also mentioned by Forster and equally necessary, is completely missing. And that is love.

Britten can certainly deal with love; it is an important, indeed an essential, element of his *Weltanschauung.* And it need not be wholly asexual. In *Albert Herring*, for instance, the heterosexual affection between Nancy and Bill is sweetly and lightly done, even if one does find it a smidgeon twee. There is, however, real emotion in the fleeting act one duet for Lysander and Hermia ('I swear to thee') in *A Midsummer Night's Dream*, while the equally brief soprano/tenor love duet (between Tiny and Slim) in the youthful, and utterly masterly and underrated – at least on the basis of the revised version – musical *Paul Bunyan*, with a brilliant libretto by W. H. Auden (1941), is delicious. But sexual passion as a revelatory force and an elemental drive intrinsic to the human animal might seem to be beyond him at this stage, or at least an attempt at it would seem inappropriate. In general, one asks oneself whether Britten is disposed to avoid the subject. For instance in the third and last Church Parable, *The Prodigal Son*, it is notable that the boy's naughty doings in the wicked 'city of pleasure' are, but for the Tempter's skills in getting him to gamble away his inheritance, dealt with in a cursory fashion. The older brother tells us that his sibling spent his time and money on 'harlots' and there is talk of the 'delights of the flesh,' but there is little sign of this in the drama. Peter Heyworth in his review of the first performance in 1968 noted that 'the Prodigal's sinful living never looks remotely like rocking the piece's moral edifice.'[3]

More remarkable still is the manner in which the critical event in the *The Rape of Lucretia*, an opera which pre-dates *Billy Budd*, is handled. Reviewing the première, Desmond Shawe-Taylor was disappointed that there was no proper violent realisation of the rape.[4] In fact the rape is hardly handled at all. It is musically and dramatically skimmed, short-changed. Nor do I think this can be entirely put down to fear of the Lord Chamberlain's censors. There is simply no attempt here to portray, even musically, violent copulation in let us say the manner of the offstage, non-rape sexual coupling between Katerina and Sergei in Shostakovitch's *Lady Macbeth of the Minsk District* (Act I Scene 3). This is not an entirely arbitrary comparison as Britten was an admirer of the work and became a valued friend of the composer. It should be admitted, however, that when filmed something very powerful and ugly can be made out of the encounter between Lucretia and Tarquinius, as is shown in the Michael Simpson direction of the ENO 1998 staging by Graham Vick which can be seen on YouTube.[5] Nevertheless. Lucretia's rape is very soon followed by her suicide and then everything is formally wrapped up in an anachronistic and, for many people, faux redemptive message as the male and female chorus sing of the coming sacrifice of Christ on the Cross. It might be remarked in passing that the general discomfort the conclusion of the opera causes – many think it has been thrown off kilter by the Christian gesture – is in some ways strange. After all, the Female Chorus makes clear the anachronistic framework at the very beginning: 'This Rome has still five hundred years to wait/ Before Christ's birth and death.' There are, however, perceptive critics fully alive to both the thematic and musical riches of the opera's final pages.[6]

In the case of Claggart, tormented by the impossibility of love, it is clear that his sick, heavily erotic monologue expresses how, in Britten's aesthetic treatment, sex and love tend to function abrasively, as alien and hostile polarities that are difficult to conjoin. Love, in short, would be contaminated by sex. Put in its clearest form, this takes us back to basics; namely the troublesome biological fact that the sexual and the excretory functions share the same bodily organs or are in close proximity. This has always been a problematic part of the human psyche in general and has generated, in particular, a difficult relationship between sensuality and religion. It once troubled the early Church Fathers mightily and led to the disparagement, demonizing even, of sex. In the first Christian centuries encratism was well-nigh the standard theological position and it decreed sexual abstinence, sometimes even within marriage. After all, hadn't Jesus, according to Matthew (19:12), celebrated those who had become eunuchs 'for the kingdom of Heaven's sake'?[7] Sexuality, it seemed, was a sign of sin rather than the royal road to, or natural expression of, love. Just as the officers on Billy's ship, *The Indomitable*, on discovering his stammer, say that nothing is perfect and that the devil is always there somewhere in the mix, so for the pious, and perhaps chaste, Christian is sex the devil's way of corrupting love. For the early theologians sex then became 'the clearest token of human bondage.'[8]

For much of his creative life Britten's solution when confronted by this dichotomy was to preserve love at all costs and to keep sex rigorously corralled. So Claggart is absolute evil; the thing itself without any erotic outlet. Several critics at the time of the première complained that he lacked motivation. But that is, with respect to both Melville *and* Britten, exactly the point. He does not need it. He is simply, naturally, diabolical.

Nevertheless he *does* need love. Moreover he is, in his own sick way, crying out for it. And Forster understands this. He understands that it is love that has gone awry. He understands that the pain Claggart undergoes is not dependent solely on the mere presence of goodness as embodied in someone else – the view we might assume that Britten took. Rather it takes added force from the self-knowledge that he can never possess it (or Billy) and that therefore his spiritual as well as his physical deprivations are insurmountable. Britten won't really get properly to grips with this problem – at least in his operas – until Aschenbach, who, it might be noted, begins as an unambivalently heterosexual character and is then confounded by a forbidden and wholly disorientating desire.

Wagner, given that a blissful and transfiguring union between love and sex is indispensable to his *Weltanschauung* and therefore kernel to his operatic project, is hardly likely to address the matter in the bald fashion suggested above. He is certainly not going to accept an inimical, or even a troublesome, relationship between the two polarities, although he is well aware that the issue is fraught with difficulties and needs explaining. Consequently he is compelled to be intellectually adventurous. This is all the more remarkable as it probably wasn't until Freud that the libidinous and affective drives were placed unambiguously in a biological and psycho-anthropological framework;

a framework that foregrounded the excretory and sexual organs in a theoretically rigorous manner. Freud argued that the sex drive (from which, of course, in the Freudian scheme love of any sort – 'Eros' – is not to be uncoupled) has as one of its original sources 'the coprophilic instinctual components' that we still see with children. But these 'have proved incompatible with our aesthetic standards of culture, probably since, as a result of our adopting an erect gait, we raised our organ of smell from the ground.' Consequently, visual stimuli take over from the olfactory ones and this places a new emphasis on cleanliness and, specifically, on the need to get rid of bodily excretions.[9] It is impossible to avoid at this point mentioning the passion of Britten and Pears for lots of swimming and cold baths. But as Freud's *speculative* theory is probably as good as any other, assuming that is we accept the assumption of a fundamental imbalance between affection and sensuality, between love and sex, we might look at the essay *On the Universal Tendency to Debasement in the Sphere of Love* from 1912 a little closer in the hope that it can be productively applied to both Wagner and Britten.

Freud pursues his argument with typical intellectual courage and trenchancy and if we follow him we must accept that the discrepancy between what we might think of as higher feelings (or at least affection) and the libidinous drive is both dynamic and creative. That will, unavoidably, have to be the case if we are also to stick with the importance of sublimation; which is to say the assumption that libidinous drives are redirected into cultural, in the broadest sense, activity. Of course sublimation was always an indispensable factor in the Freudian *Weltanschauung*, but if we are looking for clarity we could do no better than turn to the relatively late essay *Civilisation and its Discontents* (1930). There we are told that sublimation is that which 'makes it possible for higher psychical activities, scientific, artistic or ideological, to play such an important part in civilized life. . .' and that '. . . it is impossible to overlook the extent to which civilization is built upon a renunciation of the instinct, how much it presupposes precisely the non-satisfaction . . . of powerful instincts. This "cultural frustration" dominates the large field of social relationships between human beings.'[10] This should, in particular, be borne in mind in the case of Britten because it implies a double repressed drive. It is not merely a question of whether or not he was a *reluctant* homosexual, though that has been claimed, notably by his librettist

Ronald Duncan.[11] He also had public contempt to contend with. Furthermore, there was the additional problem that any mention of homosexuality, let alone anything more, was banned from the stage by the Lord Chamberlain up to 1958.[12] As an artist working in the theatre Britten was then forced into a range of alternative strategies. We might assume that in his case the function of sublimation in the Freudian sense was, as a result, especially fruitful.

If we now return to the earlier Freud essay we can then get some idea of the tangle the creative soul, let us say one very much aware of what is 'noble' and very much predisposed to create it, must get itself into when it comes to sex. We might at this point take but one example. Noble, glorious etc are the adjectives that Wagner applies lavishly to arguably his greatest and most knowing heroine: Brünnhilde. Furthermore, it is Wagner who tells us that we have, traditionally, misidentified the great theme otherwise associated with Sieglinde in *Die Walküre* act three and twice repeated at the end of the cycle. It may express 'redemption by love' (its customary title) but that is also to say that it expresses 'the glorification of Brünnhilde' and should be so called.[13] Freud, however, is not merely explaining what we might initially take to be a simple or straightforward psychic dilemma. It turns out that it gets increasingly difficult to resolve the more sophisticated and educated, indeed the more 'civilised', one is: 'There are only a very few educated people in whom the two currents of affection and sensuality have become properly fused; the man almost always feels his respect for the woman acting as a restriction on his sexual activity, and only develops full potency when he is with a debased sexual object; and this in its turn is partly caused by the entrance of perverse components into his sexual aims, which he does not venture to satisfy with a woman he respects. He is assured of complete sexual pleasure only when he can devote himself unreservedly to obtaining satisfaction, which with his well-brought-up wife, for instance, he does not dare to do.'[14] British judges shocked at the propensity of prominent politicians with immaculately respectable wives to turn to call girls could learn a lot from Freud.[15] Meanwhile I have tried to hunt up some educated friends to ask them if they feel that Freud has a point; a point, one should underline, that he explains from an exclusively masculine perspective. They tend to demur, the older ones often indicating that 1968 and all that took care of any sexual hang-ups. I confess that I am not always convinced.

Wagner, as is only appropriate for a heterosexual artist who wishes to shatter bourgeois sexual restrictions in the cause of love in its highest and most noble form, confronts this problem head on. It is interesting, for instance, how frank he is in his letters to his youthful friend Theodor Apel in 1834 and 1835. He has been sexually liberated by Minna Planer, an actress who was to become his first wife. She, not being as free of bourgeois convention as he imagined himself to be, rather insisted on marriage. Nonetheless, Wagner writing of sex with Minna automatically fuses sexual bliss with what is for him the critical phenomenon ('transfiguration') that takes the lovers out of base physical reality and into what he will later claim is the clear air of the ethereal Schopenhauerian realm. 'She has given me a couple of moments of sensual transfiguration – it was marvellous. . .'[16] In the following year, underlining the sensual abandon both he and Minna are now enjoying, he can be said to reproduce Freud's explanatory dichotomy exactly; at least he does if we remember the reputation women in Minna's profession then had. In any case, it seems there's a lot to be said for life upon the wicked stage. '. . . one can only live like that with an actress; – this disregard for middle-class values is something you can find only when the whole basis is one of imaginative freedom & poetic licence.'[17]

In case the reader infers from this a certain degree of phallocentrism and male arrogance one should confirm immediately that he or she is right to do so. All this youthful libidinous sexuality ('I have fired her to the very marrow of her being . . . she loves to the point of sickness, I have become her tyrant' and 'she is completely free with her favours towards me, almost to the point of excess. . .'[18]) is not untarnished by raw sexual egotism. Wagner's feelings are ambivalent because while they were apart Minna had 'betrayed' him. On learning this he indulged his considerable theatrical side to the hilt in melodramatic letters, notably to both Apel and Minna herself.[19] But then, when they were reconciled, he was rather ashamed of having succumbed to such a clichéd 'bourgeois' lapse. Fancy him, the great artist, being jealous and possessive. Even so, in a letter from October 1835 he contemplates betraying Minna simply for the pleasure (but of what type?) that it might give him: 'What . . . if I were to deceive her intentionally, would that not be a masterpiece of behaviour on my part?'[20]

All this is a long way from his relationship with Cosima. We will return to this in a few pages, but suffice to say now that she pulls the whole construct as close to the pole of higher, non-physical things as possible. The bestial element concerning the closeness of the sexual and excretory organs and the consequences of mankind becoming upright that are necessary to Freud's interpretation, would for Cosima simply be a sign of what had to be overcome in order that the noble work of the Master might reach its preordained heights. But Wagner himself is not so simplistic and it is to his credit that, as we will see, he struggles manfully to make the polarities merge. And no doubt he convinces himself that he has succeeded. He has certainly convinced lots of others. It is, however, as it must be, sham; no less a sham than Cosima's belief that Richard, having supposedly transcended the physical sex drive, had taken a moral quantum leap.[21] Still, she had some grounds to believe her chosen propaganda in this. After all, there were times when Richard would go the whole hog and kneel down before her; surely an extreme illustration of Freud's point concerning the sexual and emotional difficulties the educated man gets into with his respectable wife.[22] It is fair to assume that both chose to believe what they wanted out of vain self-delusion and in an attempt to establish a mutually successful modus vivendi. Nevertheless, Wagner's bogus faith in the ultimate and absolute fusion of love and sex transformed sham into great and seductive art stamped by exceptional erotic and spiritual force. And Cosima, no matter how troubled she was by his occasional physical demands, believed with her heart and soul that she understood this better than anyone else. She might well have been right.

Britten, as has already been pointed out, has no proselytising sexual agenda. Rather he wishes to push sexuality into other realms; realms that lie as far as possible from the paradigm of the naked ape and all the psycho-sexual baggage that implies. This is not to say that he pretends that he is unaware of how bestial sex can be. Tarquinius was already the 'tiger' in the forest of Lucretia's dreams long before he raped her, which reminds one of the fearsome animal celebrated in Blake's *Tyger* poem. Britten was later to set it. It is rather that for Britten there is, seemingly, nothing to be said aside from acknowledging the self-evident cruelty and barbarism that corrupts the world of innocence and pure feeling. The cruder and brutal side of sex is then folded into the general climate of sin which corrupts us as children and with which we struggle throughout our lives. For instance, while we may suspect a sexual sub-text in the relationship between the ghost Peter Quint and young Miles in *The Turn of the Screw*, it is overtly a story of innocence besmirched by eerie, certainly repressed, but not explicitly sexual, forces. As a result Britten is free to idealise sex if he chooses. In its, presumably pure, form it can be draped in elevated, benign – and conventional – clothes. Which also means that when on occasions he is confronted by what is, at least in part, the real thing, he is horrified.

In 1937 as a young man he was taken to a Paris brothel. After a while several women came into the room. Britten thought them fat, hairy and 'smelling of vile cheap scent'[23] and was appalled when they undressed completely and paraded around. His companion Ronald Duncan, who was heterosexual and who also didn't find the scene very salubrious, described Britten as 'blinking in terror.'[24] The two young men duly fled and were later, thank God, revived by the sublime sight of Notre Dame. Looking back Britten noted that: 'It is revolting – appalling that such a noble thing as sex should be so degraded.'[25] One can't help wondering whether they might have felt differently if the women had been pretty, or whether, perhaps, in those circumstances, Britten, in particular, could have found any woman alluring.

It is not surprising then that Britten was, in this matter, just as conventional and publicly bourgeois as Auden claimed he was. Wagner meanwhile, if he is to be believed, was perpetually on the lookout should he succumb to the same vice. His status as a revolutionary artist entitled to exceptional indulgences was always on show, even though he needed a very comfy and well-upholstered environment, together with the admiration of the establishment, in order to make this clear. Neither, however, was as bohemian as Auden. Britten's position meant that, officially at least, he was uncomfortable with sexual licentiousness. This made him socially very proper. Pears suggested that the puritanical aspect of his character was owed to his Anglican Low Church upbringing.[26] It was, for instance, difficult for him to accept the Earl of Harewood's divorce and remarriage (Harewood was asked to resign from the presidency of the Aldeburgh Festival in 1964), and it led to the breach with Charles Mackerras after the conductor had joked during the rehearsals for *Noye's Fludde* that Britten must be pretty pleased to have all the boys around. On hearing of Mackerras's remark through tittle-tattle, Britten carpeted him, demanding to know whether he was being accused of lechery simply because he loved children.[27] It is also this that led him to encourage Roger Duncan to preserve the 'nobility' of sex and hence to avoid 'sexual laxity', no matter that that is how much of the 'world behaves.'[28] For a moment he almost sounds like Lady Billows admonishing the unfortunate Albert Herring: 'Scorn the sweetmeats of Temptation/ Seducing you from straight and narrow ways . . . Carnal indulgence!' Still, Britten, who always wanted children of his own, was, in effect, a valued ersatz parent to Roger. This was all arranged with the encouragement and cooperation of his father: Britten's companion in the Paris brothel.

For Britten monogamy was paramount; sex, therefore could be, would have to be, kept within firm boundaries. Clearly, as John Bridcut's book shows, he became all too readily infatuated with teenage boys. True, he took up the paternal role happily and he seems to have fulfilled it in an exemplary fashion. Certainly the young men in later life remembered Britten with affection and gratitude. Yet those relationships were far from unambivalent. This is particularly clear in the erotically teasing and often passionate correspondence with Wulff Scherchen, who was the inspiration for the piano and orchestra piece *Young Apollo* that Britten later suppressed.[29] At one point Wulff calls Britten a sex maniac and Britten replies in mock Cockney 'T'aint true – Oim a good boy I am.'[30] However, while the sexual component is contained within the parameters of ironic play, there is no lack of mutual declarations of love. From our own very different perspective and time we are no doubt prone to look at all this differently – or at least to be somewhat reluctant to take Britten's protestations of innocence as wholly unproblematic. But whatever conclusions we draw as to the sexual force of Britten's feelings, we shouldn't forget that Scherchen, who went to live in Australia, later married, and took the name John Woolford, says that nothing carnal happened.[31] Paul Kildea, however, suggests that the relationship was probably consummated and claims that Scherchen dissembled in his later accounts.[32] There is, however, no evidence that this is the case.

Wulff was only one of several boys who became Britten's protégés. Imogen Holst says baldly that when Britten and the sixteen-year-old Paul Rogerson met they simply fell in love. However Rogerson, who later joined the Jesuits, made clear that the relationship was wholly chaste . . . just a goodnight kiss.[33] And David Hemmings, who created the role of Miles in

The Turn of the Screw, recalls while staying at Aldeburgh getting into Britten's bed at night when frightened by a thunderstorm or feeling lonely. He was a clued-up young fellow and already quite sure of his own heterosexual identity. He had, nonetheless, complete trust in Britten. It was only later that he found out that Pears had been 'jealous.'[34] Moreover, almost all of the boys who became Britten's protégés described their friendship with him in positive terms. It was an enriching experience. This is the case, for instance, with the young pianist and composer Ronan Magill who does, however, claim that Britten made some physical overtures in 1969, which were, as he tells it, gently rebuffed.[35] There was, however, an incident involving Harry Morris, a thirteen-year-old from a poor London family. He stayed briefly with Britten and claimed that the composer made a pass at him. It was resisted with a scream and repelled with a chair.[36] Several commentators have suggested that it might have been the result of a misunderstanding. Whatever the case, we should acknowledge that whether Britten's sexual discipline, or renunciation, is something to be admired or not, it clearly gave him the homely monogamous sanctuary he needed. He was never likely to seriously jeopardise that. In 1949, in California, Christopher Isherwood asked him if he'd ever had sex with anyone other than Pears and Britten said no.[37] All of this would suggest either a happy and untroubled marriage when placed within the parameters of popular romantic ideology, or, in Freudian terms, a considerable degree of self-denial. One cannot know, but one is struck, nevertheless, by the highly productive nature of the modus vivendi that Britten established. He knew what he needed. Mind you, others have inferred further psychic consequences to which Britten might have been subject. In fact in the case of Hans Keller 'inferred' is too weak a word. He is dealing, or so he claims, in indisputable facts.

Keller was a critic for whom Britten had real admiration; he was invited to Aldeburgh to lecture and the third and final string quartet is dedicated to him. But he took, in particular, an unusual line with respect to Britten's pacifism. He emphasized its *self-evident* sadomasochistic origins: 'It is an established fact that strong and heavily repressed sadism underlies pacifistic attitudes. About the vital aggressive element in Britten's music (as distinct from his extra-musical character) there cannot indeed be the faintest doubt, and those whose ears are not sensitive enough to recognise the sadistic component in at least his treatment of the percussion, will still be able to confirm our observation upon an inspection of his libretti, children's operas included.' Further: 'What distinguishes Britten's musical personality is the violent repressive counter-force against his sadism: by dint of character and musical history and environment. He has become a *musical pacifist* too.'[38] This may, conceivably, be the case and others have taken a similar line.[39] And even if one doesn't assume that it is an 'established fact' that pacifism generates and suppresses an unusual degree of sadomasochism, the sense of struggle that Keller detects is undoubtedly there. But then it is there, to one degree or another, in everybody, although not everyone expresses it creatively. Britten, however, was not likely to be comfortable when confronted by this sort of thing and when he read the relevant passage Imogen Holst, who worked for him as a musical assistant, recalls that he was somewhat amazed and found it terrible.[40] Nonetheless he laughed and said 'I have come to the conclusion that I must have a very clever subconscious.'[41] No doubt he had. But his subconscious would have been a good deal more than merely clever.

As already indicated, when we turn to Cosima, sex really becomes part of the problem and thus its successful renunciation an essential factor in the solution. Conversely, in respect of love she colonises the relevant emotional territory with a ferocity that is unequalled. And then, on having 'renounced' 'sensual expression', her devotion to her soulmate emerges as unmatched. All this is underpinned by her absolute faith in the unequalled and impeccable (in artistic and spiritual matters) character of her beloved Master.

Of course their initial bonding had to be sexually driven. The key declaration occurred in a carriage ride in Berlin in 1863. One assumes, however, that it was not a *Madame Bovary*-type consummation of the sort Emma and Léon enjoyed while being bounced over the Paris cobblestones. In fact, as is only appropriate with soulmates, Richard and Cosima were at first mute with bliss. And then, as Wagner records the moment for posterity in the less than reliable autobiography *My Life* (he wrote it principally for King Ludwig): 'With tears and sobs we sealed a vow to belong to each other alone.'[42] And thus he was rewarded with the love of a good woman. But he would want more than just love. She meanwhile, in terms of the higher things that were important to her, was possessive and wanted everything and, moreover, convinced herself that she had got it. Nonetheless, at first the relationship was erotic to some degree and three children were born, including the longed-for son Siegfried. All this happened before Cosima's husband, Hans von Bülow, agreed to a divorce. She and Wagner were married in August 1870. About the paternity of the first child, Isolde, there was later to be some argument and a public scandal. Following Wagner's death, Cosima claimed in court that the real father was von Bülow. However all the evidence indicates that this was a lie designed to save money by depriving Isolde of her share of income from the estate. It led to one of many vicious family disputes and a notorious and salacious court case in 1914. Isolde, in possible retaliation, later went so far as to suggest that Cosima brought on Richard's fatal heart attack in Venice on 13 February 1883. Indeed public rows of one sort or another were to prove very much part of everyday life in the Wagner family.

The erotic side of the marriage soon became, if it hadn't always been, a burden for Cosima. Even before her wedding she had noted sadly that: 'R cannot be persuaded to curb his inclinations.'[43] The following year she bemoaned: 'If only we could curb passion – if only it could be banished from our lives! Its approach now grieves me, as if it were the death of love.'[44] Sex and love simply don't belong together. And soon after the wedding she produced one of her, and his, most dubious rationalisations. On 11 November 1870 she recorded: 'For me the passionate side of love has disappeared, for R it is still alive; when with constant dismay I am made aware of this, R tells me it is precisely this which gives him the great and calming assurance that our union is blessed by Nature; . . .' We can only speculate on what this means exactly. It may be taken as evidence that celibacy in their case has been especially blessed or, conversely, that Cosima will simply have to overcome her reluctance. Given the manner in which Richard employed Nature in his theories and polemics – something which will be relevant when we turn in the next two chapters to incest – the latter seems too crude, while the former too glib. Whatever the case, he must have been aware from the beginning what a sexually and emotionally unhappy young woman he had taken to be his soulmate, his helpmate, the keeper of his flame (on one occasion when she was ill he very kindly wrote her *Diary* entries for her according to his own agenda and in her name), and on occasions his bedmate. He must have known full well that as Liszt's neglected daughter she had suffered a great deal, and that she had, with a certain dedication, resigned herself to it. He had even witnessed von Bülow striking her.[45] She, meanwhile, had told her step-sister before marrying von Bülow: 'I am well aware that it is a bad match.' As Barry Millington says: 'A masochistic pleasure in suffering and self-sacrifice came to be the determining features in her personality.'[46] In this she is like two, albeit different, Wagner heroines: Elsa in the early 'romantic' opera *Lohengrin* and Kundry in the last opera, the 'sacred festival drama' *Parsifal*.

Elsa, Wagner's most conventionally romantic heroine, is in a spot of bother. In medieval Brabant she is accused of killing her brother and needs a champion to defend her in single combat. She tells the King and assembled knights about a dream she has had of just such a shining hero. But after the trumpets have sounded and the Herald has repeatedly called on someone to step forward, there is silence and no one moves. Then, after a moment or two when things are starting to look very black indeed, something like a miracle occurs. There is a commotion at the back of the stage, whereupon Lohengrin, a glorious knight of the Holy Grail, appears on a boat pulled by a swan. Elsa has found her dream man. Everything after that goes swimmingly . . . at first. Furthermore it is all carried along by, to make a purely subjective observation, a very beautiful score. There follows a proper (bourgeois) wedding, with the famous wedding march, and then we are transported in the third act to the bridal chamber for what is surely going to be a proper wedding night and, moreover, one with a very proper wedded knight. It all looks like a staged version of the happy-ever-after ending beloved of romantic fiction. But of course there is a fly in the ointment; albeit a very odd one. It has been put there by Lohengrin himself. He insisted as a condition both for acting as Elsa's champion and for wedding her – and he makes it quite clear that he is utterly in love with her – that she is never to ask what his name is and what his origins are. In short, she is not to know who he is. At that moment she readily, and no doubt with absolute sincerity, agrees. Nevertheless it transpires that she cannot control her curiosity (at this time in his life women were always letting Wagner down, not least because they couldn't accept his conditions), and after her mind has been poisoned by the dark couple, Ortrud und Telramund, she blurts out the forbidden questions in the bridal chamber, whereupon the whole fairytale world collapses about her . . . and him.

Looking back at all this with the benefit of twentieth century post-Freudian and Lacanian theory one can easily put this story, as one can with a great many fairytales, into the context of the problematic and unstable nature of subjectivity, of the struggle to attain and maintain identity and personality, and of the arbitrary, but vital, function of naming. I don't wish to labour all that here; merely to suggest that the simple thirteenth century fable of the swan knight, which inspired the opera, is redolent with serious consequences. In other words, while Lohengrin's demands may seem in the circumstances laid out in the first act a mere formal bagatelle necessary to the plot, their implications (quite irrespective of the machinations of Ortrud and Telramund) are massive. Naturally Elsa is so much in love and, let it not be forgotten, loved in return, that she understandably sees no problem and is untroubled . . . initially. But in fact the conditions she is asked to agree to (after all, poor Lohengrin wouldn't be able to sign the church register) are a denial of his real, but magical origins and identity and consequently, as the hero's wife, a denial of her status as a subject; a subject in every sense. She just doesn't know that she is Frau Lohengrin. And while that might sound facetious – no doubt because it is – this sort of thing quite logically leads to a pathology.

Furthermore, it should be stressed that the conundrum of naming and identity is something of which Wagner is very much aware, even though he had no recourse to twentieth century French (post)-structuralist theory. A Wagner hero may well not know his name. He is certainly not likely to know who he is. This is the fundamental knowledge he must gain, often in an encounter with his particular predestined redemptive woman; a heroic female who possesses the privileged knowledge he needs in order to become the hero *he* is destined to be. This is the case with Siegmund in *Die Walküre* and with Siegfried, and Parsifal. It is also notable that both Tristan and Parsifal, and to some extend Siegmund, play with, or are confronted by, alternative designations and anagrams of their names.

In this respect *Tristan und Isolde* makes a particularly striking case because the eponymous hero and heroine meet as equals. Both no doubt need the other to discover their true deeper natures, but neither is to assume the role of the privileged mentor. Therefore their agenda is grander. The woman does not school the boy/man who then goes on his way to fulfil his higher duty. Rather, both set about the business of fusing their identities in order to make a higher psyche; a psyche that seems to have access to the deepest things to be found in the human animal. Approaching the ecstatic climax of their long act two love duet Tristan and Isolde are confronted by how they, and their names, are separated by 'this little word *and*.' Isolde imagines 'how might it be destroyed.' They then reach the point where, in effect, their names are swapped. But even this is transcended and at the climax there are: 'No names, no parting'; not even in death. Not surprisingly it turns out that death is something to be longed for. It is the guarantor that separation will be forever impossible.

Returning to the Elsa phenomenon, I would suggest that what Lohengrin/Wagner in effect is expressing, no doubt to some degree unconsciously, is the demand for complete and willing acceptance of dominant male authority. Moreover, although it was hardly part of Wagner's conscious agenda, he has created a fanciful aesthetic construct in which the nature of phallocentrism is unambiguously clear. In providing a context in which the loved woman is given every reasonable, and imaginable, incentive to accept the relevant terms and conditions and in then showing, however unsympathetically, that she cannot stick to her promise, he has unwittingly exposed the full arrogance of exactly those demands. Consequently the exceptional, in this case, character of male egotism is unavoidably unmasked. It is, after all, no small thing to deny, even by implication, who one is. And it is no small thing to keep the information of who and what one is from the person you allegedly love. In this case language is manifestly a male preserve in that the woman only gains entry by a denial of her essential nature as a woman. Interestingly, Wagner himself when he is upbraiding women – they are always failing him by not eloping when planned or not accepting his authority – employs language that recalls the complaints the wronged Lohengrin (at least that's how he sees it) directs at Elsa after she has failed to keep her mouth shut: 'O Elsa! What have you done to me?' It would, of course, be impossible for him to consider the reverse. In any case Elsa is ultimately tossed aside and duly dies at the climax.

Later, in *A Communication to My Friends* (1851), Wagner decks Elsa out in more appealing propaganda. Certainly his feelings are ambivalent and we, meanwhile, cannot fail to be bewitched by the general tone of musical sweetness and light that is associated with her throughout the opera. So in the essay he portrays her as an early, and an impossibly overburdened, embodiment of the 'unconscious' and 'undeliberate' woman who, as passive vessel, redeems the male.[47] And then he can get quite carried away. Imagining himself as having climbed, post-*Tannhäuser*, up to the pure air of the alpine summits he points out that: 'From these heights my longing glance beheld at last – *das Weib* . . . the woman who now drew Lohengrin from sunny heights to the depths of Earth's warm breast. . .'[48] and thereby Elsa can take her place as the third in the line of redemptive women central to Wagner's *Weltanschauung*. The other two, up to this point, being Elisabeth (*Tannhäuser*) and Senta (*The Flying Dutchman*). But four years earlier his feelings towards his 'heroine' were positively sadistic and he wanted to devise the harshest punishment possible for her. And that was, self-evidently, to be parted from the beloved. Indeed, what could be worse?[49] It was only subsequently that he realised that death was the best and certainly the most effective theatrical solution. He cannot, however, kill off the women who have failed him in life. Instead he has to resort to denigration in the grand manner. When Jessie Laussot backed out of an elopement she is dismissed brutally and in the Elsa fashion: 'She is lost to herself, for – she is weak!!' and '. . . she has proved herself a child!'[50] In general we are forced to acknowledge that women just don't understand Wagner. This is particularly the case with poor Minna; the marriage having gone sour very quickly. In 1850, by which time matters had got to a very bad stage, he was pointing out to her in a very contradictory letter dated 16 April, that she was simply not able to dedicate herself, 'devote' herself, to the degree – of course to the absolute degree – that he required. That is, love 'for *the man he is*.' She did not 'share' his deeper feeling. Now he is claiming that he was the one who 'insisted' on marriage because he had loved her so much. All he wanted was 'unconditional love' on her part in return, which means – Lohengrin like – she was simply to accept all the conditions he desired. And of course she has never 'understood' him properly. If she had 'she would have spoken words of comfort and encouragement.' Instead she only wanted him as a means to get 'a respectable position in the bourgeois world, a world I despise.' Therefore he can conclude that he is the one who has, again like Lohengrin, truly loved and he duly points out with self-indulgent relish how as a result he now 'suffers', and how deep the 'anguish' is.

But with Cosima, Wagner found, at least for official purposes, exactly what he was looking for. Furthermore Cosima knew it and celebrated it. She expresses the Elsa principle – or ought that to be the Lohengrin principle? – perfectly: 'A woman may and should sacrifice everything for her beloved, a man, on the other hand, can and should have a point from which he neither shifts nor wavers.'[51] In short the man's identity, his subjectivity, is never to be put in doubt, while the woman assumes hers in as much as she accepts her higher duty to him. All of this is only likely to work if the woman in question is in no doubt as to the Master's entitlement in all matters of genius and spiritual greatness. For official purposes at least, and putting aside the annoying matter of Richard's occasional libidinous demands, Cosima, as she insists again and again (the *Diaries* were written for her children), didn't entertain the slightest doubts in the matter. Just as Elsa says explicitly that she is not worthy of her knight saviour, so did unworthy Cosima know that in giving her Richard the fates had given her a near otherworldly treasure . . . albeit one with an as yet untamed libido.

The Cosima connection with Kundry is a much deeper and more complicated affair and, given *Parsifal's* exceptional status with regard to Wagner's attempt to make Christianity serve his own wilful purposes, it will play an important role throughout this book. Kundry is, however, an important figure now because she seems to, allegedly, address directly the opposed polarities of love and sex at play here. Moreover she does something sensational: she reconciles them in exactly the sublime and untroubled manner Wagner is seeking.

We can best understand this if we begin as Wagner did with his planned two female characters for *Parsifal.* There was to be an eastern-type odalisque placed in a magic garden and compelled to work in the service of her perverse lord and master Klingsor. He is a fallen knight who once belonged to the Brotherhood of the Holy Grail, so there is a clear connection with *Lohengrin.* Actually we know from the earlier opera that Lohengrin is Parsifal's son. Incidentally, Klingsor is immune to his imprisoned enchantress's otherwise near irresistible sex appeal as he has castrated himself and thereby attained magical powers. In other words he has resorted to an extreme and very partial resolution of the love/sex dichotomy. It is the solution that the first anchorites might well have approved of; Jesus too, if the passage from from Matthew 19:12 quoted above is taken seriously. But in this context it is anything but pious. As *Gurnemanz*, the most informed and authoritative figure among the devout knights, explains, it is nothing less than an act of sacrilege. Certainly in giving up sex in this radical manner he has not attained love, or indeed reached any state that one might call pure. In this we can deduce that the solution to which several of the early Church Fathers did in fact resort (Origen Adamantius for instance), and of which Wagner was well aware (although his, and indeed Schopenhauer's, principal example of sexual renunciation was to be found in Calderón's *Zenobia the Great*), just simply doesn't do the business. Quite the opposite in fact. Klingsor has, instead, acquired devilish necromantic skills and he will compel the magic garden odalisque to seduce Parsifal in the secular second act and hopes thereby to take a further step in the destruction of the brotherhood of the knights from which he is now banished.

It is important to stress that Klingsor has already morally reduced the brotherhood's leader, Amfortas, by exactly those libidinous means that he is now planning to employ against Parsifal. Amfortas, as a result, has become a tormented invalid, a type of corrupted ersatz Christ, who bleeds regularly (it is clearly menstrual in character) from the wound he received in the magic garden when Klingsor took from him the Holy Lance. At that moment Amfortas was sexually mesmerised and no doubt physically exhausted by Kundry. Gurnemanz relates that: 'In her arms he lay entranced; The Spear dipped toward him.' Klingsor was then able to take hold of what was both a 'fallen' (probably fallen in every sense) phallic symbol and a deeply religious icon. For the Holy Lance is the spear that pierced the side of the Saviour when on the Cross. Klingsor, having won it, then uses it to penetrate Amfortas in the flank (*in der Seite*). In this Wagner alters his European source material (Chretien de Troyes and Wolfram von Eschenbach and the Amfortas figure of the Fisher King). They suggest the groin or the thigh as the site of the wound. But clearly 'the side' is more apposite for Wagner because it underlines the, in part perverse (human guilt verses divine innocence), bond between Amfortas and the crucified Christ. As a result Amfortas must endure an impure stigmata; the wound that is the source of his regular bleeding. And this bleeding, we might note, takes place at the climax of the Eucharist. Although having lost the lance, the knights are still in possession of the Grail, and at the final ecstatic – and for the guilt ridden, sexually corrupted Amfortas, agonising – highpoint of the mass it glows, whereupon Amfortas bleeds. This is nothing less – but in sexual terms a great deal more – than a powerful theatrical parallel to the transubstantiation that occurred during the first Eucharist: The Last Supper. Structurally, then, we can see that this produces an opera where the first and third acts, taking place within the dying and morally diseased brotherhood, provide a compromised but clearly religious framework to the worldly, irreligious and erotic goings on in the second.

There is however a further female 'Kundry': the wild messenger of the Grail who belongs to the outer acts. She is tormented and, as we are to learn, cursed. Having conceived her, Wagner was, from the beginning of his work on the libretto ('poem'), very taken with her. He wrote to Mathilde Wesendonck: '. . . there is a curious creature, a strangely world-demonic woman (the messenger of the Grail) who strikes me with increasing vitality and fascination. If I ever manage to write this poem, I am sure to produce something very original.'[52] How right he was. And then two years later he makes the fundamental conceptual breakthrough. 'Did I not tell you once before that the fabulously wild messenger of the Grail is to be one and the same person as the enchantress of the second act. Since this dawned on me, almost everything else about the subject has become clear to me.'[53] And thus we have the composite Kundry that has come down to us; a remarkable figure who resolves a host of structural, narrative, aesthetic, and conceptual problems.

One of the most banal but also most remarkable things about *Parsifal* is that it has a happy end. In the first instance this is merely to say that all of the key principals, bar one, live. Of perhaps more importance is that the climax amounts to the seeming resolution of every moral and narrative dilemma or tension that drives the work in general and, specifically, threatens the survival of the brotherhood. This 'happy' resolution leaves the order of priestly knights intact and refreshed. At the end, after Parsifal has resisted Kundry in the second act (in, admittedly, an extremely ambivalent manner) and regained the lance from Klingsor, he returns to the knights and uses it to heal Amfortas's wound. Whereupon the ersatz saviour's sins are washed away by, we might think, the blood of the sacrificed, or crucified, lamb. The future now looks rosy.

With respect to the 'failed' seduction of Parsifal, there is a further crucial element in the complex nexus centred on Kundry that Wagner is able to fold seamlessly into both the narrative and the overall conceptual scheme. Initially Kundry presents herself to the hero as the odalisque, decked out in clichéd eastern promise. But then she takes up the persona of his mother . . . she knows his real name; he doesn't. This last step is essential if she is to carry through the act of seduction. And it is hardly unprecedented in Wagner's operas, where Oedipal desire often surfaces as part of the general incestuous agenda. Siegfried, for instance, seems at times determined to see Brünnhilde (on first meeting her he kissed her awake) as his mother. And it is only at the point when Kundry, bending over him and giving him 'a mother's blessing, the first kiss of love!' that Parsifal is able to make the decisive transformative step. Suddenly overwhelmed by the thought of Amfortas's bleeding wound he experiences a frenzied epiphany. He feels the 'burning' blood, it 'pours forth in streams!' And although he is near overwhelmed by 'sinful desires', he is able to pull back and save himself. This kiss is, therefore, of the utmost importance. It is long and sensuous and scored in some detail and there can be no doubt that with it at least one act of penetration has taken place successfully. Furthermore it is at almost the exact and decisive fulcrum of the work. *Parsifal* is balanced, but precariously, upon this kiss. It reconciles a host of opposed thematic and ideological material in what is a highly contradictory work; albeit a work that, paradoxically, seduces one by its powerful, seemingly successful, synthesis. From the kiss – a superficially carnal and a profoundly religious act – Parsifal drinks wisdom. The 'pure fool' becomes knowing. He not only learns what, in a parallel example, Siegfried learnt from Brünnhilde. He does more; he goes beyond the teaching woman. He makes her, or so he seems to think, redundant. He can then leave her rejected and distraught, telling her that she knows where to find him if she wants. And thereby he carries the opera forward to its beneficent, indeed sublime, conclusion.

It seems Wagner so well understood, or was so well aware of, the ambivalences in play with respect to the active/Kundry passive/Parsifal kiss that he was himself somewhat confused on the matter. Whatever the case, he has a hard job being clear. King Ludwig asked him to explain and Wagner replied in the extravagant language that was a feature of the initial years of their correspondence: '"What is the significance of *Kundry's* kiss?" – That, my beloved, is a terrible secret.' But he is clear that it is the point where knowledge and sin intermingle, and he duly evokes Eva in the garden of Eden where the two qualities were first conjoined. And Wagner certainly does not shirk the paradox whereby the kiss that caused Amfortas to sin awakes in Parsifal the antithesis. That is 'a full awareness of that sin' which, nevertheless, then becomes for Parsifal not a cause for a descent into decadence, but the sensual trigger of the epiphany. As we will see, Aschenbach's destiny is the opposite. For him the apple retains, overtly, its sensual quality; he praises 'the taste of knowledge' . . . twice. Although he will discover that Eve's apple – which in the iconography of both Mann's novella and Piper's libretto become strawberries – at first tastes pleasant and then, at the end 'musty.' But Parsifal is, at least for overt propaganda purposes, presented to us as unblemished. He is able to grasp the paradox and to rise above it. He now understands the innermost nature of sin and will soon be able to set off on a narrative that will end up with sin transfigured. In other words, with Amfortas's wound-cum-perverse stigmata healed and closed. In short 'Parzifal [sic] now sees deeper.' And naturally the figure of the 'redeemed' impeccable Christ 'who took upon himself the sins of the world.' is evoked.[54]

A peculiar parallel between Siegfried and Parsifal should be mentioned at this point. That is, while we may see the former as all action throughout his brief killing career, Parsifal evolves and gradually attains the status of the saint who seems – but, as we will see, only seems – to renounce the world. However, there is a direct similarity in their respective encounters with the privileged women. No only does each man confront his destined woman as an ersatz mother (Siegfried is so explicit on the matter that he seems to think Brünnhilde is actually Sieglinde, his natural or biological mother), but both have already learnt in the respective first acts of the two operas that their mother is, in fact, dead. Moreover they have received this information from sources (Mime and Kundry respectively) who were there when the mother died. It is surely a notable achievement on Wagner's part that he can employ this information as part of an aesthetic and narrative construct in such a manner that it enhances the power of the deeper, one might say spiritual as opposed to merely historical, agenda. Which is to say that the meeting with the ersatz mother attains a potency and significance not in spite of the fact that it is, superficially, based on a delusion, but because of it. To use a term Wagner was very familiar with: the deeper reality trumps the biological facts because that reality is purely 'metaphysical.'

Returning to *Parsifal*, we note that in all the other redemption operas but for, self-evidently, the comic *Die Meistersinger* the chosen heroes and heroines are likely to die. It is their natural and proper destiny. In fact it is a birthright. Of course, it is also a death raised to wished-for and ethereal heights. But in this narrow and plain context that is just another way of saying that it is not of this world. And yet at the end of the last opera (officially playing in the mountains of Monsalvat in northern Spain) it is life on this earth that is triumphant, even though the opera is placed on a piece of the planet and among a cast of characters that owe more to myth than they do to either history or geography.

The one character, however, that does not survive is the composite Kundry figure. And her death is of some significance. In the first instance, this is because with respect to the superficial ideology of the opera and its narrative form it is simply *not* necessary. Indeed it might have been, superficially considered, more practical to let her survive with her sexuality intact. After all, we know that the knights are not celibate. Parsifal at some point is to have a son and in any case Amortas's father, Titurel is still alive and singing, albeit offstage, in the first act. This necessary, but unseen sexual element (no nominal woman but the mad messenger Kundry ever appears in what Wagner calls 'The Domain of the Grail'), has naturally caused some comment. For instance Nietzsche, who broke bitterly with Wagner and attacked him remorselessly in *The Case of Wagner*, remarked sarcastically on learning that Parsifal fathered Lohengrin: '*Wie hat er das gemacht*?' (How did he manage that?)[55] A more pertinent question, however, would be to ask who Lohengrin's mother was.

Particularly striking is the radical change Kundry makes following her second act rejection; a change that could be seen as a means to make her sexuality more religiously palatable. In the third act she is shown as a handmaiden who reverentially washes, then anoints, Parsifal's feet, finally drying them with her hair. Thereby she confirms his status as an ersatz Christ and hers as an ersatz Mary Magdalene. Surely if, in this remaking of the Gospel story, the man is able to ascend to the level of the Son of God and yet remain sexually active, the woman can do something similar, even though she might not manage to climb quite so high.

It should, however, be stressed that the new Kundry becomes a good deal more than solely a new Mary Magdalene. She is even bound up, in real rather than purely allusive terms, with Christ himself. In the second act we learn that she was there on the Via Dolorosa as the Saviour made his way to Golgotha. She saw him and, shamelessly, mocked him. It is this that has left her cursed and tormented. Therefore in associating Parsifal, via Amfortas, with Christ and then placing Kundry in the innermost sanctuary of the Christian story while, at the same time, showing her seducing Parsifal in the guise of his (ersatz) mother, one of the most sensational (if conceivably unconscious) attempts to take the incestuous Oedipal drive to its limits has been engineered. Which is to say that Kundry is not just wedded to the Magdalene. She is also wedded to her namesake: Mary the Mother of God. And we should not forget that both these Marys are to be found at the foot of the Cross. Furthermore, it should also be noted that Mary Magdalene's status as a prostitute, though often assumed, is not established by the Gospels at all, and that there are strong religious traditions (the Gnostics, for instance) where she has a key role as one of Jesus's Disciples, indeed as a possible consort. This should also remind us that Wagner, according to his friend Eliza Wille, contemplated a sexual relationship between Christ and Mary Magdalene in his early and incomplete *Jesus of Nazareth* of 1848/49.[56] A work that survives as part poem (probably for an opera) and part essay, it was an early attempt on Wagner's part to colonise religion in the cause of sexual freedom. At that time he was keen to employ a certain cod socialism and to see marriage, naturally when he was unhappy with Minna, as merely an example of bourgeois possessiveness. Free love was clearly the ideal, both morally and sexually. Whatever the special pleading, it is clear that with respect to the standard bible, Mary Magdalene is given a special place in the Gospels. She is not only present at the Crucifixion, she is the first to see the risen Christ. All of these associations are exploited in a highly sophisticated and effective fashion by Wagner who, nevertheless, still summarily dismisses Kundry at the opera's end while letting both his Christ figures – the fallen but now redeemed Amfortas and the new, freshly baptized Christ destined to lead the brotherhood, Parsifal – survive. Why?

In plain language Kundry has been exhausted; so exhausted that at the end she lacks signification. As a stage presence and as an ideological construct it is as if all the meaning, all the goodness, has been squeezed out of her, not least because she has overcome her original split identity. Wagner was clear about this in the so-called *Brown Book* where he talks of the deep cleavage in the composite Kundry's character. She is a profoundly conflicted – in fact nothing less than a divided – soul (*Endlich Zwiespalt* in Kundry's *Seele*).[57] That now being resolved, she is at the end in every sense spent. She has nothing more to contribute to either the brotherhood in general or Parsifal in particular. She has made her dog-like status explicit. Her new impeccable aura (the music during which she washed and anointed Parsifal's feet, and also poured her phial of oil over his head, is ecstatic and ethereal to an astonishing degree) would probably make a sexual role in the future rather awkward. If, after all, the educated man has trouble sexually fulfilling himself with his respectable wife, how much more difficult is it going to be if the lady in question is a stand-in for the Mother of God and/or the consort of Christ?

There is one other woman with whom Kundry is associated, although it is hardly a connection that Wagner's audience would, in general, have been in a position to infer. But Kundry is a soulmate of Cosima. Like her she has become a handmaiden and like her she is the servant of a man who can be placed above all others. As the lady herself, officially giving advice to her daughters, asserted in her *Diaries*, while discernibly protesting too much: 'To wish nothing for one-self, to seek nothing, to give oneself up to *serving* . . . that, my children, is the way to freedom, believe me!'[58] Her blissful but secondary place is secure and Cosima, released from the demands of the bedroom just as Kundry is released from the obligations of the magic garden, did not fail to see her sisterhood with Wagner's fantastic, many-sided and brilliant stage creation. She certainly saw how exceptional a figure within the constellation of the opera Kundry was. As she records – at the end of October 1878 – she and Richard had a little, though rather cryptic, discussion about just this. It is, however, clear that they both understood that the core of knowledge with regard to redemption that is axiomatically possessed by Kundry, and for which the men, above all Amfortas and Parsifal, must struggle, makes her both the centre point and the mover of the drama.

But Cosima also knew that in their shared domestic world of self-delusion she was herself the redeemed Kundry. Of some importance here is what actually happens to Kundry as an active singer in the opera. She becomes silent. In the third act she is allowed a groan and perhaps a scream, for her suffering is still great. But she can only say a single word, once repeated, and that is *dienen . . . dienen* (to serve . . . to serve). There is surely no better expression of Wagner's ability to resolve the role of the woman as both a sexual object and as the fount of love at its highest than the mute Kundry he finally engineers in the last act of *Parsifal*. But in order to do so he must defeat his own sexual agenda and make his own wilful manifestation of the *das Ewig-Weibliche* (Goethe's 'eternal feminine', to whom he refers repeatedly in his writings[59]) an empty creature; all ideology and no substance. For Cosima, however, this would surely have been a welcome telos, the unambiguous triumph of all the values of love that she foregrounded over everything else; over everything she knew to be carnal and base. How happy, then, she must have been when Wagner paid her the great compliment of applying the redeemed Kundry's only utterance to her. In her *Diaries* she records him, on 16 November 1878, acknowledging her and her place in his life with the words: *dienen . . . dienen*. What woman could have wanted more?

The 'real' stage Kundry, meanwhile, can simply be got rid of, though not without doing so in a fashion commensurate with her doggy devotion to the new redeemer. At the last, Wagner instructs that a beam of light fall on Parsifal's head and a dove descend. Gurnemanz and Amfortas are to kneel in homage to him. Whereupon Kundry, 'slowly sinks lifeless to the ground in front of Parsifal, her eyes uplifted to him.' This is a brilliant resolution, flush with higher propaganda. It reconciles all the intellectual and dramatic, overtly antagonistic, elements engendered by love and sex in the Wagner *Weltanschauung*. It gives the artist what he craves while making that which would otherwise seem improper, sacred and blessed. And it is the sort of resolution that is denied Britten. That, however, might be seen by the Britten enthusiast as a state of aesthetic affairs more productive than disadvantageous.

When he was a young man Britten professed an enthusiasm for Richard Strauss. It didn't last. In 1971 he made his disgust at *Der Rosenkavalier* quite clear at a meal at home in the Red House and was dismissive of Graham

Johnson's attempt to defend both the composer and the work. Apparently what Britten didn't like was the work's 'lesbianism.' But this is rather odd, and not simply because one doesn't imagine Britten was any more disapproving of lesbianism than of any other non-violent adult sexual practice, or that he was likely to project onto female same-sex relations the sort of prejudice and repugnance that, as he well knew to his cost, many heterosexuals had always publicly directed at homosexual men. Of more interest is the consideration that there isn't, in fact, any lesbianism in *Rosenkavalier*, any more than there is, let us say, in Mozart's *Marriage of Figaro*, an opera on which *Rosenkavalier* was partly based. And Britten loved Mozart. It is simply that the character of the young male lover in both cases is taken by a soprano or a high mezzo. Octavian and Cherubino are trouser roles. True, there is no actual, explicit, sex scene in *Figaro*, while Octavian and the Marschallin are found, post-coitally, shagged out in bed together at the end of the unmistakably sexually-animated overture to *Rosenkavalier*. But one would have thought that that meagre difference was hardly likely to be the sticking point. Johnson, for instance, later concluded that Britten found 'Strauss's voyeuristic enjoyment' of the (faux) lesbianism repugnant, noting that: 'There is a salaciousness in this music. . .'[60] This may well be true, although one person's salaciousness is another person's good clean fun. And in any case, who can deny that there is an unmissable, near palpable, erotic drive to Cherubino's act one aria *Non so piu*? It concedes little to *Rosenkavalier* in the aesthetic presentation of upfront sexuality.

Even so, Johnson's inference may well be right. The sight of sexual encounters on the stage, taking to some degree a physical form, might have offended Britten's artistic sensibilities, just as the sight of the fat prostitutes in the Paris brothel upset him. In short, one cannot get around what seems self-evident; the physicality of sex posed problems for Britten. I do not mean by this that it posed problems in his private life. Speculation of that sort – of which in the literature there is a great deal – is not pertinent here and, in any case, when all is said and done we are even more ignorant of the state of Britten's marriage with Pears (although we do know that the relationship became carnal, and successfully so, at Grand Rapids in 1939) than we are of Wagner's with Cosima. The problem simply concerns what one might call the aesthetic difficulty that sex posed. One notes that conventional heterosexuality posed no problem for Britten simply because he treats it in a thoroughly conventional manner. It is sweet and safe. It is certainly not lacking, at least on occasions, in either charm or musical effectiveness but it is picture-book in character and is not going to shock either the horses or the children. For instance, but for a kiss it doesn't take us anywhere where the most prim of us wouldn't feel comfortable about going – in public at least. And when there is anything beastly it is by that very fact immediately uncoupled from any notion of true, or 'noble', sex. At best it is like Claggart or Tarquinius or *Phaedra* (the late cantata) and, in his own nasty effeminate way, the Elderly Fop in *Death in Venice*: an aberration, sex gone wrong, human sexuality degraded. Though in Phaedra's case matters, as we might expect in late Britten, are more sophisticated and there is a real sense of empathy for the woman's tragic plight. However, because the division between the noble and the beastly is, understandably, treated as an inherently moral rather than an erotic matter, Britten has no problem applying it to both heterosexual and homosexual characters. In any case, being a sign of a moral failing ill-disciplined passion is easily taken out of the framework of love – a feeling and an ethical category with which, we are presumably supposed to conclude, it has nothing to do – and placed in an entirely different, and negative, category.

All this might lead us to conclude that in general sex in Britten's operas is either violent, whereupon it loses the name of (true) sex, or sweet and amiable, whereupon it is trivialised. Which is also to say that he does not, in this matter, seem to feel any overt fellowship with Donne, a poet whose work otherwise influenced him, and who, for the purposes of seduction, pointed out to his mistress in *The Ecstasy* that everything would be fine 'when we are to bodies gone.' Britten did, however, set nine of Donne's *Holy Sonnets* and in *At the round earth's imagin'd corners blow* the question of going to bodies does crop up. But in this case the bodies to which we are to go are long dead, summoned by the souls, themselves released by the angelic trumpets on the redemptive Day of Judgement. Nonetheless, like the other sonnets in the cycle, there is much tussling in an overheated way with death and sin; with the body and with blood. And this may be a back door whereby Britten can enter into territory otherwise so awkward when physically manifested that he keeps it off the stage. Nor is it insignificant that the cycle was composed very quickly after Britten's brutal, life-changing and predictably unforgettable visit (accompanying the violinist Yehudi Menuhin) to Bergen-Belsen in 1945; a place all too replete with bodies.

From our contemporary standpoint, Britten's attitude to the physicality of sex might seem prudish. The customary response would be to dismiss it glibly as evidence that the composer had, in fact, failed; that he had, for whatever reason, bottled out. We would be inclined to talk – as is implicit in the last two paragraphs – of a problem or a lack. But should it really be seen as such? And were one to adopt such an attitude, would it not then be merely, even chiefly, a question of intellectual arrogance on our part? Furthermore, should we take such a dismissive approach, we might well fail to see the richness and the pay-offs – and the fruitful contradictions – inherent in Britten's compromised engagement with sex. Rather it is better to consider the proposition that in not attempting the passionate stories of Italian opera, or the Wagnerian higher fusion of love and sex, having, in short, no desire to portray Shakespeare's beast with two backs, Britten produces an alternative discourse that, in its own way, accomplishes at least as much as any other.

Before pursuing this I feel obliged to confess a prejudice; a prejudice that is probably the result of being brought up in a society (New Zealand) that has a close but at times antagonistic relationship to what it once called the Motherland. That relationship encourages a hostile attitude to the British class system and is highly sensitive to what it takes to be both the dangerous and the silly attitudes that it generates. I have, for instance, already used the word twee pejoratively in respect of Britten's treatment of conventional heterosexuality and I feel this colours my attitude somewhat. I also think this tweeness is very English. Moreover, it generates an antipode that leads, in the manner Freud anticipated, to very explicit and vulgar jokes. As we have seen, it is exactly such vulgarity – and he knows it is typical of the real world – that Britten is worried will contaminate young Roger Duncan.

This tweeness periodically spoils my enthusiasm for what are, otherwise, major works. Nonetheless, this does not have to be either an alien, or an explicitly working-class, response. There is the brilliant, one must say cruelly brilliant, satire *Little Miss Britten*, when Dudley Moore with pinpoint accuracy mocks the typical Britten folk song arrangement (in this case *Little*

Miss Muffet) as sung by Pear Pears. It can be enjoyed on YouTube. Moreover the great British conductor (chiefly of Wagner but also of early Britten) Reginald Goodall found Britten and Eric Crozier's treatment of the de Maupassant story *Le Rosier de Madame Husson* that became *Albert Herring* 'silly' and thought that all that 'prissy Englishness would have been knocked out of Ben if he had studied abroad.'[61] Certainly if the stage sexual liberation which Albert supposedly accomplishes (along with his ability to free himself from his mother's apron strings) is to be taken as the real thing, then the guardians of prim public morality against whom the work is allegedly directed have nothing to fear whatsoever. What he does in fact confess is trivial and even then he asks Sid and Nancy: 'I didn't lay it on *too* thick, did I?' There is, furthermore, surely a narrow and partial class element to this in as much as there is no sense of any understanding of the *social* mechanisms underpinning psychic oppression. The idea that Albert getting drunk and spending a night on the tiles constitutes genuine liberation is absurd. But, then again, more is, I dare say, not to be expected of a comic opera. Likewise there is a danger that one will make unreasonable criticisms of *The Little Sweep*, the work 'produced' by *Let's Make an Opera*. The title figure, the frail boy Sammy, is charmingly patronised by the agreeable rich children (such little dears) into whose benevolent care he has fallen. Given that these rich kids in their great house were named after the children of the 4th Earl of Cranbrook, Britten's local aristocratic family near Aldeburgh, it is not difficult to see in this the benevolent trickery necessary to Dickensian happy ends. The sweet story, however, is not contaminated by any of the novelist's deep and genuine indignation at social injustice and child labour. In some ways this is odd. Britten admired Dickens greatly.[62]

Remaining in this uncalled for, by the composer, class context one can see that Britten, like Wagner, was a theoretically weak socialist, although, unlike Wagner, his dalliance with left-wing thinking was not born of such overriding selfish needs. Wagner wanted a rationale that would allow him to be a popular radical, but national, poet as well as a man with free hands in all matters sexual. Britten, however, did not use a mixture of cod religiosity and socialism to justify his sexual appetites. Rather, sentimental socialism simply underpinned his profound sense of compassion and directed him yet more surely towards the wilful sufferings of the world. About the reasons for the suffering he was politically naïve, though not stupid. Perhaps the only exception would have to be his arguments for pacifism at the time of the Six Day Arab/Israeli war, to which we will come in the next chapter.

These are not the only examples in Britten oeuvre that are, I think, very unconvincing, and, to someone with a rough sensibility, off-putting. For instance the sea shanty episode in *Billy Budd* when the hero is sweetly chaffed by his crew mates because they assume that the ladies on shore will be making eyes at him, is about as cheesy as tweeness gets. I also rather doubt that it makes much connection with how sailors actually talk – then or now – which, given the trouble the librettists Forster and Crozier took over shipboard verisimilitude, is not an entirely unfair observation. In fact Forster really wasn't at all inclined to this sort of thing. He did, after all, confess in his *Personal Memorandum* of 1935: 'I want to love a strong young man of the lower classes and be loved by him and even hurt by him.'[63] And with respect to the sea shanties in *Billy Budd* he did, bless him, say he wanted something more bawdy.[64]

On the other hand, there is the folk song arrangement of *The Foggy Foggy Dew* when the singer (a weaver) 'hauls' the young woman into bed and 'covers up her head.' She has come to him in the night because, she says, she is frightened of the foggy dew. All this leads to a beautiful son and fond memories. Britten duly received a letter of disapproval. Apparently Peter Pears's uncle was shocked. The BBC meanwhile restricted broadcasts. Likewise, as has already been intimated, the passionate struggle between carnal and spiritual love, between the world of the body and the world beyond death, produces powerful music in the nine *Holy Sonnets of John Donne* (1945); songs that escape every sense of tweeness. Here Britten has to grapple with complex and contradictory sentiments ('Except you enthrall me, never shall be free, Nor ever chaste, except you ravish me' from *Batter my heart, three-person'd God*) and he does so with relish. Furthermore, the *Seven Sonnets of Michaelangelo*, set only a five years before, profit also from a mix of the sacred and the profane, and quite possibly also from the liberating and estranging effect of the Italian language, as the artist complains to God of the torments and cruelties done to him as an artist, and also sings of the beauty of the beloved: male but unnamed in the text. It is in fact Tommaso dei Cavalieri, a nobleman thirty-four years Michaelangelo's junior. In the case of both sets of sonnets the great questions of love and sexuality are raised again to the level of spiritual confrontations, but now with a passion that is rare in Britten.

In respect of passion and sex I wonder if the real problem for Britten starts when he tries to get this sort of stuff on to the stage. It is not simply that the stage does not so easily admit of non-conventional, let us say gay, sexuality in that what is possible in a poem or in music becomes more likely to shock when it takes conspicuous physical shape. Though it is true, as every contemporary radical opera producer knows and exploits, that all sorts of practices that we can contemplate with some equanimity in the abstract can readily become upsetting if we have to watch them. It may also be that Britten's finer sensibilities are simply too easily disturbed and the closer he gets to abstract form and discourse the safer he feels and the freer he becomes. One suspects that it was exactly this that made Harrison Birtwistle's excoriating and violent *Punch and Judy* unpalatable for him (and Pears) when it premièred at Aldeburgh in 1968.[65] As a result, the same point with respect to the sonnets made in the last paragraph might well be made about the dramatic but unstaged cantata *Phaedra.* and *Canticle V.* The latter is a setting of T. S. Eliot's poem *The Death of Saint Narcissus.* Not surprisingly, Narcissus is explicitly associated with Tadzio in Mann's novella.[66] Eliot's poem is strikingly feverish and ambivalent. There is no avoiding its powerful and unstable mix of erotic and spiritual elements, largely because its imagery conflates the Christian bishop Narcissus and the beautiful Greek boy of the same name. Furthermore, the martyred Saint Sebastian, often taken to be a gay icon, is also mixed into the work's imagery. There is much talk of blood and the saint's white body, and the beauty of his movements. 'His flesh was in love with the burning arrows' and he 'became a dancer to God' on the 'hot sand' and so forth. Britten would surely have been struck by the accidental similarity with that other Ganymede, the boy Tadzio who also dances, or plays, on the beach in the Games of Apollo, and destroys – or saves – Aschenbach. It might be noted also that Saint Sebastian is, in passing, mentioned in Mann's novella.[67] But that is at the beginning, before Aschenbach leaves Munich for the south. And though the hero is troubled, the reference to the saint is, like much else in the early pages, placed ostensibly in the context of an unproblematic notion of ideal beauty; an unsullied paradigm that Aschenbach strives to embrace . . . with his pen at least. Things will change. After all, at this stage Aschenbach is confident (explicit in the novel) 'that a man can still be capable of moral resolution even after he has plumbed the depths of knowledge.'[68] At the end he will find himself wholly at sea because he is disabused of exactly this assumption. Britten wrote the *Canticle* in 1974, after completing *Death in Venice* and after his heart operation. Eliot's indiscreet poem, meanwhile, is an early work and he later tried to suppress it. Britten, though, found it 'a beautiful, strange poem.'[69] and when sung in a non-theatrical context its sexually dangerous material, its mix of virtue and vice, of love and lust, can be thoroughly and effectively indulged.

Nonetheless, all these quibbles and exceptions should not lead us to lose sight of the proposition that the difficulties that Britten had in dealing with sexuality as a carnal, physical and theatrical phenomenon are productive of something that can stand, at the very least, in meaning and aesthetic effectiveness alongside Wagner's highly focused and goal-orientated attempt to fuse both title terms of this chapter. And this takes us into the critical Britten territory of innocence; that great moral category that stands in opposition to, but dependent on, a vulgar and brutish world. Which is to say, it takes us into the realm of children in general and boys in particular.

The chief pay-off of this move might be seen, prima facie, as paradoxical. For while there is, axiomatically, a privileged group where the consequences of the loss, or the crippling, of love as a moral force are specific and overt, the end effect is universal. Balstrode says in *Peter Grimes* that 'When horror breaks one heart/ All hearts are broken.' In this Britten is the antipode of Wagner whose agenda is, essentially, dependent on the assertion of the selected couple as the fount, or illustration, or the means, of selective salvation. For Britten, however, the matter is truly ethical in that the parameters are set as broadly as possible. He is addressing a moral force that is applicable to every human animal. And thereby his cosmopolitanism is at this point unconstrained. It is 'religious' in the least sectarian sense and, consequently, it is not to be outbid, any more than Gandhi's non-violence and compassion is to be outbid. Britten had unbounded admiration for Gandhi and the *War Requiem* was inspired in part by his moral example.[70]

As a boy in 1933 Britten was transported by the film of Erich Kästner's story *Emil und die Detektive* (*Emil and the Detectives*): 'the most perfect and satisfying film I have ever seen.'[71] And it makes a reasonable starting point for a discussion designed to justify the big claims made here for Britten's *Weltanschauung*. The story is quite simple. The boy hero, Emil Tischbein, is sent by his impoverished widowed mother to his grandmother in Berlin. He has 150 marks pinned into the lining of his jacket. On the train journey Emil meets a strange fellow who manages to steal his money. When Emil gets off the train, at the wrong station, he sees the thief and attempts to pursue him. In this he is helped by another boy, Gustav, who in turns rounds up a posse of children: the detectives. Eventually the thief is caught trying to change the money at the bank. The children are victorious.

The story, and the film, have a gritty and realistic urban setting but the whole tale is, of course, so fundamentally optimistic, so focused on the happy end (Emil is handsomely rewarded when it turns out the villain was a member of a notorious band of robbers), that it gives pleasure as a form of reassuring wish fulfilment. These streetwise children have all the nous necessary to survive, but they act in the cause of goodness. They are not ripping society off like Dickens's beguiling pickpockets, but putting it to rights. William Golding's *Lord of the Flies* it isn't. No wonder the boy Britten was taken by it. We, meanwhile, should not forget the image of 'the journeying boy' in the train. He will crop up later in 'Midnight on the Great Western', the second song of *Winter Words*, Britten's setting in 1953 of poems by Thomas Hardy. Like Emil, but yet more so, this boy is alone among strangers. He is also bereft: 'past knowing to what he was going, or whence he came.' Unlike Emil he will not soon have the consolation of other boys to reassure, to help, and, in a sense, to create for him a refuge in fellowship. We have no reason to believe that a beneficent future is waiting for him given that he is trapped in 'this region of sin that you find you in, but are not of.' Still, we might note the parallel that the journeying boy in the Hardy poem, while not having money pinned into his jacket, does wear the key to his box on a string around his neck and his ticket is stuck in the band of his hat.

If we move from the image of happy, successful Emil to the forlorn boy of Hardy's poem and then choose, by admittedly arbitrary selection, to continue down the same track we arrive at the most striking dystopian paradigm in Britten's oeuvre, at least as far as boys are concerned:

The Children's Crusade, a choral piece for boys or mixed choir. The first performance was given by the Wandsworth School Boys' Choir in 1969. It is a setting of another German work, in this case a long poem by Bertolt Brecht: *Kinderkreuzzug*. It tells the story of a group of Polish orphans in 1939. They set out to find redemption and safety and, like the most famous of the original children's crusades from 1212, they have a leader. But neither he nor they know which way to go – which is actually not so different from the 1212 catastrophe. In the end all fifty-five of them perish in the snow, as indeed did many of the earlier children as they tried to cross the Alps while believing that they were on the way to Jerusalem. The only survivor in 1939 is a dog and around his neck is neither money, nor a ticket, nor a key, but a pathetic sign that the children have written begging people to come and save them. The dog knows the way.

The Children's Crusade seems to have been unusually important to Britten. The writing is exceptionally hard for the choir, and this from a composer so receptive to children's needs. A great deal of work had to be done to get it ready for performance, but Britten was determined that it should be done, although he later suggested that two conductors would be necessary.[72] Above all, it is a grim piece; a piece from which redemption has been excluded, sluiced out from the moral and aesthetic discourse. I know of no other work in his canon that approaches it in terms of remorseless and unbending bleakness. Only horror, madness and arbitrary misfortune are to be found here. One is reminded of a letter Britten wrote Pears (9 December 1959) when he talks of a 'dream' with children slaughtered and eaten.[73] In this context we might also remember, as Brecht no doubt intended that we should, how the first children's crusade was marked by collective hysteria, and that this was not limited merely to the young people mad enough to be swept away by the prevailing climate of mass religious infantile insanity. Brecht was quite clear that the Nazi period was one in which the German nation, by putting its destiny into the hands of criminals, ended up succumbing to madness. In short, this is the world from which as an artist Britten will try to save us. It is a story fit only for pity. And while that is no small thing, not least because it reminds us of how the *War Requiem* employed pity in order that we might also win salvation and come to know love and reconciliation at the end, the loss of the blameless young in *The Children's Crusade* permits of no saving grace. Love here is wholly absent. In its place is its perverse, arguably sadomasochist, antipode. And that must be resisted at all costs.

It is not surprising if, in this context, the notion of divine intervention to save the endangered child emerges of paramount importance. After all, the consequences of failing in our duty here are profound. As the eleventh song in the late cycle *Who are these Children?* (1969), settings of the Scots poet William Soutar, reminds us: 'The blood of children corrupts the hearts of men . . . And our charity is in the children's faces.' True, the young can lose their lives in Britten. Besides *The Children's Crusade* one thinks of the apprentice in *Peter Grimes*, Miles in *The Turn of the Screw*, and the boy in the folk song *Little Sir William*. Nevertheless the key act will always be some form of redemption, or hope of redemption, so that the child may live. Not surprisingly, Christian iconography and biblical parallels will have a special place. They are self-evidently apposite and useful. While the most instructive example is *Canticle II*, which tells the Abraham and Isaac story from Genesis chapter twenty-two, and to which we will come shortly, it is important to underline the importance of the boy Christ to Britten. One of his first major compositions was the choral work *A Boy was Born*. Later he set, with great success, Christmas Carols celebrating the birth of Christ. There is also the cantata *Rejoice in the Lamb* from 1943, based on the eighteenth-century poems of Christopher Smart, who wrote them while in a lunatic asylum. The work praises all of God's creatures but at its heart is a cry against cruelty and oppression. There is also the late Canticle IV; a setting of T. S. Eliot's *The Journey of the Magi*. And surely when we are confronted by the boy child and the lamb of God, it is hardly surprising if we also think of the last act of divine sacrifice when the blood of the lamb was shed all too copiously on the Cross. Nonetheless, Britten does not turn to that final image as often as he does to the sacrifice and suffering of children. In fact it is Wagner, late in life, who becomes almost obsessed by the image of the crucified adult saviour.

All these iconographic elements constitute a fundamental moral discourse for Britten. It is a *Weltanschauung* so profound that the symbols, which for the average believer must be of unequalled power and personal significance, spring the conventional Christian framework from whence they came. They are, I would suggest, only Christian in their arbitrary iconographic origins and that, therefore, there is a perverse misunderstanding of Britten when, let us say, the Christian message that surfaces at the end of *The Rape of Lucretia* is criticised as alien. It may seem a too extravagant act of special pleading, but I would suggest it is not anachronistic at all. Further, I would point out that we know it was important to Britten because, according to the opera's librettist Ronald Duncan, the epilogue was the composer's idea.[74] The point being that the Christian notion of redemption, because it is universal and timeless in Britten's eyes, simply cannot be extraneous. The lamb as a symbol of love can no more be anachronistic than it can be sectarian.

This is also true of the symbol of the lost boy. Although we are interested here chiefly in Britten's artistic oeuvre, one can't but note how the image of the forlorn boy is central to his thinking and how big a role it plays in his emotional life. In 1932 he is deeply struck by Alfred Stevens's picture *The Dead Boy* at the Tate. It is a very tender, simple image; the boy all innocence. Britten calls it marvellous.[75] Of course one also thinks of all the young teenagers that as an ersatz father he adopted. But they are seldom thought of as lost and, inevitably, they grow up and the relationship ends or changes. But we can get some idea of the importance of the figure of the lost boy from his correspondence when on his far eastern tour in 1956. He records how a boy followed them the whole day in Delhi. They couldn't speak with him, but it is clear that the meeting was strange and significant. Britten mentions, in particular, the last sight of him waving goodbye.[76] Something similar happened with another boy, this time near Mysore.[77]

In the songs and, above all, in the operas this figure is ubiquitous and embodies great moral weight and affective power. Besides the 'Journeying Boy' in *Winter Words* he is there in the Samuel Taylor Coleridge poem 'Encinctured with a twine of leaves' from *The Wanderings of Cain* and set by Britten in his *Nocturne*. There we discover a mysterious 'beauteous boy' who has been beguiled to linger, 'Alone, by night, a little child,/ In place so silent and so wild – / Has he no friend, no loving mother near?' In the operas we might think of the orphaned Billy Budd, whom we meet as a young man 'lost on the infinite sea', or the poor Wingrave boy who, we are told, died in the haunted room generations before Owen sleeps there, or the *Prodigal Son* from Britten's last Church Parable premièred in 1968, or the

Madwoman's redemptive 'lost' son who appears at the end of *Curlew River*, the first Church Parable of four years before. This last example owes, it should be underlined, its English roots and its Christian setting to a heathen Japanese Nō play. In this it is, by implication, making the same universal argument with which *Lucretia* ends. Moreover the climactic redemption of the Madwoman is also paralleled in the second Church Parable *The Burning Fiery Furnace* (1966). There it is a boy angel who appears at the climax and rescues the three Israelites. Stylistically there is also a shared attempt at immediacy with respect to language and place. This is the reason Britten will on occasions forgo the Bible and tell the key scriptural story (Abraham and Isaac, or Noah and the Ark) in the plain, naïve, and native tongue of the Chester Miracle Plays from the late Middle Ages. Even the 'Japanese' *Curlew River* (originally *Sumidagawa*) is transposed to medieval England, and William Plomer's text duly employs a strikingly direct and simple poetic language. He does much the same with the texts for the other two Church Parables. Britten can be said to be searching for a musical and a textual discourse that, no matter how historically placed, asserts a common, unconstrained accessibility. It is the paradoxical but logical alternative to that other, but wholly related, strategy: using Latin. But while Latin also asserts a type of universality in that it is not of itself confined to time or place, it is, textually, a largely inaccessible one.

Nevertheless, by resorting to medieval and early renaissance popular texts a certain intellectual and conceptual simplification is unavoidable. That, however, fits Britten's desire for childlike clarity and underlines the precedence he gives to innocence. On the other hand, the same texts can also reduce, or simplify, matters in another sense. By concentrating on the naked (Christian) story, blood and brutality are starkly foregrounded rather than prettified. For instance, in *A Boy was Born* the massacre of the innocents is hardly likely to be skimped, and in the third song ('Herod') there is much talk of blood and slaying: 'The king slew with pride and sin/ Thousands of two year and within.' Hans Keller was clearly on to something.

Few today doubt that Britten was the greatest setter of the vernacular since his model Purcell. Even so, in this general Christian context I feel the need to confess an unbounded affection for the little Latin mass he wrote in 1959. At the end of the *Missa Brevis*, written for George Malcolm and the boys of Westminster Cathedral Choir, there is an Agnus Dei that in two minutes and by the simplest of means, conjures up in the most powerful and heartfelt manner the lamb of God who might, just, take away the sins of the world and thereby give us peace. It might even free the world for the full expression of love, although the rising pain and the touch of hysteria that is in the music makes it clear that that is, in real terms, surely asking too much.

But it is to *Canticle II*, also based on a Chester Miracle Play, that pride of place must be given. The reason is simple enough. When Britten comes to retell the story in the Offertorium of the pacifist *War Requiem*, he employs Wilfred Owen's poem *The Parable of the Old Man and the Young* to turn the moral universe of the biblical tale upside down. That is, in the *Canticle* the divine act of mercy is carried through to term and God's perverse trial of Abraham ends happily. The father does not cut his son's throat, although, as in the *War Requiem*, the boy is bound. This shared dramatic element – the binding of the boy – is surely central to the story's power and is therefore at the taproot of its unnatural, in every sense, appeal. In the *Canticle* the father tells his son sadly but gently: 'Come hither, my child thou art so sweet, Thou must be bound both hands and feet.' In the *Requiem* it is, appropriately, blunter: 'Then Abraham bound the boy with belts and straps.' The former, however, leaves an unintentional bad taste in the mouth. If overcoming this kind of sadomasochistic trial (which the Bible tells us was one of fear rather than love) is what Christians need to be reassured as to the efficacy and probity of their faith, then they are in a very bad way indeed. Moreover one's discomfort with the piece – and its touching and immediate appeal are undeniable – is not only underlined, but also in some way ameliorated, by both the naïve and simple style of the Chester Play text and the no less simple but artful manner in which Britten sets it. The overall effect is one of ingenuousness, of something childlike and immediate. But this is surely also the means by which the waters are muddied and the unfortunate implications as to the nature of God and, in this case, the nature of divine pity are fudged. In other words, *Canticle II* is also disingenuous.

If the Offertorium in the *Requiem* is disingenuous it is so on a much deeper level. Overtly nothing is fudged and its perverse climax is thrown into the listener's face. It may also be said to be thrown into the face of God.

That He should save Isaac in Holy Writ might be raised, credibly, to some kind of high symbolic sphere where it can be divested of its disturbing implications . . . although such a task is beyond me. But that the young men of Europe should die in their millions, be 'slaughtered like cattle', for what seems no good reason, is going to be harder for the religious apologist to get around. Furthermore, this climax is stamped by a visceral cruelty that threatens to rupture the work, or at least to throw it momentarily off kilter. It needs the Latin text and the boys' ethereal chorus promising eternal life and redemption for the dead souls to get the Offertorium to a decent end and to let the work continue with its overtly religious regalia still in respectable order. But it has been a near run thing and it too, though for quite different reasons from those inferable from the *Canticle*, leaves an unpleasant aftertaste. In this case, however, it is intentional. This is partly and paradoxically due to the fact that the whole thing is, *initially*, biblically impeccable. Furthermore it is more adult in that it dispenses with the childlike language of the Chester Plays. We know at the key moment that God has had his fun and that Abraham has passed his test. The ram is duly presented. In Wilfred Owen's poem this is nicely and sardonically put: 'Offer the Ram of Pride instead of him.' And then there is the ghastly pay-off: 'But the old man would not so, but slew his son – And half the seed of Europe, one by one.' Britten's setting here is ruthless. There is a relish to it. One thinks again of Keller and sadomasochism. Just how much sublimation is involved in pacifism one cannot know, but a pacifist is not by that fact alone a benign person and if he, or his friends, think he is, there will be a great deal of hostility and much poison in the human bile to process before the collective and the self are sufficiently duped as to make their utterances fit for the conventional hypocrisy of either the public world or the private sphere within which the individual safeguards his own egotistic and deluded assumptions. Being morally superior to those around one can be a bit of a burden even if one is, on occasions at least, a meek soul. As we will see, Wagner faces up to his (racist) bile towards the Jews with shameless pride (see chapter three). He is astonishingly self-aware in many things and being blessed with surpassing self-assurance, makes with seeming ease every vice into a deeper, but publicly displayed, virtue. The result is a man who is much too honest – or whose self-delusion is too grandly practised – for the comfort of his morally well-disposed admirers.

Returning to the *War Requiem* we might note that after the human slaughter has been indulged there is an ironic return to the Biblical version. That is, the Angel of the Lord proclaims to Abraham his reward for 'fearing' God. The lord will 'multiply thy seed as the stars of the heaven.' Well, we are in no doubt that the world will need re-populating. And this, too, is intimated in the final chorus of the Offertorium. After which the Sanctus and its attendant pieties can kick off, apparently in good conscience. In general it is a very unsatisfying – and certainly dissatisfying – business, and it is all the more knowingly profound, awful, and moving because of it.

Further tensions surface when we pursue the manner in which Britten employs boys to tackle and elucidate his moral and, by implication, his sexual nature. It is clear that *Death in Venice* must occupy a special place in this discussion (see especially chapter four). Nonetheless the figure of Tadzio does make clear a dichotomy inherent in the use of Britten's privileged moral, aesthetic and sexual symbol. Furthermore it should never be forgotten that in the stage works this figure will, in fact, be more than a symbol. It will also have to fulfil a narrative and dynamic role; a role that helps push the work to its end.

The dichotomy can be best appreciated in respect of two considerations. This first concerns the afterlife or the notion of a dramatic telos. Whereas Wagner's privileged heterosexual couple is wholly focused on the afterlife – albeit one that can, it seems, be corporeally enjoyed – Britten is ambivalent, at the very least, about what, if anything, follows death. Certainly the afterlife is not used in the classic religious sense of being some kind of reward for the sufferings we have endured in this vale of tears. And so while Wagner's heroes and heroines can't wait to get out of the here and now, Britten is crying out for suffering to be ameliorated in the tangible, quotidian world; the world, to quote the Hardy poem about the travelling boy, we 'are in.' As his long time friend Princess Margaret of Hesse and the Rhine said soon after his death: 'Till the last Ben had difficulty in believing in the afterlife – but was a deeply religious man as one feels in his music so often.'[78] And while this applies to orthodox Christian thinking, there is no evidence that he would have bought into a Wagnerian view of what, for the privileged characters, follows physical extinction. But Britten's position is not without aesthetic difficulties. As benevolent solutions on earth are rarely convincing and invariably evoke childlike happy ends that suggest a fairytale view of the world, the dramatic use of the privileged Christian iconography becomes problematic. Of course a naïve and benign *Weltanschauung* usually avoids death like the plague, not least because it is the real inescapable telos of life. But sometimes dramatic necessity makes the power of a final climactic death irresistible. And if it is not the death of the boy then that of the older tormented figure, although he or she (Grimes, Owen Wingrave, Phaedra, Aschenbach) is likely to have less claim on the supreme virtue of unsullied innocence. Nevertheless, it is always striking how potent, and necessary, the privileged boy figure is. In *Curlew River*, for instance, we do not just hear the voice of the dead son, he is allowed a miraculous appearance. This was a matter that Britten seems to have considered carefully, and there can be no doubt that it underlines, theatrically, the redemptive message.[79] The child sings: 'Go your way in peace, mother. The dead shall rise again. . .' and so forth. It is not unlike the consolation served up at the end of the Offertorium. In the Japanese original the mother received no such consolation. The child's spirit disappears forever.

The second consideration concerns what we might call the intellectual and moral nature of the privileged boy, or the boy collective, in the stage works. It is frequently ambiguous. How could this be otherwise? This is because the boy is not merely, or solely, a superficial symbol. As has already been claimed, he is also a mover, a dramatic force, the site where redemption can be, as in the case of *Curlew River*, made narratively effective and visible. He, or they, are not angels. They are not even angels in the religious context. For instance Britten doesn't like the way Alec Robertson in the programme note for the première of the *War Requiem* planned to describe the boys as 'angelic.' Britten feels it 'may bring some unhappy echoes of the end of Walt Disney's soupier films!' He added: 'If you could think of a phrase including the word "innocent" I should be happier.'[80] This is self-evidently of interest in the first instance simply because innocence is the key moral signifier in Britten's vocabulary. But while this approach will do for the *Requiem*, it won't do in general for the stage works. There more is necessary. Above all, the boy has to be knowing. He is not a two-dimensional, immaculate symbol, but an actor intrinsic to the narrative, no matter that he might, in some cases

(Grimes's apprentice and Tadzio), be silent. Miles, for instance, in *The Turn of the Screw* is exceptionally knowing, threateningly so, and can, on occasions, play the Governess and Mrs Grose for fools. This is simply because he has been corrupted already. As a result, the tension between innocence and knowledge is, in his case, extreme and the subsequent struggle over his soul will kill him in as much as it redeems him. It might also be added that the first Miles, David Hemmings, with whom Britten was clearly infatuated to a degree that worried Pears and threatened to cause a scandal,[81] was not only knowing but felt that this made him yet more attractive to Britten.[82]

Tadzio, however, must be the decisive example. He is not just knowing. He is also the site of knowledge deeper than even the educated man of letters Aschenbach has hitherto gleaned. In this the choreographer of the first production, Frederick Ashton, was mistaken in finding the first Tadzio (Robert Hugenin) 'too knowing.' Britten and Pears were very taken with him precisely because he was. Pears was to find the New York Tadzio dull and unalluring by comparison although he was closer to the right age and a better dancer.[83] We should not forget that Aschenbach observes early how self-aware the boy is: 'So you notice when you're noticed.' And then he is later undone when Tadzio smiles at him. As in the novella, we can safely assume it is not a harmless or an empty gesture. As Aschenbach says: 'Don't smile like that . . . No one should be smiled at like that.'

It is exactly this ambivalent quality, inherent in the privileged figure, that unlocks the deeper truth. The boy is not sealed away in the lofty world of the God Apollo. He is also an agent, as Britten's last opera makes explicit, of earthy, pleasure-loving Dionysus. He can make you mad; mad with knowledge and desire for that which is forbidden. And, particularly in chapter four, this is something of which both Thomas Mann and Socrates were also well aware.

At this point it should be admitted that much that has been tackled here with respect to Britten has broken the banks of what we might think of us as strict, or at least clearly contained, definitions of this chapter's two title terms. Certainly the comments on Britten have flooded over into territory a lot more expansive than that covered, up to now, in the discussion of Wagner. It should, therefore, be underlined again that this is the result of Britten having a less focused, a less precisely defined, conceptually driven agenda. True, with Britten sex is highly defined – sometimes to the point of apparent exclusion – not least because it is, in so many ways, threatening and disruptive. But love is free to spread itself; it is an unconstrained signifier and is encouraged to colonise as much moral and aesthetic (and dramatic) territory as it can. One of the consequences of this is that we have spent time looking at Britten in connection with religion. If this seems to some degree a digression, it is one axiomatic to the eclectic nature of Britten's *Weltanschauung*. After all, he said to Murray Perahia: 'I'm not terribly religious in my ordinary life, but when it comes to music I'm a very Christian composer.'[84] However, but for passing remarks, religion can now be, with respect to Britten, postponed to chapter four and we can return to Wagner in the firm hope that love and sex can be more rigorously locked together and placed in a more manageable framework. In taking this step, presumably the first thing we can do is put aside homosexuality for the time being.

Or then again, perhaps not; at least not until we have indulged a relevant digression. It is no doubt dangerous to pursue this matter – not least because it is so arbitrary and speculative – but it is commonly assumed that homosexuals are attracted to the opera in disproportionally large numbers. Apparently in the play *Jeffrey* by Paul Rudnick the title character says that it is not true that all gay men are obsessed with sex (everyone is), but that: 'All gay men are obsessed with opera.'[85] Meanwhile Paul Robinson claims simply, and quite possibly correctly, that 'there really is an affinity between opera and gay men.'[86] Sam Abel, paraphrasing Wayne Koestenbaum, says '. . . gay men flock to the opera in a cult of death, a glorious but ultimately futile gesture of symbolic self-immolation in the face of a hostile society and impossible love.' Abel, a gay writer and opera addict, is comfortable with the special association between homosexuality and opera, but is 'depressed' by all the theorising which concludes that gay opera fans are into a cult of sickness and death, that opera is 'nothing but a sublimation for failed desire.'[87] On the other hand, Alex Ross in the *New Yorker* 12 April 1993, argues that: 'Opera has nothing to do with the lives of most gay men, past or present. Conversely, most opera goers, fanatics included, are not gay in the least. Opera cannot serve as a synonym for homosexuality, because opera-going expresses no essential sexuality, gay or straight.'[88] This is in response to Wayne Koestenbaum's *The Queen's Throat*, an influential and wholly solipsistic book that attempts to appropriate opera exclusively in the gay cause, although to be gay in this context means to be a 'queen', and a very unhappy one at that. I admit that I know of no statistics in the matter and, for all I know, it might turn out that the same positive correlation could be made with respect to gays and football. In any case, I distrust claims of a timeless causal relationship, as though something in the DNA of gay men made them slaves to the opera. I also doubt that the phenomenon will prove itself to be either permanent or immutable. Polymorphous sexuality and changing social and cultural habits will see to that. It is, after all, not unreasonable that the most theatrical manifestations of gay identity should find for themselves a place in the opera house.

On this basis I confess – having recourse to merely anecdotal evidence and empirical experience – that I have always been struck by the apparently large number of gay men, many declaring sartorially their butch identities, at performances of Wagner's music dramas. Certainly, all the evidence is that gay men get at least as much deep and intoxicated satisfaction from the famous rapturous Wagnerian drug or Rausch as any straight opera fan. I suspect, given that the 'real' and final Wagnerian goal is not a gender specific coupling as such but the subsequent transfiguration that exactly that coupling enables, the business has an axiomatic appeal to everyone. Above all, the very language, both textual and musical, takes one into such heady abstractions, that the sexual pathway to the noumenal realm, or to just plain self-indulged bliss as enjoyed temporarily by the punter in the theatre, suddenly seems open in a non-doctrinaire fashion. Fans can believe, if they want, that all are welcome to pass through these aesthetic portals and, should they choose, to perish in the promised ecstasy on the other side.

Unfortunately for the gay agenda, that is not the way Wagner saw it. Personally I well remember several gay Wagnerians taking a critical line with me when, in an earlier book, I underlined the unbending heterosexual nature of the Wagnerian model. It is, however, inescapable and, moreover, it is also, however regrettable, interesting. Indeed a great deal of what Wagner wrote is both regrettable and interesting.

There are two key factors here that need to be addressed at this stage of the argument. The first is Wagner's attempt to get the heterosexual paradigm deep into the most fundamental epistemological and ontological categories; namely to make of heterosexual love the irreducible element of human existence. The second is the problem this creates for his intellectual relationship with his privileged and self-selected mentor: Schopenhauer. There are other relevant questions, not least those connected to the special role of blood and race, the relationship between sex and religion, the anthropological consequences of linking sex and race, and the drive to incest. But all these can, aside from passing observations, be left to the next two chapters. For even the incest question is not solely or even chiefly, at least as Wagner packages it, a sexual one. Rather it, too, is to be explained, or rationalized, in anthropological terms.

In Wagner's worldview a man and a woman are the only begetters; one might say they are the only begetters of everything. However, they are not equally so. In the theoretical essays the female is gradually manoeuvred into a passive role while the male is allowed to colonise, in a near unchallenged fashion, the intellectual territory of the active, heroic 'begetter.' This gender difference is crucial, although like much else in the argument this difference soon becomes foggy as terminology and ideas start to shift around confusingly. One does not know how clear Wagner was in his own mind about this, but in many ways the polemical goal is something approaching a fusion of the male/female binary pair. But this goal remains heterosexual, indeed it celebrates heterosexuality in this world and the next, and it certainly is not to be confused with any hermaphroditic, let alone same-sex, agenda. But in view of Wagner's inability to keep a firm grip on his theorizing, an inability clearest in *Opera and Drama*, one could say the prose attempts unsuccessfully that which the music dramas, above all *Tristan und Isolde*, accomplish triumphantly. Nonetheless, it is clear from the outset that the inevitable foregrounding, under explicitly contained circumstances, of the significance and the role of the woman is hardly going to mean that Wagner isn't sexist. As is already clear, not least from Cosima's *Diaries*, he sets the chauvinist bar as high as it will go. Even so, male chauvinism is not pursued in order to dispense with women as serious movers and shakers (although the Elsa and Kundry examples might suggest that this is often an unconscious *final* wish), but to put them in their place and to make full use of them. Wagner needs women badly and, despite his almost peerless arrogance, he also needs to fold them into both his theoretical and dramatic project. Indeed few megalomaniacal men have ever made as much of women as Wagner. And this is not only a theoretical question; a question of their conceptual importance and the explanatory uses to which they can be put, important though that is. More than this, the woman, no less than the boy in Britten, is a *theatrical* unit and has a special place in the struggle of the artist to realise a profound agenda in such a way that narrative and didactic demands are reconciled.

As we have already in part seen with Kundry, Wagner resolves these difficulties with brilliance. This is partly because the knowledge embedded in the woman is dynamic in form and function; it not only explains but directs future action. Furthermore, it also belongs in a greater story; the story of the Volk (see discussion in chapter three). But there, too, the woman's knowledge is indispensable and when she imparts it to the man she sets him off on his destined but heroic path. While it is a path that may save, in the particular case, a brotherhood of knightly monks, in the general context it is intended to redeem collectively the German Volk. Nor is this the end of the matter. Knowledge is such a key notion that the woman can only be thrown aside (as with Elsa who is ignorant and Kundry who is wise) after as much as possible has been made of/from her. Which is also to say that she is likely to continue to be a dramatic force long after she has done her initial sexual duty with the boy/man – a duty Elsa, always an exception, is not required to fulfil. There is also another significant exception: Elisabeth in *Tannhäuser* (see chapter five). Nonetheless, the true Wagner heroine will be there at the end where she is likely to find herself in the hero's metaphorical arms as both enjoy the fulfilment of mutual and transfiguring death. In other words, she is doubly productive. She remains, despite Wagner's gender bias, the key begetter of the higher ideology that transcends the phenomenal world and thereby the stage. But she is also a critically dynamic force that steers and animates the narrative that is played out on the boards. She is exceptionally useful.

Even poor Wotan is forced to turn to the female knowledge source (the Goddess Erda) when he gets into a pickle and needs advice. And yet Wotan is the most authoritative, knowing, albeit debilitated, male hero Wagner creates. Erda, however, is largely passive and appears twice (once in *Das Rheingold* and once in *Siegfried*), and she is overtly marginalised on the playing area in order to make it clear that, aside from counselling, she is not going to do anything. She is supposed to emerge at the side or from out of a cave and she is shrouded in mysterious green or blue light. In *Das Rheingold* only her upper body is visible . . . at least in Wagner's stage instructions. In short, she is all knowledge and no action. Others, however, will act and thereby hold their place in the spotlight. Brünnhilde, who takes both the conceptual and the narrative reins of *The Ring* in her hands, is the most triumphant example. As she says at the apotheosis of the cycle, she now knows all things. In fact she makes the claim repeatedly and the musical setting is appropriately dark and solemn. She then instigates the final, cleansing conflagration. This, in turn, is swept from the boards by the Rhine in full flood and the tetralogy is done with.

One can readily see that this precedence accorded the female by the chauvinist male artist is, in part, the necessary product of Wagner's penchant for naïve, even ignorant, heroes. True, they are not lacking in desire for combat, but they often need careful instruction in all the other arts and facts of life. Like Wagner perhaps, they will initially discover their deepest being in the privileged heterosexual encounter, and like Parsifal they will also imbibe profound wisdom in the process. For the transfiguration Wagner talks of in his sensual relationship with Minna amounts to more than just corporeal satisfaction. Moreover, by underlining the knowledge factor the stage encounter is not only enriched; the story is also propelled. With a lesser, and possibly a less contradictory, artist who was only interested in sex qua sex the matter would be easily short-changed and the man would go off in search of 'fresh deeds' leaving the wife behind as if she were 'her indoors.' And indeed this is what Siegfried at the end of the Prologue to *Götterdämmerung* does. But the narrative is compelled to return to Brünnhilde in her rocky cave. As Siegfried is soon drugged into ignorance and forgetfulness – the former being in many ways his natural state when outside the forest world into which he was born – it is Brünnhilde who must once again shoulder the burden of the story. This is not merely a narrative duty, important though that is. Even more decisive is the plain fact that only Brünnhilde can make the narrative's deeper meaning clear. In this, however, she is the most striking example – indeed paradigmatic example – of something that is fundamental to the classic Wagner drama.

At this point we have to address the largest and, for Wagner, the most significant of his attempts to get a theoretical handle on all of this: *Opera and Drama*. This is not always a beautiful experience as both the original and the standard Ellis translation are a slog. Of course one can in general dismiss Wagner's theoretical and polemical work – many devoted Wagnerians do, especially with respect to the nasty racist theorising – but to do so is to flunk the task of taking him seriously. After all, excluding the letters and the two volume autobiography *My Life*, but including the librettos, his writings occupy thirteen volumes of the Breitkopf & Härtel 'Complete' Edition (Leipzig 1911). Certainly indifference on this matter would have enraged Wagner. Writing to Minna on 16 April 1850 he laments: '. . . you detested my writings, in spite of the fact that I tried to make clear to you that they were now more necessary to me than all my useless attempts to write operas.' What, then, can he make of the binary pair of love and sex so that they explain everything that he requires of them? His entry point, as the title suggests, is a discussion of an aesthetic problem, although *Opera and Drama* will go a good deal further than that.

'Music is woman' says Wagner. More than this, music is 'the bearing woman.' The poet (librettist), meanwhile, is 'the begetter'; the dramatic side of the equation. It is an equation that is, at first, presented in simple, self-evident, and discrete terms. Woman is also, and intrinsically, 'love'; but a 'receiving . . . unreservedly surrendering love.' Thereafter the aesthetic marriage between the male begetter and the receptive woman is portrayed unremittingly by Wagner in sexual terms. Consequently, when the female embodiment of music duly and ecstatically accepts the male poet an act of 'fertilisation' between opera (as music) and drama (as text) takes place. Appropriately, given Wagner's greater agenda, when conception (*Empfängnis*) occurs it does so among a dense nexus of concepts and language that makes it hard to disentangle the biological, the cultural and the spiritual from each other . . . perhaps it is improper to try. A woman, for instance, is 'soulless' until 'she receives her soul through the love of a man.'[89] This also seems to result in her attaining her own 'Will', although as we will see, Wagner muddies the waters here somewhat. In passing we should also note that while the act of womanly sacrifice to the male must be embraced, and joyfully, Wagner seems compelled to add a dash of what, we might assume, is everyday reality. That is, while the woman must, when all is said and done, surrender completely if she is to be true to her deepest intrinsic nature ('the true woman loves unconditionally, because she must'[90]), she is allowed to put up an initial fight. This is only appropriate if she feels a pride in her own 'Will,' a word Wagner is using as a philosophical term before he read Schopenhauer. Put simply, the mysteriously knowing woman also knows her own worth and if, like Brünnhilde, she refuses the man at first, she is merely and not entirely inappropriately asserting that right. At the end she will, thankfully, succumb, although she might not, like Brünnhilde, end up in a roaring duet with the hero. It is hardly inapposite that this extended, feverish vocal set-to, demanding at the end a fearsomely high tessitura from both singers, celebrates the radiant joys of love and, more importantly, death: that ultimate and unsurpassable dramatic and spiritual goal.

If this seems a somewhat too straightforward account, we should also note that Wagner wants to create a proper dialectical synthesis of opposites. The woman's pride and her humility fuse in order to engender her 'prideful surrender.' Moreover if she realises this, she will also realise that she has no need of any act of deliberate self-assertion. She 'only needs *to be entirely what she is*, but in no way *to will* something.' Rather she is to 'conceive.'[91] In this way Wagner plays fast and loose with his own terminology; a problem that, after the opening pages, runs throughout *Opera and Drama.* In any case, what we have now is the, at the very least messy, idea that the act of surrender confers upon the woman her deepest ontological nature (she acquires soul and will) while raising her to the point where, paradoxically, she no longer has need of the 'Will.' Nonetheless, irrespective of the shifting terminology and all the elaborate attempts to create credible Hegelian fusions which explain everything in whatever way the author wants, it is not to be overlooked that *Opera and Drama* is pushing an elaborately and contradictorily worked-out agenda that, when all is said and done, is designed to rationalize the unlimited masculine freedom of action that Wagner needs. In this it is a pagan version of *Parsifal*. For whereas *Parsifal* colonises religious authority to turn sin into a sacrament, *Opera and Drama* uses, initially, a good deal of arbitrary philosophical twaddle to turn the violation of conventional sexual mores into acts of social and creative righteousness. It is, however, striking that in the actual music dramas the woman (whether Brünnhilde explicitly or Kundry implicitly) turns out to be a far less constrained and a far more active and determining figure than the theory, in its most upfront book form, would allow.

There is a further, narratively important, element to the package. When the woman acquires her 'soul' courtesy of her 'prideful surrender' to the hero, she is also redeemed. This is a crucial step as the redeemed woman will turn out to be the principal agent in the subsequent redemption of the male. It is as if the hero compels the woman to 'conceive' in the fundamental ontological fashion Wagner has in mind in order that he may later be saved by her, courtesy of a final act of sacrifice on her part. One might think, although it would horrify Wagner, of an insect that fertilises its mate in order that it might prove a more succulent (albeit spiritual) repast after he has killed her. However tasteless, at least in ethical terms, that simile may be, it is clear that Senta, Brünnhilde, arguably Elisabeth in *Tannhäuser* and Sieglinde in *Die Walküre*, certainly Kundry, all perform the final benediction. Isolde might be included too, not least because her opera in particular fits Wagner's later wilful rewriting of Schopenhauer. But here the fertilisation is mutual and, moreover, mutually nourishing. The two identities are dissolved into each other so that an exceptional, indeed an absolute, level of equality is engendered, one that, paradoxically, transcends male and female Wills and souls and gender difference and all the rest. And this, ironically, is the work most publicly celebrated for its unmissable heterosexual ecstasy. Nevertheless, Tristan and Isolde are, ideologically, one person; a state of affairs that they refer to on more than one occasion.

More than this, it is not to be overlooked that *Tristan und Isolde*, begun about five years after work on *Opera and Drama* (1851) was finished (the essay was written at speed), has, as would only be appropriate, taken a great deal of the essay's philosophical theorising as far as it will go. At least that is the case if we limit ourselves to the all-knowing and all-loving (hetero) sexual couple. And while alongside the glories of the music drama the intellectual labours of the essay may seem confused and improvised, one can also see in them the seeds of the stage work. For instance, faced with the problem of his initial and crudely defined binary pairings – woman/man, music/drama – Wagner is forced, once again, to fudge matters to get it all to work for him as propaganda. One notes, for instance, that the male poet must recover 'feeling', which is to say the privileged feminine element that he loses by becoming one-sidedly rational and didactic. Men, as we all know, are natural thinkers, liking nothing more than a deep cogitation in a brown study and a good chin wag down at the pub. Unfortunately, as a result drama is limited. It can only be explained, come into its own, when it is completely vindicated by feeling; and this is the dramatic poet's task, namely, 'not to invent actions, but to make an action so intelligible through its emotional Necessity.'[92] It is therefore vital to return to the womanly element so that the act of 'fecundation' can take place again.[93] In explaining this, Wagner's terminology takes us back to the essentialist notions of Goethe-based German idealism. It is to the 'eternally womanly' and that 'ur-melody' with which she is associated that Word and Poet must return so that the 'manly Understanding' can be drawn 'out of its egoism.' Wishy-washy this may be, but at least we can sense that a mysterious synthesis has taken place and all polarities have consequently been sublimely subsumed into each other. Above all, we note that it has only been possible because of the attraction of the feminine. 'This attraction is the effect of the eternal feminine. It draws egotistical male reason out of itself. And this is only possible in that the feminine excites in him that which is kindred to herself. Furthermore, it is by virtue of the kinship between reason and feeling that the purely human and the human species are created. The male and the female duly nourish themselves from the purely human and only by that is the human being created through love.'[94] And surely this is as fundamental a point as he can possibly reach, bearing in mind both the cryptic original and the yet more tangled Ellis version. The above translation is my own and must to some extent simplify Ellis, and quite possibly Wagner. They are both given in the endnote. We will see later what Wagner's synthesis might mean for the species.

The agenda of *Opera and Drama* does indeed take Wagner into the field of anthropology and the history of the Volk, and this means he will have to tackle religion again. He strides, however, into all these areas seemingly convinced that his basic concepts will allow him to cover the additional ground successfully while remaining intellectually stringent. While the arguments for accepting this are flimsy, the effort put into it is striking (see chapter three). Above all, the determination to pursue the matter to the point where incest is also liberated from taboo is, if nothing else, a measure of the great man's courage. Still, it is not to be expected that a unique and radical artist will flinch or bottle out when the task before him seems insurmountable; and especially not when he is struggling in the cause of personal vanity or self-interest.

More or less everything that has been said in the last few paragraphs can be given an *ex post facto* Schopenhauerian gloss. It was in 1854, just two years after finishing *Opera and Drama*, that Wagner was introduced by his fellow political exile in Zurich, Georg Herwegh, to Schopenhauer and he read *The World as Will and Representation* for the first time, whereupon he 'discovered' that he was a Schopenhaurian *avant la lettre*. He was to re-read the book many times and he never lost his allegiance. Nonetheless, the intellectual relationship – he didn't have the courage to go and see the philosopher personally – is not unproblematic. The problems are particularly clear when we consider sex.

In the first instance Schopenhauer takes a very emancipated view of sex. He is not prudish which suits Wagner; but he is not romantic either, which doesn't. He basically sees sex as a natural, animalistic and evolutionary thing. He links it to the great elemental driving force of life itself: the Will. This is, to take but one definition he throws out, 'a blind irresistible urge.'[95] He also says bluntly that 'the genitals are subject merely to the will, and not at all to knowledge,'[96] and 'in all sexual love, instinct holds the reins.'[97] He is, for instance, quite tolerant of homosexuality. In the Appendix, suppressed in the first English translation, to the section titled 'The Metaphysics of Sexual Love' he takes a matter of fact line on 'pederasty.' He is rather horrified by it personally – or so he says – but he believes that it is the product of nature finding a solution to a social and a species problem. He explains that it gives older men a sexual outlet while preventing them from reproducing. This is particularly clever of nature as, given the condition they are in, old men would father feeble offspring. Pederasty might also have other, perfectly reasonable, causes. Demography, for instance, in that there are societies with a shortage of women. Schopenhauer offers California as an illustration, presumably because of all those adventurers and gold miners.

As Schopenhauer is invariably celebrated by his admirers as a forerunner of evolutionary biology one should really acknowledge that the claim, while not strictly relevant for the argument here, is a bit of a stretch. His position was wholly Lamarckian. As the above example concerning the possible progeny of old men suggests, he believed that acquired characteristics could be inherited. This leads him to one of his most entertaining, yet quite possibly serious, observations. He lived in the Rhineland and was understandably curious, as no doubt were many of his neighbours, as to why southern Germans were so dull. The reason is delightful. It is because the women carry loads on their heads. This diminishes and damages the brain and, given that the male inherits his brain from his mother – as we all presumably know – the whole race turns stupid as a result.[98] Darwin this isn't. But it is quite possible that the great philosopher is not pulling our legs. At least I like to think so.

There is a further example of Schopenhauer's unromantic attitude to sex that is of some importance. In another passage from 'The Metaphysics of Sexual Love' he seems somewhat bemused by the folly of young lovers. He is in no doubt as to how powerful (instinctual) sexual love can be, how, in certain circumstances, it can overcome 'with incredible force' all obstacles 'so that for its satisfaction life is risked.' Indeed, 'when that satisfaction is denied, life is given as the price.'[99] And this leads him to a few observations on lovers and suicide. These Wagner found particularly intriguing, largely because they illustrated the difficulty, or the limitations, of Schopenhauer's general theory for the true Wagnerian. The philosopher argues that death by mutual suicide is self-evidently senseless as it denies the lovers the very thing they mean to enjoy. But this for Schopenhauer remains purely a matter for the instincts and personal gratification. We should note that he is talking about the 'common suicide of two lovers thwarted by external circumstances.' He is, in fact, asking in a rather puzzled manner whether it wouldn't be more sensible for such people to 'endure every discomfort rather than give up with their lives a happiness that for them is greater than any other they can conceive.'[100] In plain language he wants to know why they don't just indulge their libidos and take the consequences. It could hardly be any worse than resorting to lovers' leap. Wagner, when working on *Tristan und Isolde*, which clearly exists in opposition to such a baffled, even dismissive, view of wilfully chosen mutual death, took just this passage as an inducement to write to the philosopher.

One can readily see why this was so important to him. Wagner has to get sexuality onto the highest plane; it has to be for him the royal road to transcendence. But for Schopenhauer sexuality is merely a matter of species perpetuation and the exercise of the Will in its least conscious, reflective, or knowing form. And it is this that constitutes the critical bind in which Wagner was trapped. For Schopenhauer, transcendence or, to use the term he favoured, renunciation is something the exceptional individual attains by renouncing the vulgar vanities of the empirical hands-on world. The archetypal figures are the Buddha, St Francis of Assisi, Christ, and one notes immediately that they embody the type of love that Britten finds highly conducive. If Schopenhauer had known of Gandhi he would have included him too. These saintly paradigms earn their crowns in the noumenal realm because they rise above the ego. And they certainly rise above the instincts.

Unfortunately for Wagner and Wagnerians, Schopenhauer doesn't preserve the notion of the individual in the noumenal realm. It seems he is keen, as he sees it, to outbid other philosophies and to make it quite clear that the consciousness of the individual dies with him.[101] For 'death is the great opportunity no longer to be "I" '[102] Just what the noumenal means for him is therefore not always clear . . . at least to me. It is notable, for instance, that he initially plays with the notion of the 'transmigration of souls' in volume one of *The World as Will and Representation* and then in volume two he asserts it as a fact.[103] There is, however, one thing that we do know saints and mystics accomplish and it – above all – makes them fit for the higher realm. They transcend the miseries of individuation (the *principium individuationis*): that misguided celebration of, or obsession with, the self when placed in antagonistic opposition to others. This is the major source of so much of our suffering on earth. It is arguably the chief and most severe burden the human being must carry and it does untold psychic damage. Indeed, it is difficult to overstate the miserable status of the individual in Schopenhauer's *Weltanschauung*. 'He' must be overcome, dispensed with, if the will-less state is to be reached. Furthermore, once that is accomplished the true metaphysical union between the greater and deeper will (the will-in-itself) and the Kantian thing-in-itself can be sensed and enjoyed. And this means one must free oneself from egotism, sexual desire and the body.[104] This confluence between will-less-ness, or the will-less state (clearly a paradoxical formulation), together with the Kantian thing-in-itself will be looked at shortly, when it will be necessary to throw Plato into the pot. What needs to be acknowledged immediately however, is how the route Schopenhauer has marked out on the basis of the horrors of individuation and the merciful loss of the self in death is about as a-Wagnerian as one can imagine.

Wagner, after all, is the poet of the hero and the heroine, a celebrant of the ego, of the 'I', and as a dramatist 'individuation' and struggle is perforce the bread and salt of his aesthetic language and labours. Furthermore, his privileged figures enter the noumenal world in heterosexual pairs and they get there courtesy of heterosexual pairing; theirs is, initially, a hands-on world and they most assuredly 'to bodies go.' But it is in exactly this matter that Schopenhauer is unbending. Death is an absolute end for the 'I.' One suspects this is the case because it allows for the transmigration of souls. However, whatever the status of the latter: 'Death is a sleep in which individuality is forgotten', everything else 'awakens again, or rather has remained awake.'[105] And should we have doubts about this, he is keen, as he sees it, to outbid other philosophers on just this point. He emphasises that the individual is doomed. In the long story of succeeding generations 'he' is simply not worth bothering with. There is, in short, no Schopenhauerian chance of Wagner's heroes and heroines enjoying the kind of destiny the composer intends for them. Clearly, it is no accident that all this became particularly pertinent to Wagner, vis-à-vis the obvious shortcomings of the otherwise devotedly admired Schopenhauer, when he was working on *Tristan und Isolde.* Indeed nothing less than the 'extraordinary' – albeit 'gradual' – effect of *The World as Will and Representation* guided Wagner back to composition.[106] Nonetheless, it is striking how ready he is to recognise the depth of the ideological gulf separating him from the philosopher. On 1 December 1858 he had written to Mathilde Wesendonck that he had been accorded an insight, or 'insights', that have been 'reserved' for him alone; insights 'of a kind that could never have disclosed themselves to anyone else.' The key issue is: '. . . pointing out the path to salvation, which has not been recognised by any philosopher, and especially not by Sch., [Schopenhauer] but which involves a total pacification of the will through love, but not through any abstract love, but a love engendered on the basis of sexual love, i.e. the attraction between man and woman . . . The presentation of this argument will take me very deep and very far . . .' In some ways this is not new. Ten months before he read Schopenhauer, but some time after he had been told about him, Wagner wrote with near palpable enthusiasm to August Röckel on the subject of heterosexual love. He declared that '. . . all other forms of love are mere derivatives of it, originating in it, related to it or in an unnatural imitation of it. It is wrong to regard this love as only one manifestation of love in general, and to assume that other and higher forms must therefore exist alongside it.'[107] This was not something he could forgo on discovering the philosopher who was otherwise self-evidently his anointed mentor.

The actual letter to Schopenhauer is dated only 1858.[108] As already intimated it takes as its text Schopenhauer's observations on love and suicide. It seems that Wagner's reply, going by the three paragraphs he wrote, would have been a radical assault. It is hard to see how it could have been otherwise. Firstly, he politely acknowledges Schopenhauer's admission that he has not found the answer to the phenomenon of lovers giving up their lives, although he rather delicately puts the matter in the conditional (*gefunden hätten*), thereby leaving open the rather absurd possibility that Schopenhauer might in the meantime have, as it were, stumbled on the truth. He then goes on to point out just what that truth is, namely that he has discovered in the very disposition of sexual love a path of salvation that leads to 'self-knowledge' and 'self-denial of the will – and not only of the individual will.' We can infer from this that Wagner is well aware of how far he has to go. In fact the use of the term 'self-denial' here is extremely interesting and astute. It is also, depending on your intellectual disposition, either very dialectical or very hypocritical. For denial (or renunciation) in both the common and Schopenhauerian sense, is extremely relevant to the agenda of *Tristan und Isolde*. It is manifested in the character of King Marke who, on marrying the wondrous woman Isolde, does not lay a hand on her. However, this act of denial, while noble, is not of the deepest sort; that is, it is not of the sort celebrated in the scheme Wagner is foregrounding. There the privileged goal of 'self-denial' is attained by exactly those means that King Marke has forgone: sexual love. Thus it is that Schopenhauer's principle ('honour is driven from the field, as soon as sexual love comes into play. . .'[109]) is gainsaid utterly. In short, Wagner has to put the double, but mutually dissolved, will of the heterosexual couple in place of the individual ego and then claim that this Will engenders the required transcendence or renunciation. Which is also to say that it raises itself above the instincts and the ego (individuation).

And that means it has climbed to the highest Schopenhauerian state: will-less-ness.

At this point, if we are to grasp what Wagner is actually tackling, it is necessary that I acknowledge – or perhaps confess – to finding a slippery quality in Schopenhauer's terms. While this is not so extreme a phenomenon as it is with Wagner's terminology, it can lead to difficulties. Of course these difficulties may simply be the product of my own analytical shortcomings; above all my failure to appreciate fully what wonderful things dialectical thinking can engender. Whatever the case, the problem concerns – what else – the Will. Certainly the Will is the fundamental – indeed the most fundamental – category in *The World as Will and Representation (Die Welt als Wille und Vorstellung)*. But we should also look at the second term in the book's title. *Vorstellung* was initially translated as 'Idea', which was unfortunate. Idea suggests the Platonic category where reality, at its deepest (or highest) and truest, is to be found. We, however, only perceive it, to use Plato's famous analogy, when the empirical world appears as shadows reflected onto the cave wall. Consequently we let the shadowy appearance of the outside world deflect us from thinking our way through to an understanding of the abstractions, the Ideas, that inform the world. It is, however, only by thinking our way through to an appreciation of the deeper/higher Idealist reality that we can come to understand the world properly. To accomplish this means of itself a quantum leap in ontological terms. We will grasp what Being really is, partly because we will have overcome the false perceptions through which the world is otherwise mediated. Which is to say we will have freed ourselves from vulgar empiricism and the tyranny of our senses; those seemingly authoritative instruments that in fact hide and/or distort the Platonic ideas. Schopenhauer was, of course, very well aware of, and influenced by, Plato's notions. Therefore it should be clear that *Vorstellung* (properly translated as appearance or representation) misleads us in much the same manner as the shadows in Plato's cave misled the naïve observers he had in mind. As a result Will and not *Vorstellung* is the deep, truly meaningful, ontological category and must to some extent evoke – at the very least – the Platonic Ideas. Just how this comes about will be touched on in a moment.

But before we can do that, it is necessary to appreciate how nebulous the term Will can be in Schopenhauer's masterpiece. In the first instance we experience it in the egotistical manner already noted. Its most obvious form is the 'will to live' which is, as we have also noted, expressed in the sexual drive/instinct. Schopenhauer is quite clear about this: 'I have called the genitals the focus of the will.'[110] This might seem straightforward. A key qualitative shift, however, occurs when we appreciate that this 'will' can be overcome. The saint, for instance, renounces life and all its base and replete miseries. And he is chaste. Therefore, we can conclude that it is, in fact, possible to 'deny the egotistical aspect of our own being.' Furthermore, if we manage this 'there ultimately arises . . . what I call the denial of the will to live.'[111] If this is accomplished one will have risen to the wholly admirable state 'of voluntary renunciation . . . and perfect will-less-ness.'[112] And thereby the fundamental category of Schopenhauerian thought has been, by what one must assume to be impeccable Schopenhauerian means, dialectically trumped.

Yet this apparent contradiction is not the end of the matter. For while the qualitative shift denies the will, it only does so when we have in mind the will in its base, instinctual, and egotistical form. The apparent contradiction is then resolved when we realise that there is also a 'will-in-itself.' And this is the case despite the axiom that the will is 'indivisable'; that it is always the same will no matter how great the scope of its 'objectifications' may be.[113] This apparent, deeper contradiction is just something that we shall have to live with. It does not matter here. What does matter is the assumption that there is a deeper, vastly more meaningful – indeed absolute – category that not only corresponds to the Platonic Ideas, but also, as the terminology signals, to the Kantian thing-in-itself. And this intellectual confluence duly directs us to the deepest level of being; one that can never be properly known solely by the senses. For instance, Kant's thing-in-itself exists in opposition to the misleading 'phenomenological' world and, instead, leads us to consider the 'noumenal' realm. In other words Schopenhauer has adopted Kant's terminology, although he redefines it somewhat. Nevertheless, in coupling with these notions the Schopenhauerian Will preserves its paramount intellectual and explanatory status in all matters to do with ontology or being. Moreover Schopenhauer, while acknowledging that the three terms (Plato's Ideas, Kant's thing-in-itself, and his own will-in-itself) are not identical, is keen to draw our attention to their kinship. Above all, the triad should make clear to us how shallow and untrustworthy our everyday sense perceptions are.[114]

Wagner, however, does not begin with the will-in-itself as the higher form and then reveal how the miserable and benighted individual experiences it on an immeasurably lower and crippled level, courtesy of his own base instincts. Rather, he takes those base instincts and shows, or claims to be able to show, how in the context of the heterosexual couple they can themselves become transcendental. Thus he raises the individual (or the unit made up of the two loving individuals) to the point of self-denial and otherworldly knowledge, to say nothing of allowing him and her the enjoyment of sensual bliss. Which is also to say that he marginalises the ideal of the unworldly and chaste saint just as he pushes King Marke to the edge of the stage in *Tristan und Isolde*. The lovers must be the paramount site of not only physical bliss but also of philosophical understanding.

Using categories that are contingent and secondary in Schopenhauer because they postdate the will, Wagner claims that the *intellect* (and with it *perception*) must no longer 'be divorced from the will;' rather the 'intensification of the individual intellect' through the sexual experience will be such that it is raised to the level of the will 'which is the thing-in-itself.'[115] Presumably this means he feels – or would have felt if he had finished the letter – that he has got his own notion of redemption via sexuality into the heart of the Schopenhauerian system. It sits there like an alien egg in the warm and friendly nest. Whereupon Wagner would have succeeded in successfully colonising the holy grail of Schopenhaurian philosophy by a-Schopenhaurian means.

Strictly speaking the letter does not, except by strong implication, go as far as I have gone. Yet when taken in conjunction with the letter to Mathilde Wesendonck of 1 December 1858, Wagner's intentions are clear enough. In any case, he gave up after three paragraphs and the attempt was aborted. Nothing was sent at this time to the Sage of Frankfurt. Earlier he had in fact sent him a copy of *The Ring* librettos without a covering letter, merely the words 'with reverence and gratitude.' He got no reply. Schopenhauer had not been impressed. Of course it is possible that Wagner did not pursue the matter because he was in awe of the only living man he seems to have acknowledged as his master. I suspect, however, that he threw in the towel because he saw that such a fundamental challenge just wasn't going to wash. He would simply have to live with the insurmountable difference between him and Schopenhauer. What he would not do, however, is ditch the philosopher or forgo the regular instruction to be got from religiously rereading *The World as Will and Representation.* This is, for instance, particularly clear, in his last essays on *Religion and Art* (see chapter four).

Before finishing this chapter by examining, in the context of the love and sex binary pairing, two rather discursive incidents with respect to both Wagner and Britten, I wish to mention briefly a more theoretical consideration relevant to the same theme. I will limit my remarks to these the two composers, but the observations are relevant to biographical writing in general. They have been marginalised, or hitherto ignored, in this book principally because it is not a biography of either man.

The issue at stake might be called – and has, in fact, been called – 'the sexual fix.' The critic, or analyst, is inclined to look to sex as not only the source of deep meanings – a Freudian assumption with which this essay is wholly at home – but also as a site that will, when excavated, bring forth a revelation, and a sensational revelation at that. This is also, in part, a Freudian strategy in that analysis is supposed to reveal a profound hidden or denied truth. The analyst does not, on principle, believe the analysand. The latter has to be, consciously or otherwise, dissembling, otherwise what on earth would be the point of analysis in the first place. I have, however, not taken full advantage of this strategy as I suspect that it has in recent years become a rather glib gesture; although it is commercially attractive to publishers. Nonetheless, it needs to be acknowledged.

Of course once upon a time the sexual revelation with respect to Britten would have been easily unearthed: his homosexuality. But while his homosexuality might not have been acknowledged publicly, it was so self evident that it hardly required an interpretative strategy let alone a spot of Freudian digging. Nonetheless, it could be used as a code that would unlock the deeper mystery and meaning of the compositions. That strategy, simply because it was so obvious, was hardly likely to last long as an interpretative coup and would duly have to be trumped by something else. Humphrey Carpenter's book replaced it with paedophilia and the cultivation of friendships with teenage boys; something which pushed the once taboo Britten/

Pears relationship onto the margins. That the relationships with youths are important and meaningful is not, as I have made clear, doubted. The matter, in this context, is merely how far they can go in helping us to better understand and appreciate Britten's creative work. But that is not enough for the industry. There must be more sexual revelations where, perhaps, the real, or the deeper, truth is hidden. For instance, Carpenter also records that Britten was raped by a schoolmaster. This information came allegedly from a rather embittered Eric Crozier. The librettist felt that he had been unfairly put off by Britten.[116] Then there is the suggestion that Britten's father, Robert, was gay and used young Benjamin to come into contact with other boys, as though his son were an unknowing pimp.[117] Neither of these discoveries seem readily credible and Paul Kildea, for instance, dismisses them both. But when he came to write his own very valuable book on Britten's life and work, Kildea saved his clinching revelation until the end. Britten had syphilis. This is presented to us as an incontrovertible fact. Apparently it came to light during the unsuccessful heart operation: 'When Ross cut open Britten's chest and began working on the grossly enlarged heart he discovered the aorta was riddled with tertiary syphilis.'[118] However the surgeon, along with many other people involved, is dead. Meanwhile the claim has been the subject of much debate and it has not (yet) been able to establish itself as standard. It is there for the reader to pursue if he or she wants.[119]

In the case of Wagner the sexual fix and the need for a commensurate revelation has to be the process whereby his heterosexual identity is undermined. Moreover, I am guilty – if guilt it is – of making some use of it. As I do not believe that individual sexuality is either permanently fixed or unproblematic, it does not seem to me unreasonable as a strategy. His cross-dressing, about which there is, at least, reasonable speculation, his love of fabrics, of costuming, of interior design (think of the breathless and detailed letter, 22 November 1877, to Judith Gautier in Paris when he urges her to get some silk for him for a favourite couch which he will christen with her name), above all the intense theatricality of his behaviour seem to me highly relevant to his operatic project and the passionate pursuit and promulgation of an apparently rigid heterosexual agenda. To what degree the man insists too dogmatically on his sexual paradigm – even to what extent his impeccable marriage to Cosima was in fact unsatisfactory, driving him late in life to infatuations with younger women (Judith Gautier, Carrie Pringle, most notably) – is a legitimate subject for comment. Even so, I don't see that it gets us very far. Likewise, I find speculations on his (unconscious) sexual inclinations only occasionally useful, and then purely in the context of his writings and operas. After all, these days any prominent straight male can be readily put to use as a covert gay icon. In fact, the straighter the better.

I wish to finish this chapter with two incidents drawn from the creative lives of both men. They are merely anecdotal in nature, but they are relevant to the theme that has been tackled here. The first concerns Wagner and Dresden, the second Britten and Covent Garden.

Tannhäuser und der Sängerkrieg auf Wartburg was composed for Dresden where Wagner had an important and well-paid job as *Kapellmeister* at the opera house. He was officially second in command, but in fact for all intents and purposes he was the dominant figure. Minna was beside herself with satisfaction. The opera was finished in 1845 and first produced in December of that year. It was not a great success and Wagner was to make several changes, most notably for Paris in 1861. That première turned out to be a fiasco. The plot has already been touched on. We know that Tannhäuser is, when the curtains part, to be found in Venus' grotto where, in a perfect expression of Schopenhauer's will in its most basic, and base, form, he is indulging his instincts and, we must assume, his genitals to the full. So full, in fact, that he is getting bored with the whole business. It is becoming 'too much.' Venus's affections and demands are starting to cloy and we find him longing for loftier things. Now Venus's grotto is on the Venusberg, which was initially to be the title of the opera. And the title is appropriate: all too appropriate as it turned out. When the news got around town the explicit connection with the female anatomy, the *mons veneris* or *mons de venus*, initiated a lot of comment, some of it inevitably rather smutty. The local medical students, in particular, enjoyed themselves, as it seems medical students always have, with scatological jokes.

Wagner professed himself shocked; he was 'disgusted.' The medical students' jokes 'attained heights of obscenity prevalent only in those quarters' and so he changed the title.[120] No doubt he was quite sincere. After all, his higher agenda and final goal was not the pleasures of Venus' little hill – at least not ultimately – or even the singing competition on that other hill, the

Wartburg, where Tannhäuser meets the virgin Elisabeth once again. It was more likely to be something in the line of the clean and fresh air of Mount Parnassus. There, one presumes, his ideal female could be found. One notes, for instance, that Eva in *Die Meistersinger* is explicitly linked to the place. And both operas involve singing competitions. Nevertheless, Wagner's complaints are surely a smidgeon hypocritical; the gentleman is protesting too much. The Venusberg has to be at the outset what the opera is all about if one is, ultimately, to climb to the metaphorical summit and thereby to enter the higher realm. Above all, one can hardly overlook the climax of the singing competition. It had been designed to praise, as Wolfram says, the 'purest essence of love', but Tannhäuser cries out ecstatically 'hasten to the hill of Venus!' The German is *zieht in den Berg der Venus ein!* which actually evokes the notion of entry. Is it only the irreverent here who can't help thinking of phallic penetration? No wonder all hell breaks loose among the pious knights and ladies.

Probably what Wagner is most worried about – though conceivably in part unconsciously – is the necessary, and fairly explicit, carnal agenda. He doesn't want it, and it alone, thrown into his or the public's face. He needs to preserve the illusion of purity. It is not to be forgotten that so much of his polemical and artistic agenda is to colonise the animal pleasures and appetites in order to make out of them something elevated. He must always be able to enjoy, carnally, what he wants, while remaining exalted. More than that, he will actually use what others, and not just Schopenhauer, see as base to, paradoxically, reach the heights, and that not by denying the baseness but by revealing its hidden elevated nature. In the Wagner project sin and sacrament are to be as completely fused as possible to not only their mutual benefit but, above all, to his. And should the fusion work and produce the sublime synthesis, its author would be, axiomatically, invulnerable to the charge of vulgarity or lust. So while his outrage at the Dresden medical students recorded in *My Life* is understandable, consistent even, it is also self-deluded.

Therefore we have to accept that while Wagner addresses, and with enthusiasm and much labour, the question of love and sex head on, this does not mean that he is clear-sighted. At times being explicit would mean blowing away the convenient and seductive miasma in which the whole package is shrouded. It is this that makes me at times doubt that he really knew how far he was going in respect of religion and incest. In any case, the Dresden example might be born in mind when we look again at the appropriation of religion in the final two chapters, and in particular when his response to Titian's *Assumption* surfaces in the last. And as *Tannhäuser*, and the dichotomy on which it rests, is unusually instructive in the Wagner canon it, too, will crop up again there.

Britten is placed in a quite different miasma. Yet although it is also engendered by love and sex, it is not entirely of his own making. Which is to say, that while he continues to live his life diligently, working astonishingly hard as a composer, performer, and as the chief mover of the festival that he, more than anyone, put together in 1948, he can never escape a public climate in which he is the subject of snide remarks and gossip; gossip that can be at least as wounding as anything devised by irreverent medical students. Nor did it, in such circumstances, matter that he was also concerned to live well morally. That is, while he could be difficult – he was always over-sensitive and might turn on erstwhile friends – he lived as a man and an artist according to deep-rooted benign principles. Nonetheless, the hostility of respectable society could only be held at bay by much tactical withdrawal, despite his public life, and by friends and colleagues protecting him as best they could. Of course petty professional rivalry, common in the performing arts, could also play a role in all of this. William Walton, who while jealous of Britten generally enjoyed friendly relations with him, was sour behind his back and suspected, absurdly, that there was a homosexual cabal in force which meant that his own works were being sidelined. But he was hardly the only one who saw plots. Many people in the arts community professed themselves worried that the 'perverts' were taking over.[121] Meanwhile in America, Stravinsky was particularly snide. He met Britten and Pears in Los Angeles in 1949 and invited them to his home. Things did not go well, although the young Britten had been an admirer. Thereafter Stravinsky was soon making full use of homophobia, talking to friends about 'Auntie' Britten and 'Uncle' Pears.[122] Later he was to a write a famous, and a remarkably sneering, attack on the *War Requiem*.

The greater danger, however, came from the world outside the artistic community and it could be more than merely cruel. No matter how strange and lamentable it may seem to many people today, we should remember that much of the past and public revulsion towards homosexuality was not only sincere – felt, whatever its origins, as a powerful gut reaction by those animated by it – it was also a social virtue sanctioned by the law and religious authority. The vicar at Britten's local church in Aldeburgh, for instance, was not above a ringing sermon on the evils of sexual deviance.[123] In other words Britten was never going to make something saintly, or even benevolent, out of a sin that had, almost to an exceptional degree, the power to unsettle, even unhinge, British society.

This obsession with 'perverts' seems to have been particularly marked among the respectable middle classes and a section of the ruling establishment that was, militantly, anti-gay. One wonders what role the British single-sex public (i.e. fee-paying) schools system played in all of this. So many heterosexual men from privileged backgrounds were sent to boarding schools where the only mutual sexual outlet was gay. Many, it seems, having got through the experience, became violently intolerant towards 'queers' as a result. It almost seems as though there was an overreaction to something that, at one time, they must have not only confronted but have contemplated; even perhaps feeling a forbidden libidinous attraction. Whatever the complex nexus of factors may have been, there was, as the Oscar Wilde trial made flagrantly obvious, a near pathological fear and public disgust at homosexuality. And many still saw it as a present danger when Britten was growing up and making his place in the world.

On 14 July 1955 the following appeared in the *People*: 'The influence of perverts has grown beyond all measure' and if not 'curtailed soon, Covent Garden, and other precious musical heritages could suffer irreparable harm.' This was the quoted opinion of Sir Steuart Wilson, who had been (until June of that year) Deputy General Administrator of Covent Garden.[124] Interestingly, two years previously there had been much talk of Britten becoming the Musical Director. It was an idea promoted by the Earl of Harewood and entertained, for a time, by Britten himself. In the end it came to nothing.[125] Had it happened, that great cultural critic and historian of ideas, Isaiah Berlin, would not have been best pleased.

Berlin was very much a member of the British establishment. He relished his place at the centre of things, wrote prodigiously about the great and the good, and gossiped avidly. He was also not above a little bit of surreptitious back-stabbing, which he could, on occasions, take to the point of outright mendacity. For instance, in 1963 he wrote a near-poisonous private letter that scuppered the appointment of one of his bêtes noires, Isaac Deutscher, to the chair in Soviet Studies at the University of Sussex. Berlin remarked that were he to find himself in the same academic community as Deutscher it would be 'morally intolerable.' Nonetheless, when much later the truth got out he wrote to Deutscher's widow and flagrantly denied everything.[126]

Some years before, Berlin had also been fussed by the possibility that Britten might indeed become Musical Director at Covent Garden, although this was three years after the initial suggestion by the Earl of Harewood. Apparently Berlin was no homophobe ('some of his closest friends were homosexual' etc) but he nonetheless put pen to paper again. This time he sent a confidential letter to Covent Garden to stymie any possible appointment. His reasoning, while doing nothing for his posthumous reputation, is not irrelevant or lacking in significance. He argued that: 'Not to put too fine a point upon it, opera is an essentially heterosexual art, and those who do not feel affinity with this tend to employ feeble voices, effeminate producers. . .' etc.[127] What is interesting here is not the personal prejudice about the personalities of the effeminate people who 'do not feel' the correct 'affinity' but his astonishingly narrow view of the genre involved. This has to be one of the most philistine arguments ever made by a cosmopolitan intellectual with an international reputation. But perhaps it simply makes clear how reactionary the opera as a genre and a praxis could be and how narrow-minded its administrators. It certainly also makes clear how much Britten had to fight against. No wonder he set up the English Opera Group and struggled manfully for decades to keep it afloat. No wonder, either, that he embarked on the seemingly absurd idea of establishing a festival in his home town; a town that was difficult to reach, especially so in the immediate post-war years when rationing was still in force. Who, in any case, can blame him for repeatedly underlining how irredeemably philistine he found his homeland?[128]

Three

People and Nation

Britten is universally thought to have been the most important figure in the revival of his country's serious musical life in the middle decades of the twentieth century. Which is to say that during his lifetime he was regarded as Britain's greatest composer. But he was not a, let alone *the*, national composer. Wagner was. This is one of the deepest differences between them, not least because it both determined, and was the product of, radically divergent pathways to redemption. Yet, prima facie, their respective statuses might seem strange as there were many more serious rivals for the crown of leading national composer during Wagner's lifetime than during Britten's shorter one. It is not, however, a matter of deciding who sat atop the scale according to individual taste, even when that taste was shared by the majority. Nor does it matter who harvested the most public honours. Instead their respective positions with regard to their own people and nation reflect the differing agendas of both men. Those differences were profound.

Wagner's agenda was, at least as an intellectual construct, far more organised, worked-out and consciously national than Britten's. He had a notion of Germanness that he placed at the core of his artistic endeavours. He appealed to what he saw as intrinsic virtues in German language and German song and, as always, he was ready to explain all this in chapter and verse. Furthermore, these quintessential Teutonic qualities rested on a no less privileged notion of the German Volk and the German nation. He, in effect, equated the two although in his early years the modern German state did not exist. He was able, though, to watch its formation, forged through Prussian industrial and military might, as the century progressed. What is indisputable, however, is that the Volk and not river valleys or mountain ranges set the parameters of the Nation. In this he was no different from most German nationalists. 'No German-born prince ever took upon himself to mark out for his subjects as their fatherland, with mountains or rivers as boundaries, the territory over which he ruled' said the philosopher Fichte when in the first decade of the nineteenth century he called upon all Germans to take their national destiny into their own hands.[1] Consequently people – defined chiefly according to the common language – and nation constituted a homogeneous ideal; they were self-defining sibling terms. But they did not equate unproblematically to our modern idea of a state. This, logically, would produce a difficulty that was to bedevil German history in as much as it underpinned German expansionism. It is, appropriately enough, made explicit by Fichte, although he does not see it as a problem. Rather it is an inviolable first principle. Wherever the German language was spoken 'everyone who had first seen the light of day in its domain could consider himself as in a double sense a citizen, on the one hand, of the State where he was born . . . and on the other hand, of the whole common fatherland of the German nation.'[2]

Wagner rooted all this in a history that, as *he* explained it, underpinned the special status of the original native Volk. It presupposed a trek from their origins in the unsullied highlands of Central Asia to what became the European German homelands.[3] This was at the time the standard position with regard to the origins of the Caucasian people, but when Wagner tells the story it is exclusively Teutonic. Furthermore, he folds into it key symbols (hoard, dragon, etc) of the epic *Ring* cycle while revealing their, and the *Ring's* key characters', close relationship to the later Christian story: Wotan, the Stem-Father or God, Siegfried the Ur Christ. As a result myth, anthropology, and religion are dissolved into each other. For instance, of great, albeit long term, significance is the Grail. It is also part of the mix; something which should encourage us to consider how deeply embedded in the privileged *German* narrative *Parsifal* is.[4] It really has nothing to do with Montsalvat, nor with universal, racially unconstrained, Christianity. Rather, it is race based. As von Bülow, who remained a great admirer despite losing his wife to Wagner, said: *Parsifal* is 'echt Deutsch, anti-Jewish and anti-materialist.'[5]

It is also notable that Wagner gets 'Kinghood' into the Ur-mix. We should not forget that Amfortas is the 'King' of the knightly brotherhood in *Parsifal* and that therefore the notion of the King, like that of the Stem-Father,

Sun God/Apollo, and the Grail, also lies at the taproot of the German story. Furthermore, Siegfried is also linked explicitly to the same notion via his possession of the hoard. It will later 'spiritually ascend' into the Grail.[6] But in Siegfried's case Wagner takes the story as far as it can go for a German nationalist, which is hardly inappropriate given that the archetypal hero has already been decked out as Christ.[7] His earthly, and indisputably historical, royal blood-brother is the eighth century Emperor Charlemagne.[8] Yet even then there is a further step; one that takes us forward into the High Middle Ages. The Holy Roman Emperor Friedrich I is added for good measure. He, we learn, 'turned his gaze . . . toward Asia, to the cradle of the nations, to the place where God begat the father of all Men. Wondrous legends had he heard of an ur-divine Priest-King who governed there a pure and happy people, immortal through the nurture of a wonder-working relic called 'the Holy Grail.' – Might he there regain the lost Sight-of-God, now garbled by ambitious priests in Rome according to their pleasure?'[9] In the light of this it is perhaps not surprising that we find the revolutionary Wagner in 1848 somewhat absurdly trying to marry the privileged folk-based tale with Communism and, as a result, coming up with an interesting, prima facie at least, contradiction. In the *Vaterlandsverein* speech he argues inventively for a republic with a king at its head. After all: 'The farther back we search among Germanic nations for the Kinghood's meaning, the more intimately will it fit this new-won meaning and prove it . . . re-established.'[10]

That this history was – as Wagner told it – in many respects of dubious provenance did not matter a jot to him. Even those aspects that might be seen by 'schoolmen' as nothing more than folk legends were, by that fact alone, likely to be of special significance and authority. Knowledge that came from the Volk was *ipso facto* of more value than that acquired through academic study. It simply had to have its roots in a deeper and more reliable depository of truth. We should never forget that: 'The Volk alone understands the Volk . . . it consummates in truth what of its very essence it both can and should; whereas its learned schoolmaster cudgels his head in vain to comprehend what the Volk does purely of itself.'[11]

Consequently Wagner was of the passionate opinion that the German people were not only different in their own way – as all peoples are – but superior. In this he is to be distinguished from other European composers working to revive their national music. One might think of Dvorak, Janáček, Bartók, Kodály, Enescu, etc. They did not infer that their discoveries or their compositions established cultural, let alone, racial ascendancy. It is also, perhaps, interesting that all those composers were much influenced by, and often researched, their native folk music. Wagner did not. Despite his axiomatic dedication to intrinsic Volk knowledge, he imposed his ideas from above. This is not to say that he denied folk roots, but rather that he found in folk culture more fundamental things than mere tunes. For instance, in the very assonance and alliteration loaded nature of German poetic speech (*Stabreim*) he saw the fount, the Ur source, of what was to become German song in its purest and most authentic form. In particular, it is striking that Wagner takes second place to no German nationalist – not even to Fichte – when it comes to celebrating the unique status of the native German tongue and its rich, eternal character. One might think that it was something God had bequeathed to the earliest men and only the Germans had managed to hold onto it in its uncorrupted state. Late in life he rhapsodies: 'Fatherland, mother-tongue: woe to the man bereft of these! But what unmeasured happiness, to recognise in one's mother-tongue the speech of one's ur-fathers! Through such a tongue our feelings and beholdings stretch right back to early Man himself . . .'[12] We might also note that many decades earlier he imagined that he had found his 'blond young Siegfried-man' at 'the primal mythic spring' and was 'led by his hand, upon the physically-perfect mode of utterance wherein alone that man could speak his feelings. This was the *alliterative* verse . . . that *Stabreim* which the Folk itself once sang, when *it* was still both Poet and Myth-Maker.'[13]

Naturally the German nationalists in general were much fussed by the intrinsic nature of the German language. Herder, too, turns to *Stabreim* as the authentic Teutonic Ur-speech; a tongue which is, in its very nature, poetic.[14] Wagner is, however, very instrumental in the matter. It is from this speech, now written out as poems for each opera, that the music springs. In fact the music, allegedly, comes to him almost of its own accord in the process of composing the poem. In an early letter to Karl Gaillard he wants to go so far as to bind the two so closely that the causal link (text → music) almost disappears in a creative act that is simultaneously expressive of both.[15] He doesn't, however, seem able to maintain this position. In any case, it is in its first manifestation flagrantly glib and reads like self-serving propaganda. Moreover, after he has read Schopenhauer he would be naturally inclined to a different view, not least because the philosopher privileged music, without text, above all other discourses. Allegedly it has a special access to the will. As we have seen, it was immediately prior to reading Schopenhauer that Wagner had attempted the extremely complex, and at times incoherent, intellectual fusion of music and words in *Opera and Drama*. This, his longest essay, has already played an important role in the last chapter and will continue to do so. But for the moment it is enough to acknowledge that the attempt to hold onto words and music as equal sibling terms does not stand the distance. For instance, when Wagner gets to the *Beethoven* essay (1870) the causal terminology and the hierarchy have changed. Music is 'Nature infinite.'[16] It is bound up with the unconsciousness and dreams, and is then translated into language.[17] Therefore the '. . . union of Music and Poetry must always end in . . . a subordination of the latter.'[18]

Nevertheless, Wagner's job, as he understood it, was to recreate the lost heritage of the people and their culture, not merely to excavate it. Instead he would bring it back to life anew in the form of his own innovative operatic language. In this he was not typical of musical nationalists on the fringes of Europe, in countries whose native cultures had been marginalised usually due to foreign, often imperial, rule or influence. He was not the poet of a suppressed nationalist minority but the celebrant of past imperial greatness and the, admittedly mystic, harbinger of the one to come. But this did not mean that he was typical of the German revival. For instance, Herder – much admired by Wagner largely, one suspects, because he was a passionate critic of the inimical French influence in German cultural life, the despised *Gallicomanie* – lamented that the Germans had forgotten their folk music and their ancient lays. The ghastly French influence meant that princes were no longer able to speak German, or if they could it was only a language to be used with 'a serf or a servant.'[19] And had not every German court become a little Versailles?[20] Wagner shared the same opinion. In *What is German?* (1865) he derided the petty German princes tarted up in 'French livery and uniform, with periwig and pigtail and laughably set out with imitations of French gallantry.'[21] However, all this had led Herder, unlike Wagner, to compare German art unfavourably with that of other European countries and peoples. In particular he held up Scotland, a country many German cultural nationalists found attractive, as a model. The Scots, more than anyone, had preserved their old ballads.

Wagner's grander agenda, on the other hand, was not, like Herder's cultural anthropology, disposed to celebrate the democratic promiscuity of innumerable languages and song. Because he was driven by the privileged history rooted in the sublime Central Asian narrative, he was compelled – although he hardly needed much encouragement – to proclaim a dominant status for what was quintessentially German. This was largely because the Germans had preserved in essence the culture they had brought with them from the Central Asia homeland while other Teutonic peoples had subsequently lost their language and with it their unique identity. In this he was, again, repeating the passionate and militantly nationalist ideas of Fichte, whose binary pairing of the German language and the German Volk became a self-defining unit that could then be used to condemn and downgrade those Teutonic peoples who had moved on from the European lands where the migrating Germans had at first settled. In subsequently adopting other languages etc they had to all intents and purposes gone awry.[22]And Wagner, clearly of the same opinion, took it further: '. . . the German alone possesses a language whose daily usage still hangs directly and conspicuously together with its Roots.'[23]

One can readily see that this account leads, logically, to racism, and Wagner duly followed his own nose and his own 'reasoning' in the matter. He was a racist. And yet his racism was, in many respects, slightly odd because it was so culturally based – at least when it suited him. That is, although in later life he was much obsessed by the question of blood and racial purity, when he was younger and writing *Die Wibelungen* he was more than willing to accept selected interbreeding with other tribes, but only if that strengthened the stock. And even later Cosima was to record that Richard pointed out that it is all 'a matter of pure metaphysics; Slavs and Celts are mixed in with us and we have absorbed them.'[24] For when the Germans had arrived in Europe the initial Frankish and Norman blood was superseded by that of the Saxon and 'Alemanni.'[25] Yet in the essay *Know Thyself* (1881) Wagner, in a late rush of anti-Jewish feeling (he is much disturbed by Jewish emancipation), is back again talking about pure bred races.

One is doing Wagner a disservice when one downplays how intellectually alive and inquisitive he was. In particular he was an avid and omnivorous reader of the literature of other cultures and interested in foreign, musical, political and social developments. Therefore there was a strong, and one might say contradictory, strand of cosmopolitanism in his nature. Nevertheless his bedrock ideological commitment to what was German and echt became in his mind commensurate with the notion of racial superiority. Therefore, what was benign in the creative and intellectual work of other nationalist artists grew in Wagner's grand theory into a malignancy. Furthermore, in all of this he exercised a growing influence as the nineteenth century progressed. In many ways he became in his own lifetime the most influential cultural figure in his homeland. It was an influence that was to grow into an even more powerful force in the century following when the nation fell into the hands of murderous racists well able to fold the national composer, in respect of both his music and his essays, into their own ideological schemes. Of course it must be stressed that however much he had contributed unwittingly to a culture that was used by nationalist criminals as a rationale for exceptional atrocities, he would have been appalled by both them and their actions. His own failings – his anti-Semitism, his desire to wreck revenge on Paris where he had suffered so much, the anti-French satire *A Capitulation* (1870) that even shocked his friends, etc – are quite enough for the Wagner apologists to be getting on with. And while it will always be a moot point to what extent, if any, he can be held responsible for the influence he exercised after his death, that does not mean that it isn't a topic that should be pursued. It is, however, not part of the agenda here.

While for Wagner nation and people are sibling terms, as indeed they are for many German nationalists, for Britten they are divorced. People does not mean, nor does it necessarily imply, nation. Britten may well have been the poet and songster of the folk – after all, think of all those folk-song arrangements – but he was not the muse of the English, or the British, people. And if he was the muse of the folk it was a myriad and different folk, a heterogeneity of communities stretching from Britain to Ireland . . . and to France. They were each, like their regional music and their regional dialects, distinguishable. It was perhaps this that inspired his interventionism, stripping away the accretions of Victorian folk song collections drilled into children in the classroom. Britten had, by-the-way, a great admiration for that other collector of folk music and composer of works for children,

Zoltán Kodály. The admiration was reciprocated and Kodály came to the Aldeburgh festival in 1965. Furthermore, Britten was not committed to a single style and a particular formal method that could become an orthodoxy, and he was certainly not driven by a didactic message that would help forge the nation anew according to his own wilful agenda. If he wanted to improve anything it was standards of musical performance which he found deplorable. And if he wanted to revive anything it was the setting of English prosody that he felt had been in decline since Purcell.[26] Nor did he have a national ideal in mind that would express the greatness of the British people. Such a notion was repugnant to him and he despised the, often musical, imperial tub-thumping by which the British tried to convince the world and themselves of their own superiority. No wonder he relished the opportunity to parody provincial pig ignorant patriotism in *Albert Herring*. The libretto does not succumb to subtlety in this matter. An inarticulate, babbling Lady Billows declaims: 'King and country! Cleanliness is next to . . . God for England and Saint . . . Keep Your powder dry and leave the rest to Nature! . . . Britons! Rule the deep!'

Least of all did Britten have some grand theory that explained, in historical, anthropological, and racial terms, an overarching national story of which he could become the modern Pied Piper. One cannot, therefore, apply the term 'agenda' to Britten in the same way that it has already been applied to Wagner. If Britten looked inwardly, domestically as it were, at the British people it was to understand their various particularities, and if he looked outwardly it was not to admire the privileged place of the British in the world but to underline native provincialism and philistinism in the light of the cosmopolitan riches he saw elsewhere. Whereas Wagner uses German values to denigrate foreigners, above all the French (very marked in *German Art and German Polity*), Britten uses alien cultures to castigate the British. In short, his cosmopolitanism was of a more genuine stamp than Wagner's.

One could readily see all this as liberating, but it is also challenging. Above all, it is nothing like as straightforward as the – admittedly gigantic – task Wagner set himself. So many of the German composer's artistic and intellectual conundrums were solved for him because he had a specific dogmatic faith that ran along narrow, straight rails. Therefore it always knew the way to go even if it didn't always end up where he had assumed it must. Certainly Wagner would be frequently disappointed that the people and nation in whose interests he imagined he was labouring didn't seem to appreciate what he was doing for them. Towards the end of his life he often despaired and contemplated just simply leaving the place and letting the buggers stew in their own juice. Then, one imagines, they would realise just who it was they had been ignoring or had treated shabbily . . . a prophet neglected in his own country and so forth. At one time he was trying to fix up a move to the USA, but he also told Cosima: 'We will try once more with the German fatherland, with Bayreuth; and if it doesn't succeed, then farewell the North and art and cold, we shall move to Italy and forget everything.'[27] In general he became increasingly pessimistic and not just with respect to the future of the Fatherland, although it is here that his racism became most acute. Gradually he came to the conclusion that the Jews, the object of his most targeted and deep-seated racist bile, would win. In the new 1869 introduction to *Jewishness in Music* he foresaw the total victory of Jewry 'on every side.'[28] On 22 November 1881 he wrote to King Ludwig that 'there is no doubt that we Germans especially will be destroyed by them.' Nonetheless, his bleak view was also painted with an indiscriminate anthropological brush. 'The theory of a degeneration of the human race, however much opposed it seems to Constant Progress, is yet the only one that, upon serious reflection, can afford us any solid hope.'[29] One can see from this sort of thing that his racism was of an unstable and contradictory character and more will have to be said about it later in this chapter.

Britten, on the other hand, was on his own. He had no such grand theory, whether benign or inimical, to steer his work. Nor did he want one. Of course he had had advice and, on occasions, good advice. Surely that was the case with both Frank Bridge and W. H. Auden. The first was probably the greatest musical influence on his life and the second undoubtedly played an unequalled role in forming his literary taste and deepening his understanding of verse. And Britten, never the nationalist flag-waver, was to become one of the greatest setters of poetry in the history of music, comparable to Schubert, from whom he learned a great deal, and Wolf.[30] And given that the overwhelming majority of his compositions for voice were in the vernacular, that, by its very nature, made him paramount in his use of the English tongue. Herder would have been profoundly impressed.

Yet Britten still had to find his own way. He would need to go beyond what both Bridge and Auden could give him. And this may well be the principal cause of not only the eclectic and formal variety of his work, but also of his search for a community in which that work could be placed and from which it could take sustenance and find meaning. This, however, might seem, superficially, like a contradiction. It needs to be addressed.

Britten settled. And not only did he settle, he chose anything but a cosmopolitan place in which to do so. He and Pears had lived in both London and New York. Indeed in the latter case in 1940 they became members of an extremely wild and bohemian set-up in Brooklyn, ruled over grandly by Auden and made up of both a permanent and a floating population of artists whose behaviour was anything but provincial or conventional. Leonard Bernstein thought it a madhouse.[31] Yet neither of the two great metropolises exerted a lasting fascination. Britten tended to associate London with visits to the dentist or the doctor. He needed to get away to East Suffolk. Certainly he journeyed overseas regularly. He became, for a composer, exceptionally rich and could travel at will. He also had wealthy and/or influential foreign friends (for instance, Prince Ludwig and Princess Margaret of Hesse and the Rhine in whose castle at Wolfsgarten he often stayed, and Vishnevskaya and Rostropovich in Soviet Russia) who made foreign trips that much more agreeable. His five-month tour to the Far East in 1955–6, with Ludwig and Margaret, was, in particular, of considerable importance. His time in Bali had a direct effect on the musical language of the ballet *The Prince of the Pagodas* and there would have been no *Curlew River* had he and Pears not gone, without any great initial enthusiasm, to Japan. But Britten needed domestic comforts and the consolations of the Constable-like landscape around Aldeburgh. He needed peace and quiet in controlled circumstances. Stimulating company, if required, could come to him.

There is, of course, no real contradiction. Britten's interests did not shrink because he left the city. His basic disposition – internationalist and eclectic – did not become narrow-minded and provincial because he lived in Suffolk. The Aldeburgh festival was, unlike Bayreuth, anything but parochial; something that can still never be disguised in the German town no matter how exotic and elitist the audience. But there is a fruitful tension here. The great concerns of Britten's work are rooted in the particular, no matter how varied those particulars are. They take their power in part from place. The operas, above all, are exactly defined. They do not play out in the heavens or on mountain tops or on/in the Venusberg or in mythical regions in northern Spain. Two are set in great houses (Bly, *The Turn of the Screw*; Paramore *Owen Wingrave*) and the houses themselves are shown as having a perverse role in determining the mood and in influencing the narrative. 'Paramore,' we are told in a leitmotif, 'shall welcome woe.' Both operas, the first based on a Henry James's novella and the second on one of his short stories, are in effect ghost stories, and ghosts, like skeletons, come with closets. But the same is true for the towns and villages within whose parameters the other operatic works are contained. Place is critical in shaping the manner in which the stage drama unfolds. Each location is given telling musical language. Above all, it is formative with regard to the people one meets there. They are not like the unthinking but massively ego driven Siegfried and Parsifal who are equally at home or equally estranged no matter where they are, although Siegfried is at his finest in the forest. Furthermore, this Britten principle is also true, if perversely so, of the foreigners in the cosmopolitan world of Venice. They must either flee the place or succumb, properly and fatally, to the power of the sick town. And this takes us back to the first opera in that it underlines a general tendency. Grimes, native-rooted, is never going to escape the Borough and all its bigotry . . . except by death. But we have no feeling that any of the other inhabitants are either. Even the villagers in *Albert Herring* are not going anywhere. Their world is fixed; imprisoning even. In fact there is something tragic in leaving Albert in the family shop at the end. He may be master of the place now – dispensing free peaches to the children – but another librettist and another composer would have had him kick up his heels and head for the cosmopolitan freedoms, as well as the fleshpots, of London.

In this context the church parables are particularly pertinent. Their nominal *stage* settings can be exotic and their themes are certainly universal, but their context is religious and precise. They are placed in the confines of a modest church and take, explicitly, full advantage of that undisguised foregrounded fact. Their scores, for instance, exploit the long reverberations typical of church acoustics (what Britten called 'Gothic' acoustics[32]), and they draw our attention in framing devices to the building and to the monks who stage the performances. In this the parables share certain genre similarities with *Noye's Fludde.* There the great, indeed worldwide, cataclysmic event is also placed in a church. It is equipped with a basic set, hundreds of children playing and singing, and a congregation joining in the hymns. The deluge is only meaningful in the first instance because it is local. Its greater message, declaring God's mercy and applicable to all mankind, follows from that.

This emphasis on the setting, its powerful underpinning of character, mood, and narrative is hardly a matter exclusive to Britten. To some extent it has, of course, to be true of nearly all stage works. But in Britten's case it underlines a decisive tension between the universal message of pity and redemption on the one hand and the specific local site on which that message plays out on the other. Redemption is in the here and now. It should be extant, and it can be realised. For instance, the Madwoman in *Curlew River* is saved through the benediction of her son's blessing. By her last utterances – the 'Amens' – we know she is released from the torments of lunacy. It is impossible not to put some faith in this, even though we are never allowed to forget that we are watching a play within a play. In that sense the form could be said to muddy the waters in that it, theoretically, qualifies the immediacy of the message. Nonetheless, the theatrical experience is, by its very nature, empirically upfront and immediate. And with Britten, in particular, one feels very strongly that the redemptive story must be, as a matter of course, contemporary and pressing. In this it is perhaps rather like classical Dutch paintings that put the great biblical events (let us say Pieter Bruegel's the *Massacre of the Innocents*, a horror that Britten set in *A Boy was Born*) in the quotidian and palpable world known by the painter. This point is also made tellingly by Auden in respect of his, probably impractical, text for a possible oratorio: *For the Time Being.*[33] It includes a section on 'The Massacre of the Innocents.' True, some greater consolation might be found in what is to come after the event, but if there has been a tragedy its immediate moral, as well as its theatrical, presence determines the dominant mood of the piece. Surely no amount of proselytising about the coming Saviour will ever ameliorate the ghastly fact of Lucretia's violation and subsequent suicide and none of the actors in the opera pretends, at least credibly, that it could. Even the final sentiments of the Male and Female

Chorus are, despite the wonderful music, of no real consolation. By projecting salvation into the coming centuries, as though it is something we will have to, at best, wait for in hope, even though we must die before it comes, they effectively underline the arbitrary nature of the specific horror we have just witnessed. In doing that they concede everything to the here and now, making of the Christian message something that is both morally relevant for the audience yet empirically without stage purchase. No wonder they begin their perorations with a series of baffled questions.

Furthermore, is there not something disturbing about the manner in which Vere points out in the Epilogue to *Billy Budd* that he has been saved as a result of his own murderous act in sacrificing the angelic presence; an angelic presence placed precariously in the most closed of closed societies to be found in any of Britten stage works? In moral terms his failure is made only more profound by the fact that he can appeal to – as it were – arbitrary rules and laws as a justification. Of course the naval regulations in time of war are clear enough and in Billy's case their applicability is incontestable. The 'trouble' is, however, they clearly disguise and run counter to deeper ethical considerations; something which both Vere and the crew either understand or sense. The tension thus generated is considerable and the audience leaves the theatre with it unresolved.

It is hardly insignificant that the composer came to question the manner in which *Billy Budd* ended, wondering whether Vere shouldn't have embraced Billy and saved him.[34] The librettists, however, had decided to remain true to Melville, although the Prologue and the Epilogue for the captain alone were their inventions. Still, we have Vere's confession: 'For I could have saved him. He knew it, even his shipmates knew it.' How pejorative that 'even' sounds! But whatever position one takes on the matter, *Billy Budd* makes clear the power of the model. The exceptionally constricted setting, the pared down world, simplifies, in some senses purifies, both the action and its moral connotations. But for the three principals (Billy, Vere, Claggart) none of the other characters have a credible existence outside of *The Indomitable*. They are solely the victims of a great struggle that is taking place within touching distance. In fact when one thinks of the grunting chorus following Budd's execution-cum-murder, they are near wordless victims. As an overall dramatic construct, this is a highly contrived situation, forever turning in on itself. And, in being untroubled by conventional heterogeneous social life, it allows of remarkably explicit personifications of pure good and pure evil. Moreover, in being pure they paradoxically evoke the universal. Initially the moral agenda is bred in a tight hothouse from which, apparently, there is no escape. But then it reaches out in the best Britten manner until the redemptive message, however compromised, escapes into the world. The little ship may be trapped on 'the infinite sea' but what happens on board is shown, appropriately enough, as having boundless implications.

I wonder if the problems the first night audience had with *Gloriana* weren't also a product of this same tension. The placing was, in part, too specific. The great and the good in attendance wanted something grander, something more imperial. Furthermore they did not want a redemptive message, not even that of a flawed great queen who rose above herself to make a full sacrifice in the cause of duty. Instead they wanted or were expecting – and I assume this also goes for the numerous foreign dignitaries and diplomats – a pre-war, or a VE day, celebration of British might and glory; a celebration that would be fitting for the inauguration of a new Elizabethan age. They certainly didn't want a story about an invasion of Ireland (always a touchy subject) that went wrong. Nor did they want to find themselves in the queen's bedchamber when she was stripped down to her unadorned person. What must the new queen have thought seeing her namesake and predecessor without her wig. True, they no doubt expected the public scenes, though not, one suspects, so quaintly authentic musically.

It is, moreover, a moot point whether Britten and William Plomer (the librettist) got the balance between public and private scenes right. An alternating fifty/fifty split is prima facie both reasonable and aesthetically pleasing. But it hobbled the story. I sometimes think that Britten and Plomer allowed themselves to be manipulated into a similar situation that Prokofiev found himself in when he wrote his great historical opera *War and Peace*. In his case the authorities, wanting a work they could use as part of the wartime anti-Nazi propaganda campaign, demanded and got more public and patriotic scenes. True, Britten and Plomer's hands were not forced (but for the Lord Chamberlain not allowing them to refer to a chamber pot), but it is possible that they misjudged the balance not least because the audiences didn't want balance. They wanted pageantry, whereas the opera as a drama would have profited from a deeper engagement with the Essex/Elizabeth story and its tragic end . . . for both. Frankly, when Britten was told that it was dangerous to kick off the coronation celebrations with his opera and that it would be better if Covent Garden put on a ballet first, he should have listened. Nonetheless, the failure did please some people. It was given, if Tom Sutcliffe's documentary is to be believed, the sniggering Wagnerian epithet: 'The Twilight of the Sods.'

There is a further tension embedded in the structure and aesthetic landscape of Britten's stage works. It, too, implies a superficial contradiction, but it is a dramatically potent one. Despite what has been said about place and community, Britten's emblematic characters – his tragic figures – tend to be loners. More than this, one can see many of the operas as works about loneliness, a point well made by Edward Greenfield. Britten, moreover, drew attention to music's special ability to express loneliness.[35] He mentioned, for instance, 'the beauty of loneliness' in the Abschied from Mahler's *Das Lied von der Erde*.[36] And despite what one may at first think, loneliness is, in fact, very productive of dramatic constellations.

One puts the central figure in a crowded world, giving him or her a range of superficial contacts in a closed society, only to make by contrast the character's unique, possibly asocial, nature all the clearer. In some cases there will be an attempt on the part of the central character to make a relationship with one of the other figures work. But it will come to nothing. Furthermore when the characters' status as loners is most clear – even when it is forced on them – there is every reason to see the aborted but seemingly desired social bond to which they struggle as transparent and hopelessly synthetic. Often it has an element of self-delusion. Does Grimes really imagine that he will marry Ellen, or Queen Elizabeth that she can form a liaison with Essex that will satisfy her as a woman and leave her position as a monarch undiminished, and does Aschenbach imagine that Tadzio will one day actually talk to him? These are all unconvincing scenarios that take dramatic force from that very fact. Their prominent place in the psychic life of the central character only underlines his or her solitary predicament. Grimes is so inwardly turned and tormented that he cannot think critically about this. Who knows what he really believes as he psychically falls apart.

Elizabeth clearly senses that a reconciliation between the public and the private spheres is impossible. That realisation is the bedrock on which the heroic 'kaleidoscope' (Britten's term), or melodrama, that ends the opera depends. Incidentally, the device of employing declaimed text with musical punctuation was criticised as a cop-out in *Gloriana* by critics who, I imagine, doubtless approved of the same technique in the second act of *Fidelio.*

Reflective Aschenbach is, of course, only too explicitly conscious of the dangers of fantasising a kinship that is impossible. But this only makes the fantasy that much more bewitching for a self-obsessed writer prone to live in his own imaginative world. He talks of a 'relationship' with Tadzio only to observe immediately 'if so one-sided an affair can be called a relationship.' The only logical way out is the painfully authentic and absurd: 'What if all were dead, And only we two left alive?' Then it would be a singular relationship in every sense. Meanwhile poor Miles in *The Turn of the Screw* dies in part because the Governess cannot form any deep and potentially life/soul saving relationship with him. He was already beyond her help before she arrived at Bly; corrupted by the closed and fetid world of the great but haunted house.

It is also the case that to stay inside the community is tantamount to extinction. The community will unsex you, suffocate you, even if you are a great queen in possession of unequalled authority and power. Ultimately it may kill you. Balstrode brings the broken Grimes to the point where he can sink his boat and kill himself (the Borough people are, at the end, shown to be largely indifferent), Owen Wingrave accepts the challenge of the horrid family and dies alone in the haunted room, and Aschenbach duly makes his fatal, but redeeming, choice. Yet there is an awful element of parody to this last example. While destined to be utterly expelled – and surely to some degree knowing this – Aschenbach makes a last grotesque attempt to become part of the community; even to appeal to the boy. But the rouge and the hair dye merely turn him into another Elderly Fop. And that at the very moment when he contemplates what Socrates knew and, more to the point, what Socrates 'told us.'

How different all this is from Wagner. For the Wagner hero there is always a woman out there waiting for him. True, she may take some finding, largely because she is often well outside of his immediate community.

Nonetheless she must be found. A journey is necessary. Siegmund, Siegfried, Parsifal, Tristan, The Dutchman, Walther von Stolzing (*Die Meistersinger*), Lohengrin have got to travel. Several of them will undergo all sorts of extraordinary adventures on the way; adventures that they might, later, relate to us, just as Siegfried entrances the Gibichungs by telling them his life's history in the last act of *Götterdämmerung*. But the goal is always the redeeming 'eternal womanly.' In this there is an obvious parallel to the manner in which Wagner explains exogamy in *Opera and Drama*. It is, however, a very odd parallel.

Clearly the man must leave family and tribe and seek his fortune. His reward is not really a dragon's hoard, or a magic helmet. It is not even a ring or the Holy Lance. It is the woman who will teach him everything. In this way blood, knowledge and, in effect, Germanness are propagated. One might see the man reproducing in his own, humble, way something like the great trek that brought the tribe from Central Asia to the German lands. But this journey is also the means by which incest, or endogamy, is averted. Or so one would have thought. To understand this we need to accept that Wagner, initially, regards sexual love between siblings, and between parents and children, as an axiomatic non-starter . . . at least when examined anthropologically. It is not the custom or usage (*Gewohnheit*) and it is not desired. As a result the male is driven by the libido to take the vital step. The 'first attraction of sexual love is brought the stripling by an unwonted [unaccustomed] object, freshly fronting him from Life itself; this attraction is so overpowering, that it draws him from the wonted [accustomed] surroundings of the Family, in which this attraction had never presented itself, and drives him forth to journey with the un-wonted. Thus sexual love is the revolutionary, who breaks down the narrow confines of the Family, to widen it itself into the broader reach of human Society.'[37]

The great irony with this is that the desired womanly object turns out to be, when found, often nothing less than a relative, or the personification of a relative. In short the sexual union when it occurs is incestuous. Which is to say that a great deal of cod anthropology has been employed to foreground exactly that which the explanatory system was designed to factor out of the authoritative model. Siegmund finds his twin sister, Siegfried his aunt and thinks she is his mother, Parsifal ends up in the arms of a woman he takes to be his mother largely because she tells him so, and Tristan is locked in a metaphysical embrace with a woman who is, by virtue it seems of wilful choice, his own spiritually genetic double. Wagner must then devise some kind of rationalisation for this; that is, an argument which allows him to vindicate the, otherwise impossible and allegedly unwanted, incestuous act when it occurs. As we will see in the next chapter, his reasoning is specious. But given the bind in which he has placed himself by his own confused rationalisations-cum-speculations, that is hardly surprising.

These are not problems that trouble Britten. His outsiders have no redemptive soulmate. Furthermore, he was very conscious of the tension this generated. Nor was he shy about acknowledging that his dramas often involved critical figures who had lost, whether by choice or rejection on the part of their community or their families, their place within society. In the most striking example of this, *Peter Grimes*, the title character's brutishness is causally linked to the brutishness of the community. At the time of the first Met production in New York *Time* magazine reported: 'Britten regards this opera as "a subject very close to my heart – the struggle of the individual against the masses. The more vicious the society the more vicious the individual."'[38] This rather facile coupling will be superseded, or at least work itself out in more sophisticated ways, in the later works but it states a basic principle that is always to some extent in play. Incidentally, the only thing that keeps the title character of *Albert Herring* within the social webbing is that the opera is a comedy. It is merely a matter of genre. Were it not a comedy Albert would be thrown out of the community, if, that is, he hadn't died as a result of his nocturnal lunge at freedom. But it is this basic sense of sympathy with those who have been excluded that drove Britten, Pears and the librettist Montagu Slater to alter the character of Grimes as they found it in the original poem. Britten said in a 1963 interview that it 'led us to make Grimes a character of vision and conflict, the tortured idealist he is, rather than the villain he was in Crabbe.' He became 'the individual against the crowd.' Furthermore, the parallel with his and Pears's own social status during the war was self-evident. 'As conscientious objectors we were out of it.'[39] And this is symptomatic of a deeper and more comprehensive exclusion. As Pears wrote to Britten in 1963: 'We are after all queer & left & conshies which is enough to put us, or make us put ourselves, outside the pale, apart from being artists as well . . .'[40] It is not surprising then that when Britten's key characters go on a psychic journey it is to discover that they don't belong. Wagner's heroes undertake expeditions into the unknown in order to discover that they do.

If the universal has a symbolic presence in Britten it is the sea. This is perfectly understandable. As he said: 'For most of my life I have lived closely in touch with the sea.'[41] Implicit in this is an ambivalent role for the locality. The fishing town, which exists because of the sea while not being part of it, is certainly a definite place and, moreover, one stamped by its own characteristics and, as in the Borough in *Grimes*, by vibrant characters. But the sea implies a barely definable and vastly more nebulous world. As such it is present in three major operas: the first and the last (*Peter Grimes* and *Death in Venice*) and in the largest of the operatic undertakings in the middle part of his career: *Billy Budd*. It is, of course, also central to the children's opera *Noye's Fludde*. Moreover, late in life Britten planned a sea symphony and had already chosen possible poems for it. It never got written. The sea, naturally enough, implies the notion of the infinite. *Billy Budd*, as has already been pointed out twice above, explicitly evokes this. But it has other uses. It is the site of that which is unsayable. It transcends the text.

The four Sea Interludes in *Peter Grimes* tell us of things we can only be aware of through feelings and instincts. They speak to us of mysteries. One could say they embody Schopenhauer's notion of the greater epistemological power and authority of pure music, that is music without sung text ('The words are . . . a foreign extra of secondary value'[42]), and this although Crabbe has some fine passages on the sea that Britten marked but did not set.[43] The Interludes go even further than Britten's declaration: 'I wanted to express my awareness of the perpetual struggle of men and women whose livelihood depends on the sea.'[44] Rather they can be said to meet the Schopenhauer-like terms set by Auden in his 1938 sonnet, *The Composer.* While all other artists 'translate': 'You, alone, alone, O imaginary song,/ Are unable to say an existence is wrong,/ And pour out your forgiveness like a wine.' Schopenhauer claims that music is the 'essence' and the other arts mere – we might think Platonic – 'shadows.'[45] Surely, the sea takes on an identity wholly valid in itself; one that escapes the social framework of the 'men and women' in the village. Consequently the Interludes pull the opera away from the Borough society, which is the near exclusive setting in Crabbe for the title character's brutishness. In the poem he has a far more developed and incident rich history on land.

At this point I am, however, confronted by a problem. Britten would not – or at least at one time would not – have agreed with me. Andre Anderson recalls that he was not happy with the Tyrone Guthrie production at Covent Garden because 'the accent was thrown on the sea.' He wanted it on 'the people in the village.'[46] Certainly I do not wish to gainsay the power of the rich collection of Borough characters – I have said as much in the first chapter and regularly stressed Britten's ability to create a range of varied, brilliantly etched, stage figures. Nor do I wish to downplay their bigotry and provincialism. Nonetheless, Britten's position, at least on the basis of the quotations found in Brett (1983), is not wholly consistent. You cannot say that you want to create characters whose lives are a 'perpetual struggle' dependent on the sea and then say, as he is alleged to have said to Guthrie, that 'these people would be the same wherever they were.'[47] Nevertheless, in the final analysis each visitor in the theatre is likely to feel the opaque power of the sea to some degree or another. What significance he gives its unarticulated – in textual terms – mysteries is his affair.

There is a further, but related, point of debate. To foreground the sea will not always please writers who approach Britten in the specific context of 'queer studies.' They are, naturally enough, determined to have the hostile society mistreating the 'outsider' unambivalently on the first place. And *Grimes* gives them plenty of rich examples. Furthermore, they are not likely to be disturbed by the ultimate decision of the authors of the opera and, most particularly Peter Pears, to exclude the 'queerness.' He decided that it had nothing directly to do with the work's deepest themes; 'the queerness is unimportant & doesn't really exist in the music.'[48] This simply means that the homosexual theme is a subtext and an inference that must be, and ought to be, made. I have no doubt that this is, to a significant extent, the case. After all, I will shortly argue below that inference is both unavoidable and apposite in the context of Wagner's anti-Semitism. Yet I am struck by the extent to which a critic as perspicacious as Philip Brett goes in his portrayal of collective guilt. He is determined to paint near indiscriminately the animosity directed at the (ersatz homosexual) outsider in the blackest possible colour. The townsfolk must be guilty of everything. For instance, in most of his many essays on Britten he cannot resist pointing out that by knocking on the door of the hut in the second scene of act two the villagers distract Grimes and that this leads to the boy losing his footing and falling to his death. Therefore they, more than anyone, are culpable. But knocking on a door is hardly an anti-social act. True, it is vital to the moral landscape of the opera that the villagers become a mob and stage a manhunt, but this does not mean that Grimes should be divested of all responsibility for his actions, or that chance has no part in the dramatic equation, or that we should gloss over the fact that not all the villagers are bigots and join the mob.

However, when it comes to putting the Borough in the first place Brett has, prima facie, an unlikely ally. The great tenor Jon Vickers, whose portrayal of the title figure elicited much admiration and some criticism (including from Britten), claimed he wanted to get the emphasis off Grimes and onto the community. He even wanted sympathy for the crowd/mob when they set out on the manhunt, although this was in order that they should understand later 'how wrong they were.' In fact his agenda was explicitly all-embracing: 'This work is timeless and universal and it's wrong to think that homosexuals are the only ones who ever feel rejected.' Hence he was not interested in playing the character as a gay man. Furthermore, it has been suggested that Vickers was not free of homophobia. According to Charles Mackerras he was 'violently anti-homosexual' and even felt that gay producers should not direct heterosexual works.[49] The composer certainly disliked his portrayal of Grimes. Robert Tear said Britten 'couldn't bear it.'[50] Vickers, who was a deeply committed Christian, always went his own way. He was notoriously stubborn and often difficult to work with. For instance, he refused to sing *Tannhäuser* because he found it blasphemous. In the case of Grimes he changed the text and was free with the score. He was, thought Britten, too manic; he 'sentimentalises', he loses the 'visionary' aspect.[51]

Nonetheless it was a mighty and at times overwhelming portrayal. I can still remember the force and excitement of the performances I saw in the Elijah Moshinsky production at Covent Garden in the 1980s, available on video. And it is perhaps an irony apposite to this discussion that Vickers's unconventional, and arguably contradictory approach (he acknowledged that the work was written by a homosexual for a homosexual), has an ambivalent relationship to the two sides of the discussion in play here. As a victim he appeals to the promoters of queer studies, but in rejecting, more forcedly than most, the homosexual agenda he pushes the emphasis onto Grimes's brutish and culpable character. Frankly, I feel that the visionary Grimes is hard to do without, no matter how rich and many-sided the piece. Certainly if Britten felt that with Pears and his own recording he could establish an orthodoxy he did not so much underrate the accomplishments of other, future, interpretative artists, as his own. He had produced a fascinating and heterogeneous opera and central character. *Peter Grimes* would inevitably leave many questions richly open and invite a plurality of approaches.

Even so, it is clearly relevant, at the very least, that any upfront suggestion of homosexuality was expunged by the creators. This included Grimes's demand in an early draft to the boy: 'Love me darn you.'[52] Furthermore, it is clear that the title character's real torments, even if they are sublimated expressions of the composer's sexuality – which common sense decrees they must to some extent be – find aesthetic expression in the symbolic world of nature. Indeed it is just this grander context that makes them universally relevant and rescues them from the dangers of propaganda. Nonetheless, if the Anderson quote is right, the homosexual apologist will have Britten on his side when he claims that 'the natural detail is secondary to the human drama.'[53] I, however, claim that in the theatre the audience in general 'knows' that the real torments of Grimes's soul are expressed in the tonal world associated with the sea; that there is a self-evident link, as in King Lear, between the storm we hear and the storm in Peter's mind. Each member of the audience may also come to understand, or feel, that as 'no harbour shelters peace' for the abandoned soul and for the visionary, the natural world is not only a reasonable option, but also a last, if fatal, resort.

Moreover, we also note that if Grimes is a visionary he has those visions on the boat, guided by the stars, although he may well remember them when he bursts suddenly into the pub in act one and then falls into a trance. Having finished his remarkable solo ('Now the Great Bear and Pleiades', not to be found in Crabbe) his fellow villagers can only respond 'He's mad.' Perhaps he is, but he is in touch with mysteries to which none of the others can be privy. Is it the madness of the holy fool? And if so, doesn't this cloud the waters of Grimes's cruelty and brutishness? Of course, it could be seen as a cop-out or an artistic swindle in that it has shifted the emphasis to more general and nebulous things – one is reminded of the mist in *Billy Budd* that makes the sea unfit for military action and under whose cover evil can work effectively. But art should swindle; it should load the dice outrageously. What counts is the effectiveness and depth of the finished work. In the case of *Peter Grimes* I do not think the end result is shallow or ineffective. Quite the opposite. And that depth and power is unquestionably the result of marginalizing, in terms of the specific language used, the plain fact that the opera was composed by a homosexual for a homosexual. No one, however, is ignoring that. As Pears said, the opera would be read inevitably as a symbol for the 'homosexual.'[54] But it is arguable that the shift that queer studies sees as an act of cowardice, albeit one forced on the creators by censorship and the intolerant society in which they lived, is the source of the opera's greater riches and its more universal power. Whatever the case may be, it is lost on the sea where Grimes 'belongs' and not at home in a gay bar on terra firma.

The Sea Interludes also expose as hollow the pieties of the offstage church service in act two. Conventional religion with its platitudes as uttered by the sexually tormented 'Methody preacher', Bob Boles, is an absurd and shallow phenomenon when seen in the context of the oceans. Placed in such a framework, conventional religion's village Almighty is little more than a totem worshipped by moral pygmies huddled together for warmth and fearful of bad weather. Britten's religious feeling was vastly deeper and more challenging and it made him highly sensitive to, and contemptuous of, cant. There is, for instance, a strong element of pantheism in his *Weltanschauung*. Not pantheism in the classic sense of worshipping all the Gods and, even, seeing them as proactive in the world, but in the sense that Wordsworth's poetry gives to pantheism. God is in nature. But the God – Wordsworth's God – that is felt in the landscape and the flora and fauna that Britten loved, is knowable; it is exact and it is safe. It has seasons – the quality celebrated in the *Spring Symphony* – which come around on cue even while the weather is untrustworthy. It is a clear and measurable world to be seen and loved in small things as flowers and insects are seen and loved. In short, it is as detailed as the Constable paintings that meant so much to both Britten and Pears. As Britten said in 1951: 'I am firmly rooted in this glorious country. And I proved this to myself when I once tried to live somewhere else.'[55]

The sea, however, is not to be known in this way. It is the site of a different and singular God, ineffable except through music and thereby it is a realm that suggests a spirituality beyond conventional explanation.

However, if the sea is ineffable it is not impeccable. Or if it is, it is because the divine force is not exclusively benign. In *Noye's Fludde* both congregation and cast sing a magnificent setting of the great hymn 'For those in peril on the sea.' The opera is, in any case, a story of how the Almighty has used the oceans to sweep away the wicked world man has created. It begins with a plea, in another hymn, for the restoration of innocence. The Borough folk in *Grimes* likewise sing, presumably to the Almighty in his guise as a natural force, 'O Tide that wait for no man/ Spare our coasts!' *Noye's Fludde* is, of course, a childlike tale, and is without the mysteries of the stage operas, but it reminds us of just how expansive the privileged notion is. Wisdom and disease, knowledge and destruction, above all redemption and death, are naturally expressed by the sea in Britten's hands. And this complex nexus is nowhere more potent than in *Death in Venice.* We know from the novella that Aschenbach's 'love of the ocean had profound sources.' But that is merely because in the contemplation of it he had always found rest.[56] Which is to say he is not aware of just how it can intermingle enlightenment with degradation. We, however, should not forget that Asiatic cholera, which is the ostensible agency of Aschenbach's descent, was initially thought to be an overland threat. But, as the excited young man working in the Travel Bureau explains, it surprised everyone and came, in fact 'by sea', landing in the southern ports.

Aschenbach also came to Venice by sea, which is not the most obvious route from Germany. In the novella this is easily explained. Venice was not his initial destination. His first choice was Trieste from where he went on to a resort on an island in the Adriatic. But he was not happy there. Even there he felt cut off from the sea. And then it came to him. Venice was the only option. How foolish he had been not to realise it immediately. He had intended to go to Venice all along, if only he had known it. But this is also a plot device designed to, among other things, underpin the arrival by boat and it was not one that Britten or Myfanwy Piper (forgetting the train journey) were prepared to do without it. 'What romantic notion made me want to come by sea?' the perpetually self-reflective hero asks himself in the opera. And then once in Venice he is rowed across the lagoon to the Lido by the Gondolier, who does not obey his instructions and whom he does not trust. But it has nothing to do with money. The Gondolier does not charge him. Instead Aschenbach will pay a much higher price. He is, in fact, being rowed across the river Styx to the Isle of the Dead.

But it is at the end of *Death in Venice* that the sea attains its most Delphic and ambivalent expression. The wordless Tadzio signals to the prostrate Aschenbach and then wanders slowly into the waters. Aschenbach wants to follow but he is finished. On reaching the sandbar Tadzio suddenly turns 'from the waist up' and looks back to the beach whereupon Aschenbach dies.[57] We might well think that, in symbolic language, Tadzio, the 'little Polish god' who embodies 'the soul of Greece', came, not from Poland, but from the sea, perhaps on a dolphin; something which would only bind him yet closer to Dionysus. He is certainly very much of the sea in Mann's novella: '. . . beautiful as a tender young god, emerging from the depths of sea and sky, outrunning the elements.' Seeing him run from the waters onto the beach was like witnessing 'the birth of form, of the origin of the gods.'[58] Furthermore, one feels that it is in that chosen mythic yet natural element that the final knowledge that Aschenbach, near to death, gleaned is to be found. But, as will be underlined in the next chapter, this is entirely consistent with the Greek world to which Aschenbach's speculations are continually drawn. Above all, it invokes the legend of Ganymede. That particular beautiful boy is abducted by an infatuated Zeus to be his cup-bearer on Mount Olympus. Both Socrates in Xenophon's *Symposium* and Mann in the novella employ the story; the latter underlining the brotherhood between Ganymede and Tadzio.

At the very least it is to the natural world, to the sea, to which the boy god has led Aschenbach. But here the infinite wisdom as to beauty and truth – and carnal and sensuous knowledge – that make up the writer's final ecstatic peroration comes with heavy moral baggage. One might say that everything, however ethereal the music (and the solo centres on exactly that part of Pears's voice – all those Es and E flats – that Britten found so bewitching and which are also the focus of 'The Great Bear and Pleiades' aria), is now complicated. There is no flight into Wagner's clean mountain air. Rather the waters have, yet again, been soiled. One might then entertain a progression from Starry Vere's final, somewhat dubious, claim that he has 'sighted . . . a far shining sail' and that he is now 'content' (Billy uses the word often; for instance on the night before his death he says he is 'contented' and that he, too, has 'sighted a sail in the storm, the far shining sail'), to the more profound mix of moral and philosophical ingredients that kill and enlighten Aschenbach. He has attained insights that transcend the normal polarities of good and evil, transparency and opacity. We are, in short, left with a profound mess, and not with an unambiguous Wagnerian transfiguration. We really don't know where Aschenbach is going, or whether, for that matter, he is going anywhere but to his earthly grave. With Wagner's heroes and heroines we know of the (after-)world to which they are destined. Indeed we are sometimes shown it with them already settled in on the premises.

We might justifiably infer from this that if Britten's metaphorical language stretches to include the infinite, Wagner's shrinks until it arrives at the specific. Even Tristan and Isolde who can be said to be lost on the boundless sea in act one, never escape into the universal, albeit earthly, realm. They remain bonded as a privileged unit that, if it doesn't in effect expel all other considerations shows them as secondary. The sea is of no symbolic or spiritual significance. It is merely the plot device which isolates them on board the ship, while the famous philtre simply shuts them off from the world. As Isolde says to Brangäne before she orders her to prepare the potion: 'Now farewell, Brangäne! Greet the world for me, greet my father and mother!' The lovers are asocial in the profoundest sense. The true meaning and ideological heart of the opera is found in its clearest form in the preordained act of spiritual transfiguration at the end. Therefore the lovers' constricted self-obsessed, if otherworldly, megalomania is remarkable but apposite; as is their assertion of mutual 'individuation.' During the act two love duet they declare, appropriately enough in unison: 'I am myself the world.' Never have lovers been more egotistical, nor more celebrated and envied because of it.

It is, however, with the boy hero Siegfried that the shrinking – 'concentration' might have fewer pejorative connotations – intrinsic to the Wagnerian project is clearest, not least because the manner in which Wagner gets there is intriguing. He could be said to begin with the folk, finding some intellectual underpinning in communism. Subsequently he deserts this ideal, or at least he starts to water it down, until he is in a position to replace it with the hero.

It is an interesting question as to whether this is, chiefly, the result of an intellectual and ideological development on his part, or whether it is principally driven by the greater power and dramatic practicability of (stage) stories concentrating on selected individuals with a hero at their heart. Certainly the folk is not banished from Wagner's *Weltanschauung.* Rather it remains a necessary ideal – his racism means he cannot do with it – but it becomes, as we have seen, unreliable. It may well stab you in the back. It may be so petty as to want to redeem the money you borrowed from it. Worse still, it may even ignore you. Even so, in the comic opera *Die Meistersinger von Nürnberg,* with its large and ubiquitous chorus and closed urban setting in a walled town, the Volk reaches something like its true theatrical and ideological measure. There can be no doubt, however, that the hero is the genuine article. There lies redemption; for Walther von Stolzing, although he needs guidance, will engineer redemption for German art and for German society and, moreover, will do so in opposition to the odious French (*Welsch*) option. Furthermore, this is a notion and a dramatic praxis that seduces and reassures by its very simplicity. It is easy to handle and it belongs on the stage. Spotlighting the hero is straightforward; while even getting the folk in any credible form onto the boards is a problem; though Wagner might be said to have solved it, in part, in *Die Meistersinger.* In any case, doesn't the great playwright Schiller in *William Tell* state the principle clearly enough: 'The strong man is strongest when alone'? It is not surprising then if in the authentic heroic and tragic tale the tribe concedes everything to its leader. This is a consideration of which Thomas Mann gradually became aware. He found it increasingly disturbing. Wagner '. . . did not know . . . that in his tireless backward journeying to find the ultimate depths and origins he had discovered the man and the hero that he was looking for . . . *his* Siegfried.'[59] Well, if he didn't know it, he was certainly delighted to find it out.

In tracing this trajectory in Wagner's thinking – and like most things to do with his intellectual labours, one cannot expect it to be either unproblematic or straightforward – it is as well to begin with the Volk, if only in an attempt to disentangle the master's ideas. But even here, and especially if we keep in mind the Mann quote in the last paragraph, we should not fail to see that Wagner wants to ground the Volk in something deeper. At the beginning there is always Nature; that mysterious force with which *The Ring* cycle opens. And thus the Volk has to be enfolded into the great womb of the natural world, even though Wagner thought that the Germans of his time were well on the way to losing all sensory perception and recollection of this. But the Volk in its own collective fashion needs to experience what Siegfried experiences in the forest. Nonetheless, this is not the pantheism already noted in respect of Britten. Rather it is a notion of nature that can, like so much else, be employed to privilege the German people. Therefore what Siegfried dramatically embodies as hero on the boards is explained by the fundamental notion of nature to be found in Wagner's writings. For 'Man only then becomes free, when he gains the glad consciousness of his oneness with Nature.'[60] He also talks of 'the ground-view of Nature's essence' and he laments that 'Christianity upheaved the [pre-Christian] religious faith . . . and supplanted it by a new belief.'[61] Moreover, the language and imagery he uses as he describes this brutal act of uprooting is strikingly echoed in the language and imagery associated with the world's great ash in *The Ring*; the symbolic tree which, at the end, Wotan chops down to fuel the final conflagration. Above all, we should never forget how elemental this is and, consequently, how secondary everything else is. However, while it is true that Christianity, arriving late on the scene, cannot erase the past, the Volk, unfortunately, does lose 'all true understanding of the original, vital relations . . .'[62]

When Wagner wrote *The Art-Work of the Future* (1849) he wanted to underline the collective. Thus the Volk is now the royal road – indeed the only road – open to the modern, perceptive artist. It is the 'vital force' that has existed of old as '. . . the inclusive term for all the units which made up the total of a commonality.'[63] One could say that here he is dressing up Herder's ideas in his own metaphysical language and taking them as far as he can go, which is a good deal further than Herder would have wanted to go. And in contemplating this ideal he can get quite carried away. 'In fellowship [we] grow up in communion to veritable men. In common, too, shall we close the last link in the bond of holy Necessity; and the brother-kiss that seals this bond, will be the mutual Art-work of the Future . . . the Volk, will no longer be a severed and peculiar class; for in this Art-work we shall all be one, [. . .] – blissful men.'[64] Yet here also we can see how the individual pantheistic hero functions as a starting point, even if it and he are only implied. 'The real Man will therefore never be forthcoming, until true Human Nature . . . shall model and ordain his Life . . . For as Man only then becomes free, when he gains the glad consciousness of his oneness with Nature.'[65] But this is, it seems, only a first step. The hero, or the artist, 'yields himself, not to a love for this or that particular object, but to wide Love itself. Thus does the egoist become a communist, the unit all, the man God, the art-variety Art.'[66]

This sentiment is also to be found in *Opera and Drama*, written two years after *The Art-Work of the Future*. And there it underpins a further step that the left-wing radical might think consistent. The state will become redundant. But in Wagner's *Weltanschauung* it gives way not to the class, but to the tribe. The state has set up a barrier against love. 'The Going-under of the State means therefore the falling-away of the barrier which the egoistic vanity of Experience, in the form of Prejudice, has erected against the spontaneity of individual dealings. This barrier at present takes the place that naturally belongs to love, and by its essence it is lovelessness.'[67] This is very reminiscent, in both sentiment and language, of Wagner's near contemporary charge against Christianity. In *Jesus of Nazareth* (1848) we are told that because Christianity has succumbed to materialism and private property it has 'set up a dam against love's free eternal movement . . .'[68]

On the one hand these declarations might seem kosher in Marxist-Leninist terms. Marx after all insisted, above all in *The Critique of the Gotha Programme*, that the State is doomed to disappear. It is to be superseded by history's preordained and first universal class: the international industrial proletariat. This body of men (and it does seem as though it has to be overwhelmingly men) is going to reveal itself as the universal class because it will, as a result of its own dialectical evolution, attain an innate historical understanding that amounts to a quantum leap over everything that has gone before. On the other hand, however, one gets some sense from Wagner's language of just how wishy-washy his notion of communism actually was. Dialectical materialism it was not. It had more to do with the sentimental Marxism of his contemporary Ludwig Feuerbach, with whose work he was familiar and at one time admired, than with nuts and bolts class analysis. It was, in fact, the sort thing that Lenin was later to call in a famous essay on *Left-Wing Communism* 'an infantile disorder.' Frankly I don't think Britten's engagement with communism in the 1930s went, at least in purely intellectual terms, much deeper. Still, Wagner has arrived at a position that, however dependent on the pantheistic god-like individual for its initial infant steps, does indeed put the Volk in the first, all-determining, position. But he can't keep it there.

More to the point, he cannot even *put* Siegfried there. For *he* remains a loner throughout the last two evenings of the cycle, but for the union with Brünnhilde. He is always strongest – and for that matter, weakest – when alone; except, that is, when he is with the woman for whom he was destined. It is, however, notable that after the last act of *Siegfried* we only see them alone together in the Prologue of *Götterdämmerung*. The Volk meanwhile (the Gibichungs), are, at best, merely Siegfried's mindless fan club, having more in common with hooligans than the noble all-loving people Wagner has rhapsodized about in his earlier essays. In other words, in discovering that the hero is not so easily gainsaid or forgone Wagner is logically compelled to take a further step. He must accept and celebrate what is made out of the hero in both narrative and ideological terms. This is nothing less than the redeeming and paramount unit of the heterosexual couple. And there is simply no possibility, at least before *Parsifal*, of this paradigmatic ideal being unseated. In the first instance this is because the 'love' Wagner is trying to foreground – 'wide Love itself' – is really only demonstrable, in Wagner's hands, in terms of the heterosexual pair. The, folk-based, exception to this – if there is one – would be the great chorus in act three of *Die Meistersinger* when the townspeople praise Sachs, ending with *'Heil Sachs! Heil dir, Sachs! Heil Nürnbergs teurem Sachs! Heil! Heil!'* But the problem here is self-evident. We are not free of the hero/leader. The Volk has not been put on his place; rather it has, momentarily been placed centre stage (Wagner's instruction is that the Masters and the other participants 'surrender themselves' [*sich hingeben*] to the Volk at this point) so that it can proclaim the unrivalled position of the Leader. In the second instance, the matter is hopeless anyway, because after writing *The Art-Work of the Future* Wagner would have his encounter with Schopenhauer and that, however perversely, simply made him more dependent on the loving and sexual couple as the all explanatory and all redeeming unit.

This shift – though perhaps it is better called a return to the basic principles of the first redemption drama, *The Flying Dutchman* – is clear in the letter to August Röckel.[69] Suddenly the collective is *ipso facto* dismissed: '. . . we must completely abandon our search for the "whole": the whole reveals itself to us only in individual manifestations . . .' This might sound to us like a pre-echo of the struggle Wagner is going to have later with Schopenhauer's negative notion of 'individuation.' Wagner continues: '. . . we can really "grasp" a phenomenon only if we can allow ourselves to be fully absorbed by it, just as we must in turn be able to assimilate it fully within us. How is this marvellous process most fully achieved? Ask nature! Only through love! – everything that I cannot love remains outside of me, and I remain outside it . . .' And he duly goes onto to explain, as we have noted above, how all this is only possible through the love between a man and a woman. However, I would suggest that this shift from the Volk to the hero and then the couple, has been steered at least as much by dramatic needs (the business of fashioning operatic narratives) as it has by high theory.

Perhaps the most interesting aspect of this development, and one that will be examined more closely in the next chapter, is the shift in *Parsifal*. For while the Siegfried paradigm implies the Volk, although it cannot realise it, Wagner will indeed make a crucial, final step that places both the Volk and the hero on the second place. He will exceed them with something more spiritual and utterly Schopenhauerian, although he will not, as a result, sacrifice sex as the noble and necessary pathway to salvation, nor will he forgo his anti-Semitism. This shift is embodied in the, initially, active hero of the last opera and in the suffering Christ-figure Amfortas. Parsifal and Amfortas duly become blood-brothers and, as we will see in the next chapter, blood becomes a key signifier in the argument. It flows copiously and with as much relish as in the Offertorium of Britten's *War Requiem*, although in Wagner's case it does not have the stink of horror or the edgy sound of sarcasm about it. Action, meanwhile, will give place to contemplation, killing dragons to the cultivation of the soil, and Man the Hero will become the Saviour on the Cross.

In a moment we will turn again to the question of the role Wagner's racism plays in this development, but in respect of the general sketch of his work being laid out here it is worthwhile acknowledging now, albeit briefly, how disappointed Friedrich Nietzsche was with *Parsifal*. He rightly saw the last opera as a paean to quietism. He lamented the absence of the instinctual action that had animated *The Ring*, of its manliness, and of the heroic defiance of the individual who, Nietzsche thought, was by his very nature compelled to reject the pygmy societies he saw everywhere in the modern European world. In *Parsifal* Wagner had abandoned and betrayed Greek heroism – Achilles and his German cousin Siegfried both were gone – and had accepted instead the feeble world of modern Christianity. Of course Nietzsche is not going to foreground a positive notion of contemplation; he has in any case turned against Schopenhauer by this time and thinks that the philosopher is the reef on which Wagner's ship has gone aground.[70] But he does more than this. He seems to be trying to fuse the agent with the activity, so that for the hero to be and to act are simultaneous, even identical, states. Of course he really can't overcome the fact of a causal link between consciousness and action, but he certainly seems to want to give it a try. Don't ignorant people, for instance, separate the lightning from the flash when in fact they are one and the same? Likewise, there is no distinction to be made between 'strength' and 'the manifestations of strength.' Instead, the man and the act are synonymous. 'There is . . . no "being" behind the doing, acting, becoming.' 'The doer' is merely made up and added into the action – the act is everything.[71] This is a long way from the more poetic sentiment of Auden's that Britten set in *Paul Bunyan*: 'A man is a form of life/ that dreams in order to act/ And acts in order to dream.' And this, and not Nietzsche's alternative fantasy, is the world in which Wagner's great dreamers belong. There is not a hero or a heroine who does not either literally (Senta and Elsa), or metaphorically in the sense of daydreams, fall into this category. Nietzsche is, as we will see, mistaken. Siegfried is not a personification of the 'lightning principle.' He dreams constantly and longingly of his dead mother and is thereby primed for action.

Nonetheless, who is to blame Nietzsche if, in *On The Use and Abuse of History for Life*, he turns longingly to the inspiring archetypal German hero of the 1840s and 50s in order to rally the coming generations? '. . . I recognize the mission of that *youth*, that first generation of fighters and dragon slayers, which brings forth a more fortunate and more beautiful culture and humanity . . .'[72] Nothing is more apposite than this as a criticism of *Parsifal* . . . as far as it goes. But Nietzsche has no sense of the freedom in religious and sexual matters Wagner has won in compensation for progressing beyond, for transcending, *his* dragon slayer. Yet it is not to be overlooked that Siegfried has been driven from the field. At this point we might note that the Ur-boy hero, draped refulgently in nature and speaking the original Teutonic tongue, had to forge his own sword (Nothing) and that it duly became a totem in *The Ring*. On the other hand, while it is true that young Parsifal kills without thinking in the first act (his deed is instinctual and therefore very Nietzschean), he is soon brought to appreciate what a terrible thing he has done. His victim, by the way, is not a dragon but a swan. Now, however, he begins to think and understand a little – Siegfried understands more through experience than thought – and finding himself appalled and ashamed, he breaks his weapons. Meanwhile, in the relevant and contemporary essays collected in *Religion and Art* Wagner has pushed the hero off centre stage to at least the same degree as he does in the last drama. His late prose is devoted instead to the virtues of renunciation and a respect for the noble loser: '. . . our sympathy belongs not to the victor, but the vanquished hero.'[73] Above all, he is keen to foreground the cultivation of the soil, the 'tillage of the fields.' As he points out, this is the true origin of the word 'culture.'[74] Are we now to believe that Nothung has been beaten into a ploughshare?

In looking at Wagner's anti-Semitism in the context of people and nation we should make sure not to look at it from one perspective only. By which I mean, it is not merely a question of what Wagner's anti-Semitism meant to him vis-à-vis the Jews. It is also a question, and arguably a more important one, of what it meant to him vis-à-vis his own people: the Germans.

If we focus on the Germans as the defining manifestation of Wagner's anti-Semitism we will get some idea of how mistaken the strategies of the Wagner apologists are. They want to marginalise the problem. Of course the days are long gone when they could claim that there wasn't one. Even the most committed flat-earthers, and there are a lot, are aware that the anti-Semitism has to be faced. It is true that many want to contain the issue within the pages of Wagner's essay *Jewishness in Music*, initially published anonymously in 1850, as though the matter might be better got around if this were fully conceded. The strategy would then be to claim that if the poison was somehow limited to this one malevolent paroxysm it should be possible to convince the worried acolyte that it was only a single, albeit deplorable, lapse. That is, it was not at all typical. After all, we all say and do things we later regret and so forth, and artists in particular are notoriously careless in their public pronouncements. Whereupon we can conclude that the anti-Semitism is not to be made much of. It is just such a pity that it provides so much ready ammunition for sensationalist writers and Wagner haters. That, however, simply won't wash.

Once Cosima's diaries were published the plethora of racist remarks was too shocking, even for many apologists, to be overlooked. Furthermore, if attention is paid to the essays that make up *Religion and Art* (1880), and in particular the short essay *Know Thyself* that was, like *Religion and Art*, also published in the Bayreuther Blätter (1881) – although that is infrequently done – the fundamental nature and need of Wagner's anti-Semitism becomes unmistakable. And one should also note that Wagner had *Jewishness in Music* reissued in 1869, and this time under his own name. More significantly, he wrote a new introduction for it. He did not do this to dilute its message or to try to make the piece more palatable for respectable readers. There was no bashful acknowledgement, for instance, of youthful excess and so forth. Rather he wanted to strengthen the polemic simply because the older he got the greater the Semitic threat seemed to be. In other words, he was nothing less than a consistent and a bold proselytiser in the Aryan cause. And he did not lack either courage or commitment. The matter had got into his gut. As he wrote to Liszt on 18 April 1851: 'I harboured a long-suppressed resentment against this Jewish business, and this resentment is as necessary to my nature as gall is to the blood.' Therefore in the 1869 reissue of *Jewishness in Music* he was determined to show that he had himself been a specially selected target of a Jewish conspiracy and that in general 'blond and pure-bred' German art was everywhere under threat from the same dreaded source.[75]

One of the more interesting strategies of the flat-earthers is that they literally marginalise the problem formally in their own books. Dieter Borchmeyer in 1991 deals with the issue in an 'Afterword' and in his 2002 book it becomes an 'Exkurs.' Michael Tanner in 1996 gets rid of it early as though it were a bad, and definitely an irrelevant, smell. He can then get down to the serious stuff. In 2010 he leaves it to a final chapter that he acknowledges he didn't want to write. Bryan Magee (2000) devotes a long final 'Appendix' to the problem. They all conclude that it is simply not substantive with respect to Wagner's operas, no matter how unpleasant it is. Indeed Anglo-Saxons, in particular, can get quite carried away in expressing their disgust at *Jewishness in Music.* It is as if they lay it on with a trowel not merely to make it clear that they are not anti-Semitic themselves (yet who would have thought otherwise?), but to strike an implicit deal with the reader. If Wagner's guilt is played up for all it is worth in this one instance then, as a compensatory gesture, we might leave the apologists alone to enjoy the operas free of irritating references to any supposed racist content.

There are certain arguments used to underpin this strategy. They are unconvincing, but attractive to the Wagnerite who needs reassurance that the operas are indeed morally safe. The most obvious is to say there are no Jewish characters in any of the stage works and that no one says anything about Jews. Of course, unless there are specific musical quotations from well-known tunes, it is very hard to characterise any music as 'Jewish.' Some commentators have done this but as that is a matter for musicians and musicologists it is not part of the agenda of this book. It is enough to take Daniel Barenboim at his word: the music is not anti-Semitic. After all, in the operas, 'there is not one Jewish character. There is not one anti-Semitic remark.'[76] While we will return to Barenboim's position in the last chapter, his blithe assertion as to the absence of anti-Semitism can be taken as a starting point from which we can address the problem now.

One might begin with the claim, made by nearly all flat-earthers, that there are no Jewish characters in Wagner's operas. The first, but not the only, answer to this claim is simply to point out that it is just plain wrong. We know that the Dutchman is a manifestation of the Wandering Jew (The Eternal Jew) and is linked to the Jewish character of Ahasuerus because Wagner tells us so in *A Communication to my Friends.* This is not uninteresting because the Dutchman is the first of Wagner's tragic males in need of female redemption. And what is more, he is duly rewarded. In this he is not unlike the great God Wotan; a role that is vocally as well ideologically similar, although Wotan is a considerably more complex character. After all, it is Wagner who points out the – we might think – obvious parallel between the archetypal Jewish figure Ahasuerus and the God. Wotan becomes 'The Wanderer' in *Siegfried*, compelled to rove through the world and watch with mounting despair as Alberich's curse undermines all his attempts to save it.[77] It should also be stressed that Wotan fits the pattern of the Wagner hero in other ways. While it is true that there is no longer a heterosexual union open to him whereby the world can be redeemed, his glorious daughter Brünnhilde will perform the drama's last rites in order to accomplish just this. It is therefore particularly instructive to note that, according to his wife Fricka in the second act of *Die Walküre*, Wotan harbours incestuous feelings towards Brünnhilde. She is the 'the bride of [his] desires.' Wotan himself in the third act says of Brünnhilde: 'She herself was the fertile womb [*schaffender Schoss*] of my wishes.'

As Wagner explains it, the Wandering Jew is a later embodiment in the Christian era of Ulysses. As such he is a heroic, but also a doomed, figure. For, unlike Ulysses, he has no home. Rather like Grimes, he is to discover that no harbour shelters peace: '. . . death was the sole remaining goal of all his strivings; his only hope, the laying-down of being.'[78] In short, he has the same destiny as Ahasuerus, who at the end of *Jewishness in Music* is simply compelled to accept his inevitable destiny: his 'Downfall' (*Untergang*). It is significant that Ahasuerus's great sin is usually thought to have been his mockery of Christ as he made his way to Golgotha. But whereas the Wandering Jew, at least in the classic telling of the tale, is condemned to walk the earth until redeemed by the second coming, Wagner employs a 'Christianized' version of him in his first, and rather simplified – and therefore ideologically balder – redemption opera. While the Dutchman is compelled to sail eternally he is given a chance every seven years to escape the curse. He may land and if he finds the love of a good woman he will be saved. In the opera, despite, or because of, a dreadful misunderstanding, Senta – as predestined as every other decent Wagner heroine; she has always dreamt of the Flying Dutchman – proves herself to be that woman. At the climax she duly commits suicide by throwing herself off a cliff. Her dream man is in the process of sailing away with his ghostly crew, convinced – mistakenly – that he has once again been betrayed. Senta's sacrifice lifts the curse, redeems them both, and enables them to enter the higher realm as a couple. Wagner wants us to see this in a projection on the backcloth. It may be a crude version of the emblematic trope, but it will do, and with a powerful score it is highly effective in the opera house.

The reason why it is significant that in the classic version of the story Ahasuerus is cursed because he derided Christ on the Via Dolorosa is pertinent. In his last redemption opera Wagner returned to the same theme. As we have already had cause to note, Kundry confesses to Parsifal in the second act that she also mocked Christ while he was on the way to Golgotha and has been throughout the following centuries cursed as a result. And Kundry, Wagner explains, is also a manifestation of the Wandering Jew.[79] By the way, this should not come as a surprise given that Klingsor refers to Kundry as 'Herodias', and Herodias, according to legend, was also the companion of the Eternal Jew.

Arguably of more significance than the explicit references to the Wandering Jew, are the implied Jewish figures in Wagner's operas. Here, of course, we enter on territory that is both arbitrary and subjective and therefore the apologist can simply deny any association if he wants. But if he does take the line that 'This, at best, is idle speculation . . .'[80] he will have to do so in the teeth of a great deal of opposition, scholarship, and also, I should have thought, a fair modicum of plain common sense. One might here, in order to avoid the charge of banging a contemporary and fashionable drum now that there are so many critics and there is so much literature about, rewind back to a great musician who was born twenty-three years before Wagner died: Gustav Mahler. He turned to the classic case of Mime; classic in the sense that he seems the most unmissable candidate for the title of ersatz Jew. In 1898 Mahler said: 'No doubt with Mime, Wagner intended to ridicule the Jews with all their characteristic traits . . . petty intelligence and greed . . . the jargon is textually and musically so cleverly suggested . . .'[81] Certainly it is very difficult to read what Wagner wrote in *Jewishness in Music* about the mode of Jewish expression in word and song, as well as Jewish body language, and then forget it when listening to the accusations Siegfried throws at the wheedling, whining, shuffling Mime. The point is well made by Thomas S. Grey. He says simply 'one would have to be culturally tone-deaf not to see how Siegfried's attitude toward Mime reflects a great deal of Wagner's attitude toward the Jews . . .'[82] Of course all of this was argued in devastating fashion in the late 1930s and 40s by Theodor Adorno.[83]

Perhaps a more interesting example is Mime's Nibelung brother Alberich. There is one observation on Wagner's part which, one would have thought, was sufficiently clear as to make even inference largely superfluous. And Alberich, after all, would be an ideal candidate for Wagner's anti-Semitism. He looks evil, he is utterly alien, he is obsessed by money, and he is explicitly loveless. This latter state is *the* defining Jewish characteristic in the Wagner

Weltanschauung. It is the unbridgeable chasm which holds those two similar metaphysical entities, Germanness and Jewishness, irrevocably and irreconcilably apart. And Wagner is well aware of what a terrible burden it is and how, consequently, it accounts for the toxic nature of Judaism, not least because it is the Jew's tragedy that '. . . this lovelessness must ever become more obvious to him.'[84] After all, Wagner tells Cosima a few days before his death: 'Jewishness is a terrible curse; no possibility, for example, of marrying a Christian woman.'[85] But perhaps Alberich's most obvious Jewish trait is his desire and determination to take over the world. Wagner has something to say about this in *Know Thyself* (1881), which is largely given over to an attack on the Jews, chiefly the manner in which they have used money to enslave pure German society. Wagner hopes his polemic will help Germans appreciate what is quintessentially theirs. The essay was provoked, it seems, by his outrage at Jewish emancipation. With respect to Alberich he observes: 'The Nibelung's fateful ring become a pocket-book, might well complete the eerie picture of the spectral world-controller.'[86] This, incidentally, was a point not lost on the most prominent Nazi ideologue, Alfred Rosenberg. In the *Der Mythus des 20. Jahrhundert* he characterises Alberich as the blackest of Jewish demons, dreaming of gold and driven by hate. He belongs in that class of capitalists who, the Nazis always maintained, stabbed Germany in the back during the First World War.[87]

Given that those not disposed to make inferences, or to see what stands in plain sight, cannot be forced to do so, a final example will have to suffice. The arguments surrounding Beckmesser (the pedantic town clerk in *Die Meistersinger*) are, however, especially intriguing because it has been maintained that there is a coded link between the character and the title figure in the Grimms' anti-Semitic Fairy Tale *The Jew in the Thorn Bush.* In recent decades the most detailed analysis of this has been Barry Millington's (1991). It seems to have got under the skin of several apologists (Borchmeyer, Tanner, and Hans Rudolf Vaget for example) although it has stood up very well to repeated attacks.[88] Sometimes these attacks have turned out to be self-defeating. Borchmeyer, who customarily takes a broad and culturally insightful approach (he sees, for instance, an 'affinity' between the Wandering Jew and Wagner[89]) is in this instance very literal. Unfortunately he claimed, erroneously, that Wagner did not possess a copy of the Grimms' story.

Further he simply rules out any kind of code or inference and says that Beckmesser cannot be an ersatz Jew because a Jew could never have served on the town council in Nuremberg.[90] Vaget, meanwhile, is prepared to see a link between the opera and the story but maintains that it is arbitrary and therefore not determining. He also points out a supposed discrepancy because, whereas the title character in the story gets hung at the end, Beckmesser is merely ridiculed.[91] Frankly, one would have thought that a public lynching in a comedy might be asking a bit much. Nonetheless in the first (Borchemyer) case, given that the character is an ersatz Jew, it is neither here nor there whether he was eligible to fulfil certain public functions or not, and in the second, when Beckmesser is massacring the prize song in the last act, the Volk remark that soon he will end up on the gallows.

Tanner's position is especially pertinent because he wishes to preserve the joys and greatness of Wagner's operas from contemporary attacks, from critics he sees as flooding the master's works with 'sewage.'[92] To do so he resorts to privileged figures from the past. Their opinions are likely to be right simply because of who they were. This is not an unreasonable strategy and has already been employed here with respect to Mahler. No one stands higher in Tanner's estimation than Thomas Mann who 'not even once' mentions Wagner's anti-Semitism.[93] But this is pure bunkum. Mann, who incidentally knew Adorno very well, went so far as to express the view that: 'I find an element of Nazism not only in Wagner's questionable literature; I find it also in his music.'[94] Even more damning is a letter to Emil Pretorius from 6 December 1949 in which the Hitler/Wagner coupling also surfaces. Here Mann calls Beckmesser explicitly the 'Jew in the Thorn Bush': i.e. the title character of the Grimms' uncompromisingly anti-Semitic fairy tale.[95]

I do not wish to confuse, let alone shock, the reader but I feel it is only fair to say now that I see no reason why Wagner's anti-Semitism cannot be acknowledged and pursued in his essays and operas without coming to the conclusion that one cannot enjoy the music. It is this fear, however, that is behind the labours, and the myopia, of the flat-earthers and while it may seem impeccable, I believe it does them no credit. This is a point to which we can return in the final chapter. For now, having dealt with both the explicit and the implicit anti-Semitism of the operas, it is necessary to turn to what is the most fundamental, productive, and enlightening factor in Wagner's racism: what it tells us about his view of the Germans.

A useful point of entry into this part of the argument is to consider the case made by Bryan Magee. Trying to establish that there is no anti-Semitism in the operas he turns to *Jewishness in Music* and points out that there Wagner says quite explicitly that the Jews qua Jews are simply not fit for portrayal as characters on the stage. Therefore if we want evidence that the composer was not interested in dealing with the Jewish question in the operas: 'there we have it.'[96] While this is superficially logical, it surely hides a deep contradiction. To turn to an essay by Wagner that is designed to expose the bad fit between Jewishness and music by virtue of a very explicit and detailed anti-Semitic argument, in order to establish that the composer kept any anti-Semitic consideration out of his *own* creative musical work is to ask a great deal of the reader. The writer, after all, has to argue that there is no anti-Semitism in the operas because Wagner was such a *disciplined* anti-Semite. Furthermore, the essay *Jewishness in Music*, and much else besides written by Wagner, make it absolutely clear that he considered the Jewish question of the utmost importance. And it got more pressing the longer he lived. Disaster, as he told King Ludwig, was approaching. He said to Cosima late in life: 'I find it embarrassing to keep coming back to the subject of the Jews but one can't avoid it when thinking about the future.'[97] And, naturally, any consideration given to Wagner's unconscious would explode the type of strategy employed by Magee. An apologist might well point out that we have a dangerously free hand when it comes to speculations concerning the unconscious, but Wagner gives us so much evidence that it is absurd to suggest that such speculations in his case are not pertinent or that they lack underpinning from the pen of the master himself.

The point is, of course, that while no character identified *explicitly in the libretto* as a Jew 'shuffles' across the stage in the course of an opera, the threat posed by the Jewish question invests the operatic project simply because that project is, in part, motivated and driven by it. The anti-Semitic desire to set something before the public that is *not* infected by Jewishness is, as Wagner tells us repeatedly and Magee knowingly underlines, one of the chief drives that animate him. This is the case simply because Germanness is so often defined as being in opposition to weaker European racial and cultural types (above all the French or *Welsch*) or to the Jews. And hence the Magee type argument ends up establishing the very thing it is supposed to expose as invalid and irrelevant. For everything that is positive and German in the operas is so because it is *not* Jewish. It positively screams (or sings) its non-Jewish being and, moreover, Wagner goes to great lengths to explain, theoretically, how this is the case and how far-reaching its consequences are for the German nation. So even if we reject the two arguments already presented – that Wagner does in fact have identifiable Jewish characters in his operas in that *he* identifies them explicitly in the essays etc, and that he also employs ersatz Jews anyway – we might expect to find the Jewish problem present in the form of its beneficent antipode. And that antipode is Deutsch and echt. It is what Hans Sachs, in effect, sings about throughout *Die Meistersinger* and then turns into an explicit nationalist hymn to German art and the German Volk at the end: 'Scorn not the German masters and honour their Art.' This is the art the Jew simply cannot produce for he can never, even after generations, escape his racial identity. He will, for instance, always expose himself in the degenerate manner in which he speaks German.[98] Although a good mimic, he is no more able to pull the trick off convincingly than is Mime.

Therefore the real hero fighting the anti-Semitic cause in Wagner is Siegfried. He and the likes of Walther von Stolzing are the true anti-Semitic characters; as indeed are all the glorious heroines who redeem them and their like. (Sinful Kundry, as we have seen time and again, is a special case.) Perhaps the chief virtue of Siegfried, at least in this context, is that he is not fooled by Mime, 'his' ersatz Jew. Neither is Walther von Stolzing. Despite all the chicanery devised by his ersatz Jew (Beckmesser), Stolzing finally comes into his full voice and establishes the new musical language while paying homage to the greatest of all German masters: Hans Sachs. It is, of course, wholly apposite that Beckmesser is exposed in word and song by the Prize Lied that Stolzing and Sachs have mutually put together. Faced with the task of interpretation and performance Beckmesser can only produce what Wagner in the essay calls *Gelabber*: drivel or gibberish.[99] Like those Germans who have gone awry by aping all things French (the ubiquitous Wagner and Herder accusation), the Jew attempts, but mercifully fails, to pass himself off as genuinely German.

Central to this undertaking is Wagner's insistence on not only the special status of the Jewish *naturel* (tongue, whether in speech or song), but also of Jewish blood. This is an interesting position for him to take up and it exposes a contradiction – but a necessary one – in his thinking. Whereas he is, perhaps surprisingly, broad-minded when it comes to German blood – as we have already had cause to note – he is not when it comes to Jewish blood. So it is not only with respect to the Jewish tongue that he is unbending. But this determination is based on the need to be absolutely clear as to the identifiable threat to German life and German art. So while he was quite prepared to tolerate – indeed to welcome – the intermingling of German blood with the sturdier races of Europe, in the case of Jewish blood there must be no concession whatsoever. The plain fact is, Semitic blood is 'corrosive.'[100] One must have nothing to do with it. In *Know Thyself* he states the principle in the most unbending terms possible: Should a non-Jew marry a Jew, 'a Jew will always come to birth.' This is all very peculiar as the usual accusation thrown at the Jews at this time – in particular very prominent in the work of the highly influential historian Heinrich von Treitschke – is that the Jews don't assimilate. Yet Wagner seems terrified that they might. In fact he assumes they already have, and moreover wherever the diaspora has taken them. Therefore, unlike the German: 'The Jew . . . is the most astounding instance of racial congruence ever offered by world-history . . . [he is] . . . without a fatherland, a mother-tongue . . .'[101] In plain language Wagner is nothing less than obsessed by what he calls, with his customary self-revealing frankness, the 'dreaded power' of the Jews.[102]

It will be necessary to remember this in the next chapter when Wagner's near frantic determination to keep Christ free of any association with either Jewish language or Jewish blood will be addressed. For the time being it is enough to suggest that the apologists are going to have their work cut out if, in the face of Wagner's passion on the subject and its overriding importance to him, they remain determined to put a firewall around the operas in the hope that they can keep out the poison. And while their reasons for doing this can now be left to the last chapter, one might at this point be satisfied with the awful suggestion that art – even great German art – sometimes needs poison, and that the Germanophile may well end up killing the thing he loves if he insists on adoring a chimera and running away from the real object of his fascination.

We are, of course, in the very position that Wagner didn't want to be in, in that for us what the Germans used to call the 'Jewish Question' is simply a normal part of life, irrespective of whether we are Jewish or Gentile, or indeed whether we are aware of such a question at all. By which I mean that irrespective of the extent and practice of anti-Semitism, we do not, in general, feel the need to compartmentalise in the manner that seemed to be a matter of national survival for Wagner. Yet Wagner must have had some strong sense of the alternative to his black and white *Weltanschauung*, not least because Jews, at least from Meyerbeer onwards, often played prominent roles in his creative life. In real, lived terms the Jewish question was never a matter of yes or no, with Wagner uncompromisingly in the no camp. He had Jewish colleagues, Jewish assistants, one of his favourite conductors (Hermann Levi) was Jewish. And then there was the sad case of Josef Rubinstein, the self-hating house Jew at Wahnfried during the last decade of Wagner's life. Of course Levi was insulted and patronised (Wagner wanted to devise a pseudo-Christian ceremony that would spiritually cleanse him so he would be fit to conduct *Parsifal*[103]) and Rubinstein was accused by Cosima of displaying 'all the dismal characteristics of his race' when she and Richard were not happy with his behaviour.[104] But Rubinstein, a fine pianist and musician and of much use to the Wagners, was utterly devoted. He could not go on without the master and duly committed suicide a year after Wagner's death. It is certainly striking that Wagner did not live in a *judenfrei* environment, not least because once he had been financially rescued by King Ludwig he might have done so had he wanted. It seems, however, that the necessary and metaphorical gall he mentioned to Liszt was indeed something that he could not live without. Surely this was because it was an indispensable ingredient in his creative life. It had to be kept nearby.

Consistent with this last supposition is a further consideration. In putting the Jews, no matter in so uncompromisingly negative a manner, at the centre of his *Weltanschauung* Wagner was compelled to build his intellectual life in the essays around the Jew as a symbol and as an empirical threat in much the same way as he built his philo-Germanic (anti-Semitic) ideal in the operas around Siegfried as its blond, blue-eyed, flesh-and-blood manifestation. The result means that instead of simply ditching his Christianized Jew, the Flying Dutchman, and moving on in manner that transcended, even ignored, the Jewish question, he ended up continually deepening the relationship. He cannot, of course, be as uninhibited in the matter as Nietzsche, who said that all artists and geniuses are Wandering Jews,[105] but he sees a perverse brotherhood – one might call it a negative blood-brotherhood – nonetheless. As we have seen, he regarded the question of German (if not Jewish) blood as 'a matter of pure metaphysics.'[106] But he can go further than this. In a letter to Nietzsche he confesses that he has 'succumbed to a curious scepticism which leaves me thinking of "Germanness" as a purely metaphysical concept, but, as such, it is of immense interest to me, and certainly something that is unique in the history of the world . . .'[107] All of which is fair enough. But does he not finish the sentence in order (knowingly) to contradict it? '. . . its only counterpart being Judaism.' I suggest it is impossible not to conclude that Wagner was profoundly and productively entangled in the whole Jewish business, whether we are talking about pure anti-Semitism, or his awareness of an unwelcome, but unavoidable, and above all creative, kinship.

None of this sort of stuff ever troubled Britten. Distrusting the notion of a nation and reducing the people to the local community, whether benign or, as in *Grimes*, largely horrid, he might be said to have escaped the bonds of nationalism. And yet he cannot have been indifferent to England, and quite possibly to Britain. He indulged in enough generalisations as to the backward characteristics of his birth nation's social and, more immediately relevant, musical life as to suggest that he had no ready or honest escape into the uncontaminated life of a near recluse, stuck out in the country and only concerned with his immediate fellows; almost all of whom would have had to be seen as simple but authentic chaps making their living as fishermen, shopkeepers, farmers and whatnot. The whole *Gloriana* project would have been anathema to him if he had been, in fact, so abstracted from the land of his birth. Nor should it be forgotten that once he had accepted the proposal for the opera he was most insistent that it should be given the exclusive status of a command performance, or at least that it be 'officially sanctioned.'[108] Nothing – certainly not a ballet – was to interfere with this, even though Lord Harewood, the Queen's cousin, advised him against it, and Peter Pears entertained serious and mounting doubts throughout work on the piece.

As a result, we might well infer a deep ambivalence in Britten's relations with the great and the good, not least because he enjoyed and cultivated such relationships. Royalty, British and German, were his friends. This went so far that his enemies and rivals could with some legitimacy accuse him of being a 'court composer' and suggest, with perhaps less justification, that their own compositions and careers were adversely affected as a result. Apparently Britten said to his friend Michael Tippett: 'I would be a Court composer but for my pacifism and homosexuality.'[109] Certainly he seemed on occasions hungry for status. Awards and honorary doctorates were collected. Then there was the peerage. Many, including perhaps Pears, thought it a strange business. Why on earth did he need that in his dying months? It was this sort of thing that led several commentators and artists – some like Robert Tear had worked for him before being turned out for assumed disloyalty – to suggest that he was timid and bourgeois; that he had gradually fudged his role and sold his integrity cheap.

On the one hand, it could be said that the honours and his status were proof of his success in improving the musical life of his country. After all, he had been once a fierce and, one might say, unpatriotic critic. As a self-consciously radical young man he had said of Elgar's first symphony: 'I swear that only in Imperialist England could such a work be tolerated.'[110] If he was now rewarded, then it was because he had exposed all the dyed in the wool traditionalists as redundant. He had, more than any one, pushed British musical life into the European world, he had given it an operatic identity, and had encouraged a school of new composers. His reaction to the scores sent to him by younger composers (and also to those sent by older ones such as Otto Klemperer) was unfailingly practical and encouraging. He had also shown the degree to which music making could not only be great on the national scale, but also effective in the community hall and classroom.

On the other hand, one might suspect that the two asocial blemishes that would always to some degree stain his character in the public mind – pacifism and homosexuality – were a constant very present danger; a danger that needed to be dealt with and, if possible, defused. While the first could be paraded publicly as a perfectly admirable moral position, albeit one with which the majority of his fellow countrymen and women could never agree, the second was a crime for most of his life and a subject of public derision, contemptuous humour, and endless gossip for all of it. Therefore it was advisable of Britten to embed himself among the establishment great and good, not least because he could. His world might have exploded at any time. Moreover, it is not clear how he could have been any bolder than he was as a homosexual and have remained true to himself as a man. In truth he did not like the gay scene, he didn't even like the word 'gay',[111] and he certainly didn't like 'queenery.'[112] But he did regard his sexual life as permanently settled once he and Pears became lovers in Grand Rapids. Pears said that Britten 'really was one hundred percent homosexual.'[113]

Auden may well have disliked Britten's 'lack of daring',[114] but it is arguable – indeed I would suggest that it is self-evidently obvious – that the psychic repressions Britten accepted as a matter of course, even though they may have been forced upon him by the society in which his public life took shape, would turn out to be vital and productive forces in his creative life. It will be argued later that precisely because these matters were sublimated and not turned into sloganising they found richer and deeper expression. Britten may have been a committed but not a banner waving pacifist, but as a gay man he was as honest as circumstances allowed. Of course he could have changed those circumstances, but he would not have had the career he wanted had he done so. Surely Auden appreciated that a poet in order to work and to see his work produced needs only himself and a publisher. He does not need the performing apparatus that is a matter of life and death for the composer, and particularly for a composer of stage works. Even so, Britten's 'marriage' was an open secret. In real terms he hid nothing. It is hard to argue that Auden's relationship with Chester Kallman was more blatant than – let alone as daring as – Britten's union with Pears. Yet Britten was never going to assume the more colourful, and flagrant role of a Quentin Crisp; someone who confirmed, to his own satisfaction, every public stereotype of the 'queer' as queen.

In general, it is a moot point as to why Britten was not more active politically. Why didn't he speak out more often? Was his timid response to political matters born of naïvety, or a feeling that he would be out of his depth, or perhaps a deep appreciation that a public role would cost him too much as a creative artist? Conceivably he might have believed that he could accomplish more by being silent in the public sphere and working behind the scenes. He was certainly upfront about his pacifism. But that was unavoidable, forced on him as a result of his chosen status as a conscientious objector during the war. But he took no part in protests against the Soviet Union when his Russian friends, above all Rostropovich and Vishnevskaya, were given a hard time. And on a Soviet Tour in 1963 it seems, in an interview in Pravda, he gave the impression that he was praising Soviet ideology by underlining his support for the notion of the artist in the community. But how could he have said otherwise given that this was an indispensable principle of his own thinking? Nonetheless, wanting to keep his Soviet contacts, he refused to protest publicly against the 1968 Soviet invasion of Czechoslovakia.[115] It could be argued, however, that in his private correspondence and dealings with Ekaterina Fursteva, the notorious and intransigent Soviet minister responsible for cultural affairs, he was adroit, flattering and manipulative. He duly won trips abroad, above all to Aldeburgh, for the Russian artists with whom he had formed close creative relationships. Yet the public options he chose were soft. There was a commissioned anthem for the United Nations, *Voices for Today* (1965), and bland pronouncements. Furthermore, as we shall have cause to underline, he can hardly be said to have faced up stringently to the intellectual conundrums born of pacifism.

No doubt there was also a biographical dimension to this. His life history marked out a gradual, but largely inexorable, development from youthful radical to grand old man of British music. Naturally after *Grimes* things got easier. And when the militant wartime hysteria inevitably diminished after 1945, pacifism became more socially palatable because it was no longer seen as undermining the nation at a time of crisis. In any case, hadn't Britten and Pears at least come back during hostilities? Their friends Auden and Isherwood would always be attacked because they never even made that gesture; and given that it would only have been a gesture they were probably right not to have trivialised their respective principles by doing so. Auden, by the way, was not a pacifist and registered for the draft in USA in 1942 but was rejected on medical grounds. His homosexuality also excluded him. Britten, meanwhile, might be said to have had the courage of *his* convictions. Moreover, under certain non-belligerent circumstances, conventional patriots can quite like pacifists. They are assumed to be morally good, although quite possibly misguided. For establishment figures, even military men, it is nice to have a few pacifist friends. It always makes a worthwhile subject for dinner table discussion – as it does for schoolboy essays – and provides a ready opportunity to show how broad-minded one is. Nothing pleases a high-ranking army officer more than the chance to point out that only men who have seen action truly appreciate the degree to which war is hell and how, therefore, it should be avoided at – nearly – all costs. So there is nothing bizarre in the *War Requiem* becoming Britten's great national, quasi-religious, composition. It is, after all, a far more open and knowing appropriation of the religious world than the more subtle, incest-based, and quite possibly self-hypocritical, invasion engineered by Wagner in *Parsifal.*

To put the matter plainly, I think that Tear and the others who appear in Tom Sutcliffe's television demolition job are in this respect wrong. Britten did not capitulate and prostitute himself at all. Indeed his selfishness speaks for him. He was wise to tart his opinions up with a bit more wishy-washy religious decoration when he appealed against the decision of the first tribunal on his application for exemption as a conscientious objector. That successful appeal freed him from any type of war work whatsoever. He did not belong in jail and martyrdom would have been humbug. He was wise to do what he could to get out of it. And surely the comparison with Tippet is exaggerated, at least when it is used to berate Britten. Tippett's two months in Wormwood Scrubs speak for his integrity in refusing all work that could be construed as assisting the war effort, but it does not make one composer a saint and the other a hypocrite. Their relative positions were very different. Britten was already established as a national figure; questions had been asked in Parliament during his time in the USA. In fact during Tippett's brief prison sojourn Britten gave a concert there. Tippett assisted. He also arranged a church commission for him. In any case, it was perfectly clear that Britten and Pears could do far more for national morale in Britain as touring performers – tasks they carried out assiduously – than working as civilians in civil defence etc. Surely even pacifists could have lived with that. Although there is a real problem here; a problem as to where to draw the line. Tippett, for instance, would not work as a fireman. But don't firemen and, for that matter, hospital porters et al, make a greater contribution to saving lives than singers, pianists and composers? In this context one could argue that there is a *reductio ad absurdum* inherent in the strict pacifist position. It necessitates either prison (Tippett felt very good about entering Wormwood Scrubs and was happy to be there) or life as an anchorite. For pursued stringently, in a time of total war pacifism makes any communal activity whatsoever, sabotage excepted, morally impossible. Moreover, we are also surely entitled to ask how does Tippett's unbending attitude to the establishment during the war sit with his later collection of grand national honours?

As we will see shortly, Britten, too, was confronted by the difficulty of making sense in practical terms of pacifism as a moral and philosophical position that otherwise seems so serenely clear and untroublesome when expressed as a self-evident absolute. What we can, however, say with confidence is that the final wartime decision of the tribunal to exempt Britten wholly was right, and the qualified decision on Tippett was wrong.

Britten is certainly caught in several anomalies that result from the professed fundamentals of his thinking on both moral and practical problems. After all, although the nation was placed lower on his scale of priorities than the community, that of itself did not sever the two notions. For instance, he might well have agreed privately with Forster that it was better to betray one's country than one's friend, but he was, like Forster, unable to compartmentalise community and nation so that there was no emotional or intellectual traffic between them. Rather the former has to imply the latter. This may lie at odds with the connotations of the argument otherwise being made here, but it is nonetheless an inevitable state of affairs. Britten can no more put a firewall around the Borough than Wagner can around Nuremberg. And, more to the point, neither composer wanted to. The Borough stands as a condemnation of England's (if not Britain's) provincialism and dangerous small-mindedness, just as Nuremberg declares with overweening confidence the glories of the German nation and people as expressed in their unique 'holy' art. Celebrating the community always implies a relationship with something greater, no matter whether the community is portrayed as typical or exceptional. The mere fact that Britten engaged with people and places that he knew, or felt close to through literature, meant that he could not avoid evoking the nation within whose frontiers those communities were situated. Tippett's operas, however, with their exotic settings (stretching to outer space in *New Year*), elaborate (often Jungian) mythological and psychological terms of reference, and 'foreign' pseudo-American jazz and blues influences, are not held within that kind of framework. Nor are many of his other works, most strikingly the late Oratorio *The Ascent of Man*. There the agenda is explicitly universal, and historically near unconstrained.

This returns us to an earlier theme in that it underlines just how far-reaching Britten's attachment to the loner-cum-outsider has to be. This is chiefly because that loneliness is not expressed in terms of an overt asocial existence. These loners are not solitary in the literal or superficial sense. They are neither hermits nor desert mystics. Rather they are outsiders that stand among, and often for good dramatic reasons in the middle of, the community. That is the source of their tragedy. The community should be, but usually is not, their salvation. If we want to find the loner as a true solitary we can do so in Auden's 'Look Stranger' (or 'Seascape') set by Britten in his collection *On This Island*. There the stranger, like Grimes, belongs not to his fellows, and quite possibly not to the island nation as a whole, but to the precisely given place: the 'small field's ending pause', the chalk cliffs that resist the tide. After all, limestone, the subject of one of his most celebrated poems, and not community, might be seen as the bedrock of Auden's England, just as the local fauna and flora were of Britten's Suffolk. It was Britten's great theatrical task, however, to make the community talk and sing; to make it tell.

Perhaps the most remarkable example of this is a creation of Britten and Auden's when working together: Johnny Inkslinger in *Paul Bunyan*. He is in many ways the most impressive of all Britten's outsiders, not least because he is surrounded by his mates in the lumberjack camp. In fact with respect to nation and people, he is arguably the greatest tragic creation in the Britten canon; something that is only made bearable by the light, near Broadway, genre in which Inkslinger finds himself. He is condemned to a happy end and the cheers of his fellows, although he well knows that he does not properly belong with them that he will never bond with them in any deep sense. It does not matter that he claims, no doubt honestly, that 'It isn't because I don't love them.' It is that 'The company I have to speak to/ Are wonderful men in their way/ But the things that delight me are Greek to/ The Jacks who haul lumber all day.'

Inkslinger is also the intellectual equal of his tragic cousin Aschenbach. The two men bookend Britten's stage works. Of course he is not to share Aschenbach's confrontation with a type of love that will lead to his wholly unexpected encounter with a parallel type of self-knowledge of which he had been up to then unaware. And he is most definitely spared Aschenbach's fall. However, thanks to Auden, Inkslinger surpasses Aschenbach in literary and poetic terms in the context of a stage work. Grimes though – and no doubt thanks to Montagu Slater – can stand alongside him. In fact Grimes can be regarded as his wholly non-intellectual, but equally reflective, blood-brother; one who in his visionary moments talks only in poetry. But, while the fisherman goes under, Inkslinger goes to Hollywood. He leaves to universal acclamation, though one doubts that he will find there a suitable environment in which to write the novel 'with which Tolstoy couldn't compete' . . . or anything like it. Still he can, and does, dream. His great solo is among the finest things Auden and Britten did together. How much of them as artists and homosexuals is sublimated in it is a matter of pure speculation; but it is speculation that the responsive listener might advisably indulge to the full.

The structural and intellectual tensions that I have tried to outline here underline another aspect of Britten's creative output. It was suggested at the beginning that his moral landscape implies the universal; it evokes values that are unconditional in that they are not constricted by nation or tribal affiliation. Instead they reject all such constraints and assert their absolute character. In that, they declare their purely ethical nature. One might now place this matter in the – superficially contradictory – framework which lays out the rival claims of place and a seemingly free-floating realm. These do not prima facie appear as sibling notions. It has, however, been argued hitherto that Britten requires the former in order to ground the ethical weight of the latter in the most immediate and potent manner possible. They are, therefore, held together by a structural and ideological binary force. In other words, in respect of *Peter Grimes*, I do not see that either the Borough must be sacrificed to a universal and mysterious totality as expressed in Grimes's 'Great Bear and Pleiades' solo and the Sea Interludes, or that the dramatic immediacy of the coastal village and its sharply drawn and varied inhabitants, turns the spiritual heart of the opera into a lot of wishy-washy extraneous moral pontificating. Wishy-washy it may be – such things probably must be to some extent – but extraneous or pontificating it is not.

The parallel with Wagner is again interesting. Although his theorising is often both nebulous and lacking in intellectual stringency, the model he is using allows him to be clearer in nuts and bolts terms. This is because, while the nominal universal is implied and sometimes shown, it is wholly expressive of the nation or tribe. In this it is quite unlike the, we might think, more authentic universal to be found in Britten. Moreover it is also a remarkable – and megalomaniacal – state of affairs. After all, one would have thought that the *avant la lettre* Schopenhauer enthusiasm, the relatively unproblematic marriage between the pure Wagnerian idea of redemption with the pure Schopenhauerian notion of renunciation, the passion for the noumenal, and so forth, would have made the otherworldly very culturally heterogeneous indeed. Have the right feelings, do the right things, forgo egotism (ironically, impossible for Wagner), and one would benefit from an open door policy that wasn't at all interested in national passports . . . let alone blood and language. The sublime post-death realm should on principle be potentially available to all. We mustn't, for instance, forget that Schopenhauer's archetypal saints – those souls fit for the non-phenomenal realm – range from Christian to Eastern sages.

Wagner, however, although he might have been inclined at times to think otherwise, was no multi-culturalist. True, he did contemplate an opera (*The Victors*) based on the Buddha and his favourite pupil Ananda. Nor is this without either relevance or interest, not least because Ananda was to enjoy a revelatory Parsifal-like sexual experience. As a consequence the whole structure of Buddhist teaching would be moved within the parameters of the Wagnerian *Weltanschauung*. For instance, not only is the Buddha to 'open up the community to women', he has to 'acquire a new insight.' He will do so via his pupil and courtesy of the standard heterosexual union and the concomitant dramatic encounter. Which is to say that it will be Wagner and not Ananda who will be instructing the Buddha. Thus will the master in the east reach 'one last remaining stage in his development.' In this way Wagner will have, in the enlightenment stakes, out Buddha-ed the Buddha.[116] The end result of such a shift would be, of course, a purely Germanic ideological tract, albeit a tract typical of the master's last, less belligerent, years. It would also, one imagines, be animated by wonderful, ethereal music. And in fact this is exactly what happened. *The Victors* was abandoned and the project evolved into *Parsifal*. And while we might see this as a shift that does not so much enhance as merely indicate the pacific nature of Wagner's last engagement with religious and philosophical thought, it does, more significantly, also point to the deeper and inherently German, rather than exotic, agenda of Wagner's last opera. Above all, we should not forget that 'Germanness' is, like German philosophy-cum-religion, 'a purely metaphysical concept.'[117]

It is therefore a folly, though one popular in some quarters, to rewind and see *Parsifal* as an encoded Buddhist work. Such an approach may show an appealing enthusiasm for, allegedly, revelatory hermeneutics, but it flies in the face of any understanding of Wagner's invasion of Christianity. That is, it does not do justice to his embrace of the dominant, and supposedly impeccable, ideology; an embrace that allows him to remake conventional religion so that it becomes fit for his own megalomaniacal and unconventional needs. Whether part of a conscious programme or not, in *Parsifal* he turns a violation of the incest taboo into a Christian sacrament. One wonders if the failure of Wagner's most committed fans to do him justice in this case is an unintentional recognition of the remarkable skill and subtlety with which the appropriation has taken place. It is seductive in a manner that has no equal on the musical stage. Perhaps the greatest test of its success is the astonishing number of acolytes who see *Parsifal* as a self-evident, indeed as an impeccable, religious work, whether Christian or Buddhist. At Bayreuth the small band of reactionary faithful are still appalled if lesser devotees, forgetting that they are in a secular church and have just witnessed the miracle of transubstantiation, applaud after the first act. On the other hand, any attempt to drape *Parsifal* in priestly Buddhist robes pays no attention to either Wagner's, in effect, a-Buddhist attitude as explained by him in the letter to Mathilde Wesendonck quoted from in the last paragraph, or his struggle at the time, clearest in *Religion and Art*, to come to terns with a new and irenic notion of the Saviour. This last consideration can be left to the next chapter, but the matter of the essential tribal nature of Wagner's after- or other- world remains apposite.

We can be in no doubt as to its Teutonic character if we turn from the overtly religious *Parsifal* to the overtly pagan *Ring*. In fact *The Ring* implies a great deal of Christian thinking just as *Parsifal* suggests a pagan freedom inimical to any conventional notion of Christian dogma. That, however, need not bother us at this point. Of more importance is Valhalla. Brünnhilde in *Die Walküre* attempts to sell the Germanic after-world to Siegmund in the famous and solemn *Todesverkündigung* of act two. In a profound sense Brünnhilde has come to take the German hero home and there is no reason why he should find anything alien in the non-phenomenal world to which he is now destined. Of course, as soon as Brünnhilde starts to put some very phenomenal flesh on the picture we can no longer hold onto anything that is really noumenal; certainly not in the pure idealist sense that Schopenhauer had in mind. No matter. What is important is that in the other world Siegmund will meet his beloved but mysterious father. And he will not be short of company. 'Dead heroes/ in a splendid body/ will embrace you kindly/ and welcome you solemnly.' Most enticing of all, his hedonistic needs will be well taken care of. 'Desirable maidens/ abound there in splendour./ Wotan's daughter will gladly give you your drink.' Here it is Brünnhilde and not Ganymede who becomes the God's cup-bearer. In any case, it would seem that as soon as Wagner addresses the extra phenomenal world to be enjoyed in the afterlife, it turns out to be very corporeal indeed. In fact it sounds more like a holiday camp than anything Schopenhauer – or the Wagner of *Parsifal* – might have envisaged. Though it should be acknowledged that by the time he got to *Parsifal*, Wagner has more or less succumbed to, or engineered, the ideal of a mythical, but ersatz German, world in which the pleasures that Siegmund is offered in Valhalla are enjoyed in the here and now because the here and now, at least as far as the priestly knights of the Brotherhood in Monsalvat are concerned, is the 'after-world' paradoxically present on earth.

The irony is that in dismissing Valhalla Siegmund is asserting a higher class of love; the love he feels for Sieglinde, who is not allowed through the gates of the heavenly castle. While Siegmund's rejection superficially violates the usual Wagner trope, it is also based on a remarkable irony. For we might well feel that the kind of self-sacrifice (and renunciation) that Siegmund now proclaims is closer to the Schopenhauerian ideal than anything Brünnhilde has to offer. And Brünnhilde comes, in effect, to the same conclusion. Whereupon she duly disobeys Wotan and takes Siegmund's part in the upcoming fight with Hunding. He is to live and remain with his pregnant partner. It is, however, a vain gesture, but it has mighty consequences. And these consequences underline several paradoxes that are kernel to *The Ring*. These come about simply because by beginning at the end of the *tetralogy* and working back (at least as far as the libretto/poem is concerned) Wagner ended up producing a mighty work imbued with his deepest evolving philosophical interests throughout the long period in which he struggled with the project. And these developments over the twenty-six years of, interrupted, labour on the cycle became of such significance that it was beyond the original libretto of *Siegfried's Death* (*Götterdämmerung*) to bring them, but for a certain number of grand and musically effective gestures, to fruition.

One of the paradoxes follows, quite logically, from Brünnhilde's historically radical and world shifting act. The *Todesverkündigung* is, after all, the balancing point on which the cycle as a, would-be coherent, unit turns. In adopting an earthly and a human notion of love Brünnhilde loses her godhead. Wotan takes it from her as he sets her in a sleep from which she can only be awakened by a fearless – but again human – agent. Both Wotan and Brünnhilde – and of course we – already know who this is going to be. Yet the love that is put into the world by virtue of the *Todesverkündigung* also has to be the high spiritual road that leads to the final redemptive act of sacrifice and immolation at the end of *Götterdämmerung*. It trumps anything that Wotan or the gods, and Brünnhilde in her original state, represent. This is problematic because in sticking closely to *Siegfried's Death*, Wagner is lumbered with a knockabout plot line, dependent on a drugged and manipulated puppet Siegfried, that can no longer realise the high agenda that *The Ring*, in the meantime, has taken on. This does not matter for the moment. It is, however, apposite, if somewhat contradictory, that this time the final projection suggested by Wagner shows not the other world in the form of the redeemed heroes and heroines, but the destruction of Valhalla. We have therefore good grounds to infer that the love that triumphs is not the love that normally leads, Dutchman and Senta-like, to the noumenal realm. Their love was always heading that way and really had no practical place on earth. But the sexual love of the Volsung twins, Siegmund and Sieglinde, is not only of this world, it is also consummated in this world and produces a son, Siegfried, who is more deeply embedded in the German natural world than any other of the heroes.

Wagner, however, is ambivalent about the last pages of *The Ring*. He sketched five endings. In the first from late 1848 he wants a largely happy, love-drenched climax, and Siegfried and Brünnhilde are indeed to be seen in the afterworld, Dutchman and Senta-like. This is, however, soon abandoned.

Nevertheless, putting aside the incoherence, or contradictions, into which the final opera collapses, we are surely justified in concluding that triumphant love is in this case not only an essentially earthly matter – in dramatic terms it is usually that anyway – but that it transcends, or at least takes precedence over, the other-worldly love to which it normally gives rise. We might, therefore, infer that not only was Brünnhilde ignorant of the depth of passion and devotion that Siegmund and Sieglinde felt for each other, she was also not aware of how constrained an after-world Valhalla and Wotan represent. But, trapped in the contradictions of the last opera, she will never be able to express the lesser status of the world Wotan has had built, courtesy of the giants, for the dead German heroes. But though she cannot express it, in the later endings of *Götterdämmerung* she can certainly dispense with it. Valhalla burns. Furthermore, we have no need to lament its obliteration.

None of this, of course, undermines the self-evident fact that no matter which version is chosen the ultimate resolution of *Götterdämmerung* and with it *The Ring* reflects the privileged position of the German tribe. The folk who gather in awe around the fringes of the flooded 'world' during the last pages of the score (at least in the most common staging) are clearly German. Moreover the complete *tetralogy* with its gods and mythological creatures, along with the forest and the Rhine and the baleful and primitive Gibichungs in the last opera, has always been an exclusive German story. Nor is it clear that the business is over. We know, for instance, that not only are the Volk still present but neither German nature nor Norse myth, nor the thirteenth century Nibelungenlied have disappeared from the world. And of course the life-giving totemic river is, and always will be, with us. And, more significantly, so are its three 'natural' children: the naïve, life-loving Rhine daughters. The ring, meanwhile, has itself been purified in the conflagration (the curse is gone) and returned to its original, natural and thereby uncontaminated state. It is once more the Rhine Gold. Thus is innocence put back in the world. Wagner has, thereby, taken ostensible universal values to do with love and redemption in order to explain the Germans to themselves. Consequently, if they are perceptive and grateful – and, as he well knew, they were often not – they would gain a better understanding of what the privileged notions of people and nation really should mean to them. Thus might we not infer that the mythical story could be told again, but with a different, and benign, outcome. It is, despite all of its faults and anomalies – and its ideological and racist poison – truly Wagner's great national bequest.

Because Britten's *Weltanschauung* is not embedded in, or formed by, a national story he has a freer hand in the deployment of universal and spiritual values. But this also means that he faces more difficult and challenging aesthetic problems. One could say he goes from the local – upfront and empirically present – to the great abstract moral themes with little in between. No doubt this is in part because he has no ready dramatic or philosophical framework to do with nation and people in which to work out his themes in such a way that he can move easily from the specific to the all-embracing. There is no national myth or legend to hand that give him the incipient material from which he can fashion the fundamental themes he has in mind, not least because national myth is what he does not want. It would constrict and contaminate exactly those themes that are most important to him. In this he can be said to be true to the advice, which he later quoted, given him by Auden in his 'New Year Letter' of 1940. Composers must 'accept their loneliness and refuse all refugees, whether of tribal nationalism or air tight intellectual systems.'[118]

It is perhaps in poetry, above all, that Britten finds ample material to do with innocence and redemption. Poetry speaks to him in an exceptionally intense manner. And given a poem's specific and contained character it is structurally relatively undemanding. It is hardly surprising then that Britten is readily inspired to song throughout the full course of his career. The operas, of course, must be more formidable undertakings. But this is not merely, or even chiefly, a question of length. True, going by his own comments, that was the case with one stage work; the ballet *The Prince of the Pagodas*. The sheer quantity of music to dance to that he needed to produce made the composition burdensome, even painful. The operas, however, need a more developed and coherent structure, a narrative that will facilitate a dramatic and evolving expression of the values that have brought Britten to the project in the first place. Britten's intellectual and aesthetic demands are, therefore, considerable and his difficulties are not simply typical of those faced by any composer or librettist making operas . . . any operas.

We might draw a comparison here with classic Italian opera. We can say that in Britten's case it was not the essential, and certainly not the sole, task of his librettists to produce narratives that threw up exciting possibilities for numbers (solos, duets, ensembles etc) driven by clear emotions (love, revenge, jealousy, torn feelings and so forth) of the sort that shape, let us say, the operas of Verdi. Britten was surely well aware of the particular narrative structures that had attracted Verdi and about which he was often explicit, and demanding, in his correspondence with his librettists. After all, Britten admired Verdi's operas and learnt a lot from them, above all, I would suggest, in formal terms. When, as was noted in the first chapter, he talked to Copland about the importance of mastering 'the ability to write many kinds of music – chorus alone, chorus with orchestra, soloists separately, soloists in ensemble, and so on',[119] it was exactly the skills that Verdi showed in such large measure that, we might think, he had in mind. But Britten needed more than this. Therefore, it is not solely that he isn't looking for something like Wagner's national agenda in which legends and chronicles and ballads (their origins do not have to be unambiguously German) are employed to explain the deeper nature of the Volk and its special history. He also does not have at his disposal the national agenda of Verdi at the time of nineteenth century nation building, of the Risorgimento. The grand choruses, the call to battle, the struggles of the people, the tales of heroism and betrayal, the love of a character on one side of the nationalist divide for someone on the other . . . none of this will really do. Britten needed something more sophisticated, far-reaching, and ambivalent to work with.

It is not surprising then that for his operatic raw material he often turned to, or was directed to, literature, above all to short stories and novellas. It is true that on one occasion he had recourse to a 'ready-made' play, but, on that occasion, he was under great time pressure. He had to have a new work in short order for the next Aldeburgh Festival (1960) so he and Peter Pears, very successfully, cut down Shakespeare's *A Midsummer Night's Dream*, adding next to no text of their own. With its three intermingled plot lines, the wide variety of characters, and the tension between the supernatural and the earthly realm, it presented Britten with a series of rich opportunities to display his inventive and technical brilliance. The score he produced is wonderful. But the work does not engage as deeply with his privileged themes as do the other literary-based operas. The *Dream* is a comedy and all problems are appropriately resolved at the end. But the narratives he was usually looking for and found in, above all, *Billy Budd*, *The Turn of the Screw*, *Owen Wingrave*, and *Death in Venice*, grapple with innocence and redemption head on. In other words, they engage with the guts of the moral disposition that steered and formed his creative life.

This is also to say that these stories had to deal with and dramatically realise evil as well. Innocence, after all, is pertinent and meaningful because one sees it everywhere corrupted. It is fragile, like goodness itself. Moreover evil must be shown and fought (quite possibly unsuccessfully) in that we might have some idea what redemption – more nebulous in Britten than in Wagner – might mean. In the operas, therefore, the means that are found to stage evil within the framework of a dramatic narrative are of the utmost importance. And it is certainly no disadvantage that in dramatic terms evil is readily productive of plot. Bad people make things happen; they make for drama and conflict. Consequently, for the Britten project to work morally, evil must be seen and heard. Claggart (*Billy Budd*), Quint (*The Turn of the Screw*), the Wingrave family (*Owen Wingrave*) are all evil and all consequently formative, unintentionally, of redemption. Furthermore, we might note that both Billy and Miles cry out 'devil' at their fatal, climactic moments. Billy before he lands the blow that kills Claggart and Miles in what seems to be a desperate gesture to free himself from Quint.

With respect to *Death in Venice* the matter is, as always, more sophisticated and ambivalent. Evil we might think is somehow co-opted and weaved into the redemptive message itself. And in being wedded to knowledge and sickness and desire it transcends specific characters, even those seven agents, all sung by a single baritone, who do not merely guide Aschenbach to the edge of the abyss, but also help him gain some, seductive, insight into what is to be found therein. Therefore, while Britten's major sources – and they were all of a high literary order – presented great opportunities, one can get some feeling for the demands placed by him on his librettists. Like Verdi he employed a lot, putting aside some and returning to others. It was no easy task to make the literary originals not only fit for the stage in dramatic terms, but also effective in underlining and developing the privileged values. For the innocence and redemption that Britten foregrounded always amounted to both a cerebral simplification and a spiritual and emotional enrichment of the literary source. The former is always inevitable in opera which cannot as sung text argue, speculate, or analyse as prose can. The latter, however, is the product of both Britten's genius as a musician and of his wish to give the moral values in play the widest possible terms of reference. In that, they spring the parameters of the literary works from which they were fashioned.

One of those moral values was pacifism and it turns out to be very instructive. It should be stressed that pacifism is relevant not because it is of itself a fundamental ethical component of Britten's *Weltanschauung*, but because it *expresses* an ethical disposition. Pacifism is the *product* of a given attitude towards goodness and evil; it is a conscious position taken up by the individual on the basis of a presupposed moral, and thoughtful, disposition. But it is not itself that disposition. It can, however, be an unmediated emotional response to something very upsetting. One thinks in this case of Britten's shock when he was first confronted by the sound of a boy being beaten. 'I can remember my absolute astonishment that people didn't rush to help him.'[120] In this context one inevitably recalls the pained and compassionate music Britten wrote for the Novice after his shipboard thrashing in *Billy Budd*.

In some ways this explains a fundamental difficulty inherent to pacifism. It is fine, we might think, when we meet it as a sweeping, arguably fundamental, axiom of correct behaviour. That axiom or principle is plain enough in that it underpins values for which everyone not inclined to fascism – or to something similar – feels some innate sympathy. Violence and killing are self-evidently wrong and in a morally good world would not occur. But that is also to say that the virtuous pacifist position is a reflection of the simple fact that neither the world nor the human being is, in fact, exclusively – if at all – virtuous. This banal fact, however, soon becomes, paradoxically, part of the problem. That is to say, it becomes part of the problem that pacifism itself seemed, prima facie, to solve with such sublime self-confidence.

I recall, for instance, a famous poster from my youth with the slogan 'What if they gave a war and no one came.' Although not word perfect, it was, apparently, drawn from a poem by Carl Sandburg. To many students of my day its implied argument was thought to be so self-evidently irrefutable that it simply swept the board of any objections. Yet when the pacifist position is applied to specific situations, and if the pacifist is prepared to acknowledge that these situations vary, are historically conditional, and mix good and evil in different ways, the grand universal principle becomes very problematic. One option for the creative artists – but it is an easy option – is to choose a story that is already placed in a spiritual context, that is contained in itself, and from which the appropriate moral can be readily drawn. This is the case with Britten's *Cantata Misericordium* (1963), which is a Latin setting of the parable of the Good Samaritan from Luke chapter 10. It may not be a specifically pacifist work as such, but its kinship is clear enough. Above all, its narrative is exactly defined, it has a clear message, and it allows of no extraneous considerations.

However, when pacifism engages with historical reality and attempts to make its grand and intellectually intolerant principle fit across the board, it can only maintain its probity by denying the decisive relevance of the differences that confront us everywhere and all the time. Hence the fundamental generalisation, axiomatically allowing of no exceptions, collides with common sense. Whereupon, it can only get out of the resulting dilemma with its original rectitude intact if it dismisses the empirical reality of specific horrors and specific crimes, or simply downplays them so that the killing of the single individual is equal to the slaughter of millions: in other words the adoption of an impeccably moral position that is utterly disengaged from reality. Were one, however, to engage intelligently with the specificities of history and its horrors, or for that matter, with the evil intrinsic to some degree in every individual, it would put the initial imperturbable generalisation – that under no circumstances may one be violent – under more pressure than it could probably bear. Pacifists are more or less compelled into an act of withdrawal – whether literally or inwardly – from the world. At least they are with respect to the dualism made up of combat and non-violence. Hence, if they acknowledge historical conditionality, or face up to the complexity of relative barbarities, it is only to dismiss them as secondary. It appears that under no circumstances must such thinking be permitted to contaminate the clear shining principle that indiscriminately outlaws all bellicose behaviour.

Under these circumstances it is very difficult for the committed believer to avoid, in effect, putting his head in the sand. Yet Britten was not disposed to withdraw. Rather, as a creative artist he engaged. In his case pacifism was deeply rooted in, and took sustenance from, core values that steered his work as an artist. Hence one infers that he must not only have been aware of the anomalies to which this gives rise, but must also have been periodically confronted by them.

There was, for instance, an occasion when Britten and Pears, on their way back to Aldeburgh, visited Hans Keller in London. It was at the time of the 1967 Arab/Israeli Six Day War and Keller and several of his other guests were, not surprisingly, concerned about the fate of Israel. Britten, as a man of principle, did not give way and maintained his pacifist stance, at one point going so far as to suggest that Israeli soldiers should prostrate themselves in front of the Egyptian tanks. This, as might be expected, did not go down well. Keller records that Britten 'stalked out of our house.'[121] They did, however, remain friends.

Surely this is a glaring example of the bad fit – or of no fit at all – between the principled pacifist position and common sense. Furthermore, as Keller points out, it is all very well to advocate suicide for oneself, but it is quite another matter to recommend it to others. Presumably Britten thought – although one can hardly be confident in the matter – that mass Israeli sacrifice without any military gain would deter the Arab armies. If he did, he was a fool. But whether foolish or not the result of military defeat for Israel at that time was likely to have had extreme consequences for both the Israeli people and the Israeli state. Without foreign intervention the latter, at least, was likely to have been extinguished. But it could have been very much worse. And Britten, of all people, was in a position to appreciate this. He had visited, with Yehudi Menuhin, Bergen-Belsen shortly after its liberation in 1945 and had been, of course, profoundly shocked. This, however, had only served to underpin his unconditional anti-war posture.

Perhaps of more relevance here is the inability of the proposed, but faux, solution (suicide) to actually address the problem at issue. The above example is, admittedly, extreme but it is hard not to conclude that when dilemmas of this sort occur the pacifist, while surely entitled to hold firmly onto his principles, would be wise to hold his tongue as well. And yet holding one's tongue is not, customarily, the *raison d'etre* of a deep belief that expresses a lofty moral position. If one is right and one wishes to save the world from violence by the blanket application of voluntary non-violence, what more logical option is there than the act of proselytizing? One's philosophy can only have social significance in as much as it shared by as many people as possible. Therefore let it be shouted from the rooftops. Well, that was hardly Britten's style. But he was a creative artist who dealt knowingly with the issue nonetheless.

And it is here that the problem only seems to get more intractable. Firstly one should note that the non-violent figures whom Britten admired were in quite different historical and political positions from the one he was in; or, for that matter, the one the Israeli soldiers of June 1967 found themselves in. Britten admired in particular Martin Luther King[122] and Mahatma Gandhi.[123] But the former was conducting a social revolution in a nation that was, officially, under the rule of law as determined by democratic principles. It was a society in which social justice was an acknowledged right, however much it might have been in respect of African Americans more honoured in the breach than the observance. Nonetheless, a non-violent strategy had excellent chances of success. It was, in other words, a calculated campaign and not just a blanket moral position uninfluenced by the prevailing historical and social circumstances. Furthermore, its purchase among the African American population depended as much on that (as well as on specific strategies such as bus boycotts to which it gave rise), as it did on the Christian paradigm from which many drew moral and emotional sustenance. King was never going to recommend to his followers that they throw their lives away. Gandhi, meanwhile, was conducting an explicitly nationalist campaign aimed at expelling the colonial masters. The fact that Mother India was an extremely multifarious and potentially unstable social and economic construct was merely, in the first instance, a factor that influenced strategy. Passive resistance was essentially a tactic. Furthermore, in being a nationalist, Gandhi is in some ways more easily placed in Wagner's belligerent *Weltanschauung* than in Britten's pacific one. Yet he too, like King, played his cards cleverly and can be said to have gained – partition aside – what he wanted. Had, however, a more potentially violent police force been available, or employed, the colossal loss of life that accompanied partition and the migrations between India and Pakistan in 1947 could have been avoided or radically mitigated. Neither man, we might note, committed suicide or sought death. Both were gunned down by rogue individuals.

In the operas the dilemma is largely absent simply because pacifists qua pacifists are not driven to action. As a result they are not nearly as useful as villains. Invariably they assume passive rather than proactive roles. And if they become dramatically powerful it is usually because they have elicited hostile reactions in others. This is, of course, the scenario of *Owen Wingrave*. Actually Henry James did attempt a stage dramatization of the story himself – *The Saloon* – but Britten's librettist, Myfanwy Piper, made little, if any, use of it.[124] As one would expect, she and Britten simplified the original short story's argument and discursive observations. But, unfortunately, they largely failed to enrich its moral content. In allowing less subtlety than is found in James, the element of propaganda, the remorseless weighting of the tale in favour of the hero (a more unambiguously heroic fellow than in the literary original), dominates. The musical realisation of all of this is often gripping, and the opera contains many striking things. But the argument for pacifism is no argument. It is a piece of mere placard-waving given dramatic power by the family curse and the haunted room.

There is an interesting parallel here with the other James adaptation: *The Turn of the Screw*. There the supernatural is properly dramatized and the ghosts have, as a result, real purchase. True, this may also be seen as a simplification given that the novella allows us, even encourages us, to consider whether the whole business of Quint and Miss Jessel isn't the product of the Governess's overheated imagination, itself born of her sexually repressed infatuation with the absent father. Readers of Henry James when they confront the opera often want to take advantage of this scenario, but Britten, who decided that the ghosts had to sing, has cut a good deal of the ground from under them. A speculation that works quite well if one is reading a book alone, seated in a comfy armchair, is not so easy to sustain when one is surrounded in an auditorium by hundreds of other people, all following the fortunes of flesh and blood figures on the boards. Nevertheless, the end result is that the struggle for Miles's soul – the attempt to recover his innocence and remove the curse of Bly – is massively enhanced simply because in dramatic terms the Governess can be seen, exorcist like, to enter into one-on-one combat with Peter Quint. At the climax of the opera she *knows* he is there. We, of course, don't need to be convinced. We can see and hear him.

But while the ghosts of Bly are extant, those of Paramore are, at most, imaginary. The business with the haunted room is, consequently, difficult to take seriously. It is really little more than mumbo jumbo. Even Kate's challenge to Owen to spend the night there is positively silly if one escapes the seductive power of the score. For many it is silly even when experienced in terms of the music and the drama. As a result the pacifist theme becomes banal.

This is only underlined by the Wingrave family in general. Miss Wingrave and General Sir Philip come across as pantomime heavies employed to demonstrate that Owen must be right. To be opposed, and then rejected, by such people amounts to a confirmation of one's own righteousness. Certainly there is no chance in the dinner party scene at the end of the first act that Sir Philip will show himself to be one of those broad-minded army types who like to initiate a conversation on pacifism in order to show how liberal they are. No family member in this company is going to talk of the horrors of war with anything other than lip-smacking relish. The trouble with all this dice loading, however, is that it undermines the pacifist case and the pacifist disposition. Of course there is nothing wrong per se with loading the dice. Art does not have to – nor should it – play fair. An opera is not a philosophical tract. But if the emotional appeal that is thereby generated is found to be both shrill and banal, the moral argument it was designed to underpin – realise, even – is prostituted.

The *War Requiem* is probably the most powerful pro-pacifist composition in the Britten canon. But it is so because it does not make the case for pacifism, either intellectually or emotionally. Rather it makes the case against war, which is by no means the same thing. Its subject is, as Wilfred Owen said, war and the pity of war. The poetry, we are told, is in the pity. And surely we feel at the end of the piece that it is at least as much in Britten's music as in Owen's verse. All this works wonderfully because, as we have already had cause to note, Britten is ruthless (conceivably, if you believe Keller, sadomasochistic) in his aesthetic indulgence of the horrors. Innocence and redemption take their full measure because evil is in the world. Furthermore, it bears repeating that the manner in which the poetry and the score subvert and enrich the religious text is, in particular, intensely powerful and disturbing.

Perhaps Britten doesn't handle war effectively when he is dealing, theatrically, with the group. There is, for me, something exceptionally vapid, for instance, in the chorus the crew of *The Indomitable* sing in *Billy Budd* as they prepare for the aborted engagement with the French ship: 'This is our moment, the moment we've been waiting for.' It is hardly one of Forster's most inspired lines. Unfortunately it is set to music that is at least as trite and hackneyed. Mind you, that may be the point. Perhaps Britten is simply telling us how crude and jingoistic war is. And yet I doubt it. It would hardly fit within the conceptual framework of the opera and, in any case, it is not the aesthetic or intellectual vulgarity of war that horrifies Britten but its cruelty and gratuitous horrors. When we put aside the group, however, matters become much more formidable. As is customary with Britten, it is the particular that tells. There, above all, are universal values truly felt and understood. It is this that makes the tale told in the Offertorium so disturbing and the final poem of the *Requiem*, 'Strange Meeting', so moving.

In fact I confess to being at times deeply upset by Britten's ability to portray the particular, even the seemingly small, act of suffering. The *cri de cœur*, the threnody, that he makes out of the Scottish ballad 'The Bonny Earl O' Moray' (especially when sung by Peter Pears) is something that grips you by the throat. Meanwhile 'The Choirmaster's Burial' from the Hardy song cycle *Winter Words* might, one sometimes thinks, cause a revolution if properly sung. Certainly Pears's performance has a tinge of justified hysteria about it that, if let loose among the folk, could be dangerous. The song tells the simple story of a choirmaster who is not given, by the pedantic small-minded vicar, the burial he had surely earned a thousand times over. He is denied the music, above all the hymn 'Mount Ephraim', that he desired. But this local tragedy assumes grand unconstrained spiritual proportions. When in the dead of night justice is done and 'A band all in white/ Like the saints in the church glass' is seen by the vicar playing over the fresh grave, the music attains the same sort of potency, rich with accusation, that is found in 'The Bonny Earl O' Moray.' There is deep injustice in the world and it is most powerfully experienced in terms of the individual soul who is, as a result, so arbitrarily and indifferently discarded. When we experience this sort of thing in its most intense form in Britten it can evoke the sound, and with it the mental picture, of tumbrils on the cobbled streets.

Four

Religion and Philosophy

Wagner is blessed with a philosophy. And what's more he knows it. Britten really isn't. I find it hard to believe that were you to ask Britten what his philosophy or his *Weltanschauung* was, he would be in a position to give a coherent answer. Or indeed that, even if he liked you and thought you worth the effort, he would want to try. Wagner, assuming he had found a ready audience, would be hard to rein in and it wouldn't be long before you were secretly wishing that you had never brought the subject up in the first place. You would have been wiser to stick with his fascination with interior design, his sensational night gown, and his detailed specifications for Cosima's silk knickers. And it wouldn't be any different if you were curious as to his religion. Wagner would be able to overpower you with the same confidence as to the righteousness and profundity of his opinions. Actually it would be easy for him because there would be no effective category difference in his mind between his philosophy, even when given the widest terms of reference, and his religious disposition. This would be entirely logical in that his religion was always folded into his, very flexible, philosophical system. Therefore he did not in this matter, as in others, remain faithful to Schopenhauer, who attempted to maintain a rigorous distinction between religion and philosophy.

Wagner did not employ religion to disrupt, or to challenge what he chose to believe, or to question either his ego or his inclinations, but to confirm everything he wanted confirmed and, in addition, to give it the necessary patina of piety. Naturally this would, in particular, have to be the case when the views and desires that formed his *Weltanschauung* were not in the least pious. Britten, on the other hand, might well have been able to say something about religion when asked. It was a question that he addressed. But if he were to assume a philosophical position, it would take second place, or at least have to conform to, the ethical qualities that invested his general, quasi-religious temperament. Above all, he would not be in a position to drag in all sorts of cod anthropological, historical, and nationalist theories in order to give the whole business a faux scientific – and very Wagnerian – gloss.

We know that Britten told the tribunal considering his application for complete exemption from war work in 1942 that he was deeply influenced by his Anglican upbringing but didn't believe in the divinity of Christ. He was, to quote Peter Pears again, 'an agnostic with a great love for Jesus Christ.'[1] The trouble with this – or possibly its greatest strength – is that it is prima facie wishy-washy. It's a feelgood position that allows one the appropriate expression of Christian virtues without taking on the burden of Christian dogma, let alone obedience to the church. This is all very well in itself, but it raises the question – among many – as to what Britten actually thought as to the purpose of life and even whether he did in the end, following his instruction from Bishop Leslie Brown, entertain the prospect of an afterlife. The two notions are, after all, linked for most believers; indeed the latter underpins the probity of the former as well as, to put it crudely, functioning as a consolation for enduring the sufferings of the world and as a reward for faith. To be an orthodox Christian is to believe in the incarnation, the resurrection, and the Ascension. Whereupon we might note that wilful, even heretical, Wagner not only, at various times, accepts all three, but can be said in his operas to dramatically manifest them, both literally and metaphorically. Siegfried in the allegedly pagan *Ring* cycle is probably the clearest example. In *Die Wibelungen* he is an Ur-Christ and we can in *Die Walküre* witness his conception, which, being exceptionally incestuous (his parents were twins), is certainly immaculate in Wagnerian terms. Therefore he is, when he finally rushes onto the boards in the first act of *Siegfried*, a magnificent incarnation of Aryan theology born of a 'marriage' natural in Nature, albeit engineered by the Stem-God-Father (Wotan). Following his death in *Götterdämmerung* he comes, apparently, back to life when his arm rises to prevent Hagen from taking the ring. And, of course, a subsequent ascent into Valhalla was, initially, to be his self-evident destiny.

As to the Ascension, we will have cause in the final chapter to underline how Wagner was overwhelmed by the assumption of Mary.

In this context it seems fair to entertain the view that Christianity does amount to a coherent system of thought, that it proselytizes an allegedly homogeneous body of beliefs. Which is to say that it can be said to provide consistent answers based on, it is assumed, sound premises, although one would think that it needs to put the notion of faith as a more or less necessary, and of course largely unproven, given on the first place. After all, not everyone, we must assume, is going to be accorded a sensational, visionary epiphany let alone an utterly doubt removing encounter with the Almighty Himself. Yet even given this proviso, Christian apologists will argue that the dogma is cogent.

A system, however, is exactly what Britten does not want. Wagner, however, is determined to have one, but it will be very much his own bespoke intellectual construct. And he duly cobbles together a highly wilful and made-to-measure intellectual edifice. Fortunately it turns out to be fairly malleable in that it always permits a certain degree of free, or arbitrary, dismantling and reassembling. Furthermore, as with many religious apologists, Wagner is always prepared to move the goalposts, and in an untroubled manner, in order to preserve the necessary axiom: namely the axiom that does not so much proclaim that one is always right, but that one can never be proven wrong.

This distinction between Wagner and Britten has important consequences with respect to the determining, and mutually shared, idea of redemption. Wagner is always going to be in a position to tell us what *Erlösung* means. The word is ubiquitous in his writings and in the opera libretti. Appropriately enough it seems to colonise the spiritual (and sexual) landscape of the first redemption opera, *The Flying Dutchman*, where, equally appropriately, it and its derivatives are uttered exclusively by the Dutchman and Senta. It is not clear, however, that Britten could actually tell you what he meant by redemption. Though I suspect that he could isolate the virtues that are missing in the world and the vices that are present that make redemption a profound, desirable, and pressing need. One might therefore conclude that whereas Wagner is upfront, clear, and flag-waving on the matter, Britten is uncertain, nebulous and somewhat confused. One might further infer that the notion of redemption plays a more soggy role in Britten's thinking and in his creative work. It is, however, one of the goals of this chapter to question the confidence of the Wagner position and to argue that, despite appearances, redemption functions in Britten's work in a substantive and deep manner.

Religion and philosophy are much concerned with death. Operas – at least tragic as opposed to comic operas – are likewise deeply in hock to the idea of death and, more to the point, its power as a dramatic event. Wagner, it might be said, is drenched in death. It is, for his higher characters, a consummation devoutly to be wished. More even than this, it could be seen as itself a causally related consummation to sexual consummation, in that the latter can be said to lead to the former and thence to all the wonderful things that are associated with death. This is no doubt clearest in the so-called love death (*Liebestod* – not, it should be said, Wagner's term) that ends *Tristan und Isolde*. The heroine's peroration is, paradoxically, all about drowning while ascending ecstatically to the, nominally, 'dead' Tristan. She sees him 'soaring on high.' But it is a vision and a higher melody that only the chosen can apprehend, although Isolde seems surprised that those around her do not see and hear as she does, '. . . see, friends! Do you not feel and see it? Do I alone hear this melody. . . ?' And it is here we realise that while all this records Isolde's entry into the non-phenomenal world, it is for her a corporeal, an empirical, experience. It is, as she makes clear repeatedly, of the senses. In this it is the most striking manifestation of the sensual invasion of Schopenhauer's idealist thought that Wagner engenders. For us agog in the theatre, however, it is a wholly spiritual, though a conceivably orgasmic, experience and woe betide the perfect Wagnerite if his fellow punters suspect that he does not feel wondrously drained and elevated at the end of it.

Perhaps the business with mortality and love is clearest in *The Ring*. The significance of its (ambivalent) pagan character will surface repeatedly in this chapter, but for the moment what counts is how consummation, whether of sex or death, will work on a large, and indeed sprawling, canvas. The first consummation among the higher characters about which we can be sure – and enjoy – is that between the twins Siegmund and Sieglinde at the end of the first act of *Die Walküre*. And it is placed wholly within nature. Spring floods into Hunding's hut and, with both siblings erotically charged, the brother takes his sister bride in his arms as if the whole business were self-evidently blessed by Nature itself. And indeed it is. It is a tremendous moment.

Meanwhile, when something similar happens between their son Siegfried and Brünnhilde, the ecstatic copulation is explicitly linked to death. In this case – at the end of *Siegfried* – love, sex, and death come together in a riotous outpouring of human passion. Siegfried and Brünnhilde throw themselves into sex while exulting about both it and the grandeur of death. This is not, as some commentators have always assumed, an innocent – ignorant even – acknowledgement on their part that they are doomed because of Alberich's curse, neither is it an example of dramatic irony that works because the audience knows more than the lovers. Rather it is an expression of the promise that must be inscribed in both love and death. It is because the couple are death-dedicated that they know they are blessed. We, meanwhile, can only hope that when they – along with all the other higher characters of *The Ring* – do die they can experience a similar joy in the noumenal world to which both consummations, sex and death, have opened the door.

The most striking consequence of this is that for Wagner death is not a problem. This is not merely to say that death is the perfectly proper final event as experienced in the Natural world of forests, mountain tops, and rivers within which Wagner is likely to place his heroes and heroines. Rather, death is free of any grim associations. It is not tragic at all. In this way the Wagner redemption drama adopts the mantle of the tragic opera as genre while wholly subverting it in praxis. The deaths of his higher characters may well be dramatic (the villains, of course, are always dispatched with theatrical and musical flair) but they are not, despite Siegfried's funeral march, cause for grieving among those who are true believers. And surely even Siegfried's funeral march is unmistakably more exultant than distraught. In this way the Wagnerian death of a chosen one does, propaganda-wise, more than Britten's pantheism ostensibly can . . . or possibly should. Of course Wagner's works make pantheistic appeals too – *The Ring* is a near axiomatic pantheistic work – but that pantheism is always focused on a privileged afterlife. Wagnerian death does not mean we return to nature's compost heap, rather that we rise above it. In Britten matters are not so straightforward.

Certainly there can be a sense of an afterlife in Britten. Billy Budd's body is given to the deep, but we are led to believe that his soul is among the birds; after all 'the sea fowl shadowed him with their wings.' And hadn't he as foretopman always belonged, by implication, in the heavens? In

Melville the matter is clearer in that the metaphors are taken further. In chapter twenty-six it is underlined that he 'ascended' to the point on the ship from which he was hung, whereupon he 'took the full rose of the dawn', the light being 'shot thro' with a soft glory as of the fleece of the Lamb of God.' Salvation and Billy are conjoined. Aschenbach, meanwhile, muses on the higher Platonic realm courtesy of Socrates' *Phaedrus* before sliding down into death. Whether that means he must go right to the bottom of the abyss while the Ganymede boy is scooped up by Zeus the eagle and set down on Mount Olympus, is surely not clear.

If one describes death as ambivalent in Britten, this is not to draw attention exclusively to the uncertain feelings of the composer as to an afterlife or to his ambiguous relationship with Christian teaching. It is also, and arguably more importantly, to address the nature of redemption when placed in the context of death. In the Wagner coupling redemption makes of death an un-death. It upturns the customary narrative and causal relationship. In Britten the ambivalence as to death and redemption is real and more contradictory. Death can certainly on occasions take on the full force of inconsolable grief, something that can be heard in the threnodies of the *Sinfonia da Requiem* and, at least for this listener, in the grim sonorities of the *Cello Symphony*. But it can also generate consolation, above all when it is married to sleep. We will turn to this last point in a moment, but if we are to do justice to the death and redemption coupling in arguably its most striking expression in Britten we ought to stay with *Death in Venice* for a little longer. Furthermore, we also, as a result, need to pay some attention to the final string quartet that post-dates it.

The last movement of Britten's *Third String Quartet* (1975) is a passacaglia, entitled, like Venice itself, *La Serenissima*. It contains five quotes from the opera. The last is the 'I love you' motive which, at the end of the first act, signals Aschenbach's brutally honest recognition of his real state. It follows the aborted attempt to flee the city and, subsequently, his knowing acceptance that in Tadzio he has found the human being where knowledge and beauty and all the dangers and insights therewith implied are, irresistibly, embodied. Although I am not qualified to produce a technical analysis, which would anyway lie outside the parameters of this essay, in this case it needs to be said that the relevant theme is in the diatonic key of E major. This is the scale most closely associated with Aschenbach in the opera. At the end of the string quartet it is heard in its pure form, in that the diatonic scale is not invaded by semitones foreign to it. Perhaps, then, at this point, the declaration of love in the opera attains its true redemptive, and unambiguous, aura. Of course the string quartet has no recourse to the dramatic ambivalences intrinsic to knowledge and beauty as they are worked out in the stage drama, and in that sense finding an optimistic and redemptive close in the chamber music piece might seem a touch too easy; even if we are not troubled by the reduction of the opera's philosophic agenda which such a resolution must entail. Nonetheless, it is agreeable to believe that David Matthews is right: 'We cannot but feel that the redemption of Aschenbach which began in *Death in Venice* is completed here.'[2] And even if a final inference of this sort is glib – after all, in these matters we are, when everything is said and done, at the mercy of wholly subjective sentiments – love, we might think, is not a bad solution. Certainly, in this case it is not going to be either a cliché or a cop-out. Whatever the opera and the novella have accomplished they have not turned love of knowledge and love of beauty into the cheap currency indulged habitually in the opera house and in kitsch literature. Even so, it is impossible to put the matter in terms that are both concrete and worthy of it. Matthews, at the end of his discussion of the string quartet is understandably imprecise. 'What lies beyond death is beyond the scope of most artists, but Britten, close to his own death, came as near as anyone to providing a clue.'[3]

For those who not only want an irenic ending because it is both nice and civilised but also because they believe that such an ending is most likely to fulfil the agenda implicit in redemption, there is comfort to be had from Britten's last months. As is underlined in the final pages of the sixth volume in the *Letters from a Life* series, knowing that he was about to die his mood became resigned and loving and he was remarkably kind and generous to all his circle. Furthermore, he tried to mend fences with those he had previously called his 'corpses'; friends and colleagues with whom he had once quarrelled and then put off. I, however, suspect that this general line, because it is so impeccable, rather diminishes redemption. This may seem idiosyncratic. After all, the standard model makes of redemption something unblemished, or at least suggests that it can't be seen in any light other than an ideal one. As was conceded in the Preface it implies resignation, salvation, knowledge.

This is no doubt self-evident. But inbuilt into this essay is not only the notion of a redemptive struggle engendered by the creative tensions born of qualities that function abrasively. There is also a potent degree of uncertainty, suspicion even, as to the final sublime telos. No doubt this view is profoundly irreligious, but to reach the telos of redemption, as it is commonly imagined, means to sacrifice much of the fruitful content of the struggle that gets one there. In order to end up with impeccable and clean bathwater the baby, or babies, have to go. Whereupon the bath has probably to be given a good scrub and then refilled from the finest unsullied springs. In short, happy ends are reductive. They are also likely to be banal. And should they be emotionally and intellectually effective, they are so only for the moment. But those who are attracted to a benign narrative that is destined to end in a peaceful and resigned death with all dilemmas resolved will not be disappointed by the story of Britten's lasts months. And in respect of his creative and intellectual life they can make the same inferences as David Matthews with a clear conscience. I, however, suspect that Britten's greatness is better appreciated in the compromised, contaminated even, redemptive struggle itself. Aschenbach is the most remarkable manifestation of this.

In returning to the final opera we return to something that is always ambivalent. As we will see later in this chapter, there is a struggle for Aschenbach's soul between Apollo and Dionysus. And even if Dionysus, pleasure-loving and sensual (Socrates would say 'swinish'), is regarded as the ultimate victor – although I believe he isn't – the fact that Apollo was in the game leaves the other, ethereal, door open. At least it is in Myfanwy Piper's ideological scheme. But all this promise of something that exceeds the life we experience empirically and corporeally is impossible to pin down, not least because one feels that librettist, composer, and quite possibly novelist, are as uncertain in the matter as we are. The dramatic, if paradoxical, upshot is that death in Britten tells; it has purchase. It has about it the real feel of tragedy and not of special pleading. It is embedded in life. At the end of *Tristan und Isolde* or *Götterdämmerung* the receptive punter may be exhausted, but he is in ecstasy. At the end of *The Turn of the Screw* or *Peter Grimes* he is distressed. At the end of *Death in Venice* it may well be impossible to disentangle the nexus of emotions and thoughts in whose web the sensitive member of the audience is now entwined and entrapped.

There is one phenomenon that is often linked to death that Britten, and of course the poets and writers on which he drew, make use of. It is sleep. Fortunately, given the quality of his literary sources and the work of his librettists, Britten is hardly going to reduce death courtesy of sleep to the banal euphemism in which the grieving talk of their loved ones having, as it were, merely nodded off for the duration. We should note again here that sleep does not play such an important role in Wagner. There it is made redundant by the triumph over death engineered by the composer. But as we have had cause to note, Schopenhauer does make something of it, equating it with death: 'Death is a sleep in which individuality is forgotten.'[4] This is probably a result of his increasing interest in the transmigration of souls, the key point being that the individual is erased. In the context of Britten's oeuvre, however, it is not simply a matter of sleep keeping open both possibilities, namely the Christian afterlife and the pantheistic extinction of the self through natural bodily decay. Rather, sleep also suggests something that has not been accomplished; something which remains unsettled. It does not give up on the world. It implies an awakening. It raises the possibility that the suffering and cruelties we have witnessed are not in themselves the end of the matter. If we have failed to see redemption realise its agenda to the full, we are not, in general, left without hope. And we imagine that we can certainly – perchance – dream. The great cycle *Winter Words* ends with the ethereal song 'Before Life and After.' It suggests that the time of nescience (not knowing, or true unsullied innocence) can come again – but 'How long, how long?'

Perhaps in dealing with sleep in this manner one is guilty of a dishonest strategy. For the idea, seen in this light, seems of itself to promise redemption without explaining how this happens or even what redemption amounts to. It just asks the sort of questions that are put at the end of *Lucretia*, which are also versions of the 'How long, how long?' question. No doubt it implies spiritual qualities well enough, but it does not show them. There are no meaningful projections on the backcloth at the end of a Britten opera. But unless one is promulgating a given, explicit narrative with an equally given, explicit redemptive telos, that is the price of a sincere spiritual disposition. Moreover, in Britten's hands it turns out to be a potent business. And however much Britten may be concerned with peace and redemption in the here and now, sleep cannot but also imply something potentially transcendent.

Nonetheless it is not unproblematic. Sleep is often associated with longing and struggle, something surely very clear – even though there is no text – in the remarkable variations and passacaglia on 'Come Heavy Sleep' that make up the *Nocturnal after John Dowland* that Britten wrote for the guitarist Julian Bream in 1963.

In the Shakespeare Sonnet (43), which Britten set in the *Nocturne* (1958), the paradoxical nature of sleep is axiomatic: 'When most I wink, then do mine eyes best see.' It is in dreams that the poet perceives the beloved most clearly. In the Keats sonnet 'O soft embalmer of the still midnight', the last poem set in the *Serenade for Tenor, Horn and Strings* (1943), sleep is a consolation that momentarily releases us from the sufferings of the world. It may bring death . . . but it may not. Dreams here are not, as in the most famous of *Hamlet's* soliloquies, a threat. Rather the poem underlines, longingly, exactly that which Macbeth loses in killing Duncan. It is the solace and respite, bestowed by sleep that 'knits up the raveled sleave of care.' Macbeth, and for that matter his wife, will never experience it again, and it is this that Keats desires. Britten's setting is beautiful, flooded by a yearning for release. The problem, or the most pertinent consideration, lies in the fact that we are probably likely to assume that that release can only come definitively with death together with a final, wholly unambiguous, redemption, which is not what the poet, or the composer, has chosen to praise.

Dreams, meanwhile, are ambivalent. On the one hand they drive Lady Macbeth to madness and death, just as Aschenbach's dream – in the novella, even more of a nightmare – guides him to the ambivalent abyss. But they can also be unambiguously refreshing and a liberation. Furthermore they can lead to new insights. When in Britten's only Shakespeare opera the four lovers awake after the exhausting trials that Puck has put them through, they are astounded to discover that they see each other anew. Britten makes a good deal of Shakespeare's text at this point, appreciating fully the qualitative shift that has taken place. He takes Helena's lines 'And I have found Demetrius like a jewel/ Mine own, and not mine own' and fashions a quartet, changing the proper name and giving the same sentiment to each lover in turn. There is a real element of wonder in the setting. It is clear that a degree of folly and possessiveness has been overcome and the love they now feel is both deeper and more adult. Their midsummer dream has been wholly beneficial. The 'raveled sleave' of care, in this case, has been more than merely knitted up.

The final Wilfred Owen poem employed in the *War Requiem*, 'Strange Meeting', ends with the two dead enemy soldiers reaching some kind of reconciliation. At the close they sing together: 'Let us sleep now.' It may be a banal and self-evident point, but in this constellation, in which the baritone and tenor soloists can be said to stand at the middle point, death – appropriately replete throughout a work commemorating mass slaughter – is in a sense already overcome. And during the last pages of the *Requiem* the repeated utterances of 'Let us sleep now' are interwoven into the Latin text for the dead; a text that is shared between the main choir, the boys' choir, and the soprano soloist. Of course, the Latin text also promises rest and peace. But that peace is the peace of the grave. No doubt for the orthodox the promise of resurrection is substantive, but Britten, it seems, wants nothing to do with it. His agenda is more immediate. It is surely not insignificant then that 'Let us sleep now' is the last sentiment we hear in the vernacular.

This final promise, or perhaps entreaty, is also employed by Britten in another 'religious' work composed shortly after the *War Requiem*: the *Cantata Misericordium*. This is a dramatic retelling of the Good Samaritan story, composed to a Latin text by Patrick Wilkinson. It is also for two male soloists (tenor and baritone) and was recorded by the two singers (Pears and Fischer-Dieskau) who made the first recording under Britten's direction of the *War Requiem*. Here the notion of amity is, if anything, stronger. The act of benevolence in giving succour to the victim potentially reconciles Roman, Jew (in Wilkinson's text the Traveller is identified as a Jew; something that is not clear in Luke), and Samaritan. The theme, or message, is, of course, as direct and as obvious as possible: 'Love . . . thy neighbour as thyself.' (Luke 10: 27) And when the Samaritan has provided for the Traveller he leaves him in a tavern, having paid the bill, with the words: *Quis sim, unde sim gentium, parce quaerere. Dormi nunc, amice, dormi: iniuriarum obliviscere* (Who I am, and what my people, ask no more. Sleep now, my friend, sleep: forget your injuries).

Naturally the cantata is a simpler, more single-minded work than the *War Requiem*, which is another way of saying that it is also less problematic and disturbing. Sleep here is not an end; it comes instead with the promise of recovery. And while the horrors that are the flesh and blood of the earlier work cannot, in Britten's hands, entirely erase the possibility of redemption, in the later piece there is nothing to fear. Ultimately everything is radiant and no special effort is required to convince oneself that redemption is in the world. It is not even necessary for us to entertain the notion of hope. Instead the successful redemptive act is made the very stuff of the drama and we become witnesses to how love and comradeship, uncontaminated by prejudice or tribalism, make the universal Christian message real. Sleep here is entirely benevolent. And maybe because of this the attendant notion of redemption is reduced, or diluted.

Perhaps the *Cantata Misericordium* is too simple. Written for the hundredth anniversary of the foundation of the Red Cross, is it too much like propaganda, an exercise in wish-fulfilment? But this is a harsh, even a mean spirited, question. It does, however, readily come about in this context largely because the cantata is so closely related to the greater work, and that work is anything but simple or pat. Pears, for instance, says of the final pages of the *War Requiem:* 'It *isn't* the end, we haven't escaped . . . we are not allowed to end in a peaceful dream.'[5] This underlines powerfully the struggle and the ambivalence that is essential to Britten's greatest works. Their emotional punch is born of the hope that good can be done in a world that is bad. One may not want to believe that the world is bad, and there is in Britten much joy and beauty and peace to be had; most of it born of his pantheistic and humane disposition. But in the end we will have to struggle hard to find a space for human kindness and for the spiritual qualities that are held dear by most people. As always, Britten – even when, perhaps particularly when, he is writing ostensibly religious works – is dealing in the here and now, in present suffering. He may not have a system, but his philosophy, such as it is, is practical in intent even when it is absurd in common sense terms; something which was made much of in the last chapter regarding his pacifism and the Arab/Israeli Six Day War. However, with respect to the end of the *Requiem*, Pears, is, of course, right. There is no easy way out. The matter is neither over as a tragedy nor resolved as a religious programme with an irrefutable and final redemptive promise. It is much too disturbing for any of that. Indeed, it was much too disturbing for many in the audience, who were, as many have been since, left in tears. At the première Fischer-Dieskau himself was, as he records, an emotional wreck, 'completely undone.'[6]

There is another notion that, while not directly related to either love or death, can be added appropriately to the mix. It is extremely important to Wagner and it is both dramatically and intellectually potent. It is blood. Clearly its critical significance for Wagner is due, at least initially, to its fundamental defining role in arguments as to race. For even though it has been underlined that Wagner is not – always – unbending on the matter of race and blood, allowing an enrichment of German blood from sturdier peoples once the Ur-tribe arrived in Europe, he does in his last essays tend towards the pure bred position. This is clearest in *Know Thyself.* But even in his final, and incomplete, essay *On the Womanly in the Human Race* – he was working on it the day he died – he is forced into praising monogamy (something he otherwise kicks against) because polygamy is likely to lead to racial degeneration. For instance, the white race must have been monogamous 'at its first appearance in saga and history.' And therefore one must now see Goethe's eternal feminine as not only the individual object of 'ideal love' but also as the 'fountainhead' of the species; by which he surely means the white race.[7]

Blood, however, is clearly of great dramatic, or operatic, power and Wagner makes full and brilliant use of it. The measure of his brilliance is that blood is always more than just a theatrical splash of colour. It is loaded with deep significance. One might consider the drop of blood that falls on Siegfried's hand after he has killed the dragon Fafner. It burns and when he puts his hand to his mouth something miraculous happens. He suddenly realises that he can understand the song of the Woodbird. It's a fine move on Wagner's part as it allows him to fold Siegfried more deeply into the natural world; something which is essential to the agenda of the second act of *Siegfried.* It is, however, a strategy that is bound to come unstuck. For Wotan's scheme to work – his grandson Siegfried is to regain the ring, remove the curse, save the world – the hero has to be his own man. This is no doubt one of the reasons why he must remain ignorant until he meets Brünnhilde. Were he to know how the dice have been loaded, the points already set, the narrative pre-written, there would be no case to be made for him as a psychologically free agent. Even so, Wagner can make some of this work, although one assumes here that he is, as it were, fighting on the side of his – I would suggest obvious – alter ego, Wotan. But Siegfried does make his own sword when he forges the shards of Nothung. In the second act of *Die Walküre* Wotan had shattered Nothung, leaving Siegmund defenceless before Hunding. The sword had been, in effect, placed so that Siegmund might stumble upon it as a ready-made, but bespoke, object. In *Die Walküre* it only had to be found. But having reforged it and rechristened it in the first act of *Siegfried* the hero can move off to kill the dragon Fafner, who guards the ring. In the second act he muses on nature and on his dead mother while sitting before Fafner's cave. Both – forest and cave – might be seen as womb symbols. And it is while dreaming of his mother with longing and pain, that he hears the sounds of arboreal nature, famously conjured up by Wagner in the passage known as Forest Murmurs.

All of this amounts to a formidable accomplishment and Wagner realises it wonderfully. It is the high-water mark of the a-Christian pantheist agenda and the point at which Siegfried the man seems most likely to realise what Wagner wants of him. But Wagner/Wotan has not got rid of the essential problem, which is that the allegedly unblemished and glorious hero is really just a puppet in the hands of others. Wotan does not – because he can not – play fair. This is the accusation that Alberich throws at him at the beginning of the second act, in effect repeating the argument that Wotan's consort Fricka employed ruthlessly in the second act of *Die Walküre*, and it is incontrovertible. It was soon after this that Wagner put the *Ring Cycle* aside for more than ten years. When he returned to it, he got through the third act of Siegfried but was then stuck with the knockabout farce that is *Götterdämmerung*, whereupon the higher intellectual agenda could only be retained in a flawed and incoherent fashion. King Ludwig, however, insisted on the completion.

But if blood is an effective heathen symbol in Wagner's *Weltanschauung*, it is even more potent in his, arguably faux, religious work *Parsifal*. The irony is hardly likely to be missed but, then again, it is an irony inscribed within Christianity itself. The Lamb of God, a universal symbol of peace and love, bleeds copiously. Christianity in fact plays out in the Mass – itself based on an actual event when Christ dined with his Disciples for the last time – the Freudian ceremony which followed the posited Ur deed of Vatermord and cannibalism. That is, the supposedly first act in which the primal Father is killed and then his blood drunk and his body eaten. This, Freud argues at the end of *Totem and Taboo*, is the *fons et origo* of civilisation;

a term – or better said, a notion or an event – that is applicable to the whole story of human history irrespective of tribe and culture. Yet there is no more striking, if unintentional, illustration of the primal event than the fountain-head ceremony of a religion that stands in opposition to everything that Freud maintains. The radical explanatory and narrative trope that emerged when Freud dragged psychology into the field of anthropology is thereby ironically underpinned by a dogmatic World View that celebrates a wholly different, and opposed, ontology, as well as its own equally alien, privileged and narrowly focused narrative. Furthermore, hovering above all of this is the ultimate icon of the Saviour on the Cross, bleeding and given over to gratuitous and perversely indulged suffering. And we, meanwhile, are instructed by our priests to accept and give thanks for what is in fact – or so *they* tell us – the incontrovertible proof and manifestation of the love of God, of the blessings of peace, the virtue of gentleness, and the promise of redemption. Yet what is most striking in this perverse business is that this time the Old Testament story of Isaac and Abraham is carried to term. Furthermore, before the Lamb of God is slaughtered it/he has to be tortured at length. And this is all related in fine poetry stamped by sadomasochistic relish. What Britten, courtesy of Wilfred Own, throws in our faces in the Offertorium of the *War Requiem*, is here given to us as a Christian apotheosis; they very proof that 'God so loved the world . . .'

Wagner, when tackling this heady brew in *Parsifal*, does not let us down. The dramatic potential of the Catholic Eucharist is not underplayed. And blood is ubiquitous. The more there is of it the more our faith in the love of God is, one would think, confirmed. Even the Youths officiating at the Eucharist in act one are blood-devoted, or blood-addicted: 'For the sinful world, with a thousand pains, as once His Blood did flow, now to Him the Saviour with joyful heart my blood be shed . . .' Actually this is rather reminiscent of Britten's Canticle III 'Still falls the rain.' The poem, by Edith Sitwell, portrays the crucifixion, and ends: 'Then comes the voice of One who like the heart of man/ Was once a child who among beasts has lain—/ "Still do I love, still shed my innocent light, my Blood, for thee."' It is, of course, not surprising that Britten is happy to put the emphasis on the innocent child. But in Wagner's opera it is Amfortas's regular bleeding, bound to the glowing liquefaction of the holy blood contained in the Grail, that raises the matter to the artistic and philosophical heights; the latter taking full advantage of the non-intellectual, creative freedoms of the former. It should also be noted that Wagner is quite clear about the multiple terms of reference of the Grail, although he is mistaken in thinking that this is just a wilful idea of his own. He tells Mathilde Wesendonck that the Grail is not merely the chalice used by Christ at the Last Supper, the Ur-Eucharist when the first transubstantiation presumably took place. It is also the goblet 'according to my *own* interpretation . . . in which Joseph of Arimathea caught the Saviour's blood on the Cross.'[8]

It has already been pointed out that Amfortas is, in effect, a fallen Christ. And it was not long after having completed a prose sketch for the possible opera that Wagner realised that he had underestimated just how important he was. He wrote to Mathilde Wesendonck that: 'Looked at closely, it is *Anfortas* [*sic*] who is the centre of attention and principal subject.' Consequently he is, or becomes, ever more deeply embedded in Wagner's *Weltanschauung*. Wagner also realised that Amfortas is a blood-brother to the Tristan of the third act of the earlier opera. Tristan too was a sinner, but only when judged by worldly standards of morality. Amfortas is a sinner in both worldly and spiritual terms. Nonetheless, Tristan is also a copious bleeder. His wound, like Parsifal's, won't heal . . . or 'close.' Wagnerian knowledge, we might speculate, is attained through sex, but knowledge can be dangerous, even sinful, and there is no return to the original state of virginal innocence. Well, or so we might have thought. But as was pointed out in chapter two, Amfortas's wound does close courtesy of Parsifal and the magic/Holy Lance. The bleeding duly stops and thus is the unblemished Ur-state restored. But while the comparison between the two is telling (Amfortas is, according to Wagner, Tristan 'inconceivably intensified'), such is the potency of the Amfortas figure that he can only be properly compared to Christ; that is, to the Christ who, unlike Amfortas, cannot, by definition, sin. This pairing can drive Wagner to rhapsodic language. This is very upfront in the letter to Mathilde Wesendonck. Amfortas's '. . . only solace lies in the benediction of the blood that once flowed from the Saviour's own, similar spear-wound as He languished upon the Cross, world renouncing, world-redeeming and world-suffering! Blood for blood, wound for wound – but what a gulf between the blood of the one and that of the other, between one wound and the other!'[9]

Thus with the imaginative and fictive creation of Amfortas on the stage Wagner has engineered a deep fusion between the arts and faith. Amfortas's recovery should remind us that miracles belong in art just as much as they do in religion. Wagner's trick is that he manages in *Parsifal* to employ both discourses – secular and divine – to realise his aims, intermingling them absolutely and seductively so that each profits from, and is enriched by, the qualities normally ascribed exclusively to the other.

Wagner provides some kind of theoretical underpinning for this strategy in the essays collected under the title *Religion and Art*, originally published in 1880 in the Bayreuther Blätter; a journal for Wagnerians founded by the master in 1878 and edited by a devoted disciple, Hans von Wolzogen. Art will have to save Religion, to rediscover the deeper meanings of the religious rites that have over the centuries been corrupted to the degree that the deeper truths they once enshrined have been lost. 'One might say that where Religion becomes artificial, it is reserved for Art to save the spirit of religion by recognising the figurative value of the mythic symbols which the former would have us believe in their literal sense, and revealing their deep and hidden truth through an ideal presentation.'[10] It is, of course, quite consistent of Wagner to argue that Art must excavate and refresh the lost import of Religion as encoded in its rituals and symbols. That is, it is not solely a matter of a convenient propaganda shift that allows him to place *Parsifal* above contemporary religious practices and thereby to seal the opera off from charges of blasphemy. After all, we should not forget the wilful anthropology of *Die Wibelungen* thirty-odd years before. There culture (and religion) was explained on the basis of a pre-Christian narrative and pre-Christian symbols that were later colonised and, in part, corrupted by Christianity. All of this is clearest 'today' in the decadent practices of Rome.[11] One might conclude from this that the restitution that Art makes in the ostensible interests of Religion will, in a manner quite consistent with the Freudian narrative mentioned above, end up pulling Christianity back into the pre-Christian (or pre-Christ) period of human history. Freud, it might be noted, was a passionate amateur archaeologist and fully conversant with a process of discovery that excavated and revealed the real (and chronologically deeper) roots of current practices. In many ways the 'talking cure' is an intellectual and therapeutic undertaking wholly archaeological in character.

There is a further consideration that must have played an important role in the Wagnerian brew whose principal ingredients were religion and philosophy: aesthetics. It is mentioned here only in passing not because it is unimportant, but because a proper treatment of it would overwhelm the theoretical parameters of this book. It cannot however be avoided, and must at this point interrupt the more focused discussion of Wagner.

Aesthetics was a special category in German thought. Moreover it was matter of great weight and much discussed. The key text was probably Kant's *Third Critique: On Judgement.* This affords aesthetics a unique epistemological role in that it is seen to offer a means of grounding idealist thought in provable axioms. Which is to say Kant maintains that it can be established that certain 'synthetic' statements are of themselves true; that is *a priori* true. This is a quality that up to then he had ascribed only to so-called analytical statements which are, in essence, tautologies. 'All objects occupy space' is just such a statement simply because it is true of itself. It is like saying the bachelor was unmarried. But synthetic statements such as what is the right way to behave, or what if anything we can say about the external world that is not wholly determined by our perception of it through the senses, are a different and a more important matter. Enquiries into such matters need to be freed from the exclusive sensory and subjective intellectual prison in which vulgar empiricism traps them. Kant argues therefore that there is in fact an intrinsic mental capacity, a 'cognitive faculty' in the mind of us all, that lies deeper than individual sensations of pleasure.[12] Following an elaborate analysis, in which aesthetics has the decisive role, he comes to the conclusion that certain moral values (tied up to the notion of the greatest good, the *summum bonum*) are, indeed, *a priori* true. This is because 'aesthetics judgements' are to be found 'in the class of judgements of which the basis of an *a priori* principle is the distinguishing feature' and thus they can be introduced into 'transcendental philosophy.'[13] The final section of his book, on teleology, goes even further than this, asserting that man must have been created for 'an end' and then inferring the existence of a God or an 'Author.' The arguments for this are not strictly relevant here, though it should be pointed out that Kant's use of the word teleology is in simple terms the same as that used in this essay. Namely it is a narrative explanation focused on an end: a telos.

Schopenhauer, in particular, was a great admirer of Kant and, as we have already seen, keen to marry his own terminology with his. But whatever the details of the case, Wagner could not have been either ignorant of, or indifferent to, the discussions on aesthetics that were – and were to remain – an essential and privileged component of German idealist thinking. In placing religion under the umbrella of art he was simply reflecting this.

Not inappropriately, the late essays from 1880 also try and take Schopenhauer into the territory of *Parsifal*. Once again, having made the colossal intellectual investment of the early 1850s, Wagner shows himself consistent in his determination not to ditch his privileged source of philosophical authority. However he is not consistent – surely because it is not possible – in the polemical strategies he employs to arrive at the conclusions that are important to him during the *Parsifal* period. In general, Schopenhauer has to be remade constantly in order to be fit for whatever 'contemporary' purpose Wagner wants of him. It has already been underlined how well aware Wagner is that the sensual, heterosexual encounter so essential to his own philosophical system violates the fundamental tenets of Schopenhauerian thought. Frankly, I suspect that when he finds himself in these sorts of difficulties, he is helped, not surprisingly, by the foggy nature of the Will and will-less-ness in the Schopenhauerian system. In this case (*Parsifal*) Wagner can devolve upon his notion of the Redeemer an inherent status that Amfortas must strive towards and can only reach when the second Christ figure, Parsifal, performs the climactic miracle. Wagner, ostensibly employing Schopenhauer's terminology, explains; 'As the Saviour himself was recognised as sinless, nay, incapable of sin, it followed that in him the Will must have been completely broken ere ever he was born, so that he could no more suffer, but only feel for others' sufferings; and the root hereof was necessarily to be found in a birth that issued, not from the Will-to-live, but from the Will-to-redeem.'[14] Furthermore, this pre-ordained act of self-sacrifice on the part of Christ takes us back appositely to the richly theatrical, and deeply religious, image of bodily torments. It also, however, draws our attention once again to the Oedipal connotations of the Mass. '. . . his own flesh and blood he gave as last and highest expiation for all the sin of outpoured blood and slaughtered flesh, and offered his Disciples wine and bread for each day's meal: 'Taste such alone, in memory of me'.'[15] Of course, we are simply free to reject any Freudian connotations as we please. Nonetheless, should we entertain the proposition that Freud is right, Wagner must have had, at the very least, some inkling of the forbidden, above all Oedipal and incestuous, desires. The operas suggest that he felt them very profoundly indeed. However, he cannot, pre-Freud, have thought of, or analysed, them in the way we can.

The appropriate, but rather bizarre, counterpart to this over-indulged redeemer-based corporeal agony follows quite logically if it is remembered that it has been contained within the religious milieu, albeit in its most theatrical form. In other words, the ideology celebrated by all the slings and arrows and suppurating wounds is, in full stylistic contradiction to itself, pacific and loving. At least that is what it is supposed to signify for us who, as it were, live in the real world; which is to say that we live for the most part in the world outside the temple and the theatre. But then we are forced to ask ourselves how is it that our world is torn asunder by actual strife and killing. Presumably we would hope that all the symbolic blood-letting celebrated with such relish in both the Wagnerian playhouse and the house of God, would allow the Prince of Peace to rule untroubled in the 'real' world, itself redeemed by his unparalleled agonies and his tremendous sacrifice. Wagner's answer to this conundrum is consistent enough, but hardly credible. It is not the God of the Christians that brings war into the world but – what else? – the God of the Jews: 'Manifestly it is not Jesus Christ, the Redeemer, whose pattern our army-chaplains commend to their battalions ere going into action; though they call on him, they can but mean Jehova, Jahve, or one of the Elohim, who hated all other gods beside himself, and wished them subjugated by his faithful people.'[16]

This is surely an instance when Wagner is asking us to take too much on credit; even if we can accept the general disposition of his own wilful, allegedly Christian, faith. And while it is true that the faithful at Bayreuth don't seem to have any problems with this sort of thing during a performance of *Parsifal*, this is because they would be disinclined in the context of the drama to make use of the polemical opinions kernel to the contemporary essays. In general they clearly don't feel, or wouldn't feel, troubled by the anomalies foregrounded here. Nonetheless, despite their unperturbed attitude, it is all part of a piece. The anti-Semitic agenda is necessary if the whole package is not to come apart. For Wagner it is incontestable that the immaculate Man/God phenomenon is under palpable threat everywhere in Germany. The Aryan/Christian paradigm needs to be defended if 'we' are not to go under. After all, is not Christ free of Jewish blood and the Jewish language? These are matters on which he is insistent. In *Jesus of Nazareth* (1849) he has the Saviour pole vault backwards over the Jewish phase. He is no longer of the House of David but of the 'lineage' of Adam.[17] Then he repeats the point thirty years later in *Religion and Art*, softening the tone and adding a touch of 'reasoned' (pseudo) historical verisimilitude, '. . . it is more than doubtful if Jesus himself was of Jewish extraction, since the dwellers in Galilee were despised by the Jews on express account of their impure origin . . .'[18] In other words, Jesus is the Son of Man and not the King of the Jews. Presumably it is unthinkable that Adam could have been a Jew.

Meanwhile, on the language issue he can get quite hot under the collar. On 27 November 1878 Cosima records in her *Diary* that a 'heated' Richard is simply not going to give way in the matter. Jesus just didn't speak 'Syriac-Chaldean.' He was also very concerned that she might, naïvely, accept the dependency of Christianity on the Jewish historical precedent. He warns her that it is a false relationship.[19] And, in any case: 'If Jesus is proclaimed Jehovah's son, then every Jewish rabbi can triumphantly confute all Christian theology.'[20] He needn't have worried. Cosima was even more virulently committed to the anti-Semitic cause than he.

Nonetheless, this taste for blood is handy. It can also be employed to underpin the a-Christian element in Wagner's work, or at least Wagner can employ it to this end. It vindicates his pantheism in that it foregrounds Nature as the greater, pre-Christian, God and it establishes, though contradictorily, the case for incest. It is incest, above all, that will give us a better idea of how free from stringent thought, and how arbitrary, both his philosophical and his religious theorising is.

It was pointed out in chapter two that there is a deep contradiction at work in Wagner's use of incest. It is unmistakable if we look at the operas in the context of *Opera and Drama*. Whereas the book length essay seems to rule incest out as unnatural in that such desires do not customarily, and psychologically should not, arise within the family, the operas are likely to tell a story whereby the male, compelled to leave his kinsfolk and go on a quest, ends up in the arms of a chosen woman who either is, or represents, his sister or mother. Nor can this be got around by arguing that the couple are ignorant of the blood relationship. The opposite is usually the case. The acknowledgement, or discovery, of the potentially forbidden consanguinity is a vital inducement to its actual consummation. Therefore the argument in *Opera and Drama*, which one supposes was designed to provide rigorous intellectual scaffolding for the freer creative and theatrical use of the theme, doesn't do anything like justice to the erotic state of affairs found, in fact, in the music dramas.

Wagner does, however, develop the incest theme in the essay, taking it further than we have hitherto acknowledged. It is striking, for instance, that fifty years before Freud and *Totem and Taboo* he looks at the case of *Oedipus Rex*. Sophocles' play was, of course, very popular and Wagner, like Freud, was a great lover of literature. Both men were keen students of Greek culture, and had Freud not been wholly indifferent to music he would have found in Wagner opera an additional haul of material that illustrated, even vindicated, his theories. He might well have uncovered operatic examples richer and more meaningful than those he inferred from his chosen literary sources: *Oedipus Rex* and *Hamlet*. Nonetheless, Wagner's reaction in the essay to the Oedipus story was conventional. 'Still more violently was roused the public horror, by the circumstance that Oedipus had wedded his own mother and begotten children of her.'[21] It seems that such repugnance would have been entirely normal; intrinsic to human nature. Further: 'The intuition of the essence of family-love and its distinction from the love between the sexes is therefore an instinctive one, inspired by the very nature of the thing: it rests upon Experience and Wont, and is therefore a view which takes us with all the strength of an insuperable feeling. Oedipus, who had espoused his mother and begotten children of her, is an object that fills us with horror and loathing, because he unatonably assaults our wonted [customary] relations towards our mother and the views which we have based thereon.'[22]

So what one sees here in the essay is nothing more than the conventional position underpinned by Wagner's probity, or self-image, as an analytical thinker. *Opera and Drama* is his big book and it is to establish that he is a serious intellectual. Therefore it is not surprising that what we call the taboo has been taken on board as a self-evident and proper phenomenon, wholly the product of instinctual human feeling at its most unproblematic. As a result he is not at all surprised at – nor disturbed by – the horror that follows the violation of the taboo. In other words. he does not consider the Freudian proposition that we are horrified precisely because we *desire* to do that which Oedipus has done. This was a 'discovery' that dawned on Freud in the 1890s and was to lead to *Totem and Taboo* fifteen years later. A keen theatregoer, he recorded, with some excitement, the initial moment of insight in a letter to Wilhelm Fliess on September 21 1897: 'Everyone in the audience was once a budding Oedipus in fantasy and each recoils in horror from the dream fulfilment.'[23]

Yet how different it is in the operas. There, liberated by imaginative freedom, the desire to break the taboo is near ubiquitous. The major examples have already been mentioned, so we might just note here that the same theme even crops up in the comic opera *Die Meistersinger* when Eva toys with the idea of marrying the older Hans Sachs. He, too, has contemplated the same thing. His relationship with her has always been loving; he carried her in his arms when she was a baby and we might think of him as her second father. *He* certainly does, and duly draws the obvious conclusion. Picking up on Eva's teasing suggestion, he observes that should he woo and win her he would then have 'a child, and wife too: that would indeed be a pleasant pastime!' But by the same token she would have a husband and a father in one, or, in other words, she would fulfil the unconscious wish of the Electra complex, the female expression of the universal Oedipal drive. As Sachs says: 'Yes, you have thought it out well for yourself.'

Wagner must surely have been aware of the discrepancy between the manner in which he explains incest in his writings and the way he employs it in the operas. And he does make a further move in *Opera and Drama* that might be seen as an attempt to get around the problem. It fails, but the attempt is, inevitably, revealing.

In this case the argument is drawn from nature and it might, consequently, be thought of as a parallel move to the great shift that occurs at the end of the first act of *Die Walküre*. At that moment, as we have already mentioned, the natural world envelopes incest, revealing it to be an intrinsic part of itself. And thereby it confers its impeccable benediction on the union of the twins Siegmund and Sieglinde. Surely we have good cause to believe that the Will, in its grandest form, is in the world at this point. We cannot fail to see that Siegmund and Sieglinde, drenched in Spring, are free of the pettiness of human society and all the meanness of purpose and egotism that normally animates the individual; that is to say they are free from the moral debilitations that follow from Schopenhauer's negative notion of individuation. However, Wagner's argument in the essay is also drawn from intentionality and ignorance, whereupon it cuts right across the case for incest as a force of nature as found in *The Ring*.

In the first instance the polemic drawn from nature is, it seems, easily established. 'Did Oedipus offend against this Human Nature, when he wedded his own mother? Most certainly not. Else would revolted Nature have proclaimed her wrath, by permitting no children to spring from this union . . .' This is of course an odd argument, for it does not simply declare that incest is okay if the children are healthy, but that somehow Nature herself consciously decides in the matter; that a pantheistic judgement is, as it were, handed down from high Olympus. Presumably we must conclude that if no children are born, or if those that are turn out to be weaklings, incest, in those cases, had been a bad thing morally. But then it can have nothing to do with incest as a cultural construct at all. It is merely a matter of biological health. Moreover this is, with respect to the Greek story, made manifest in Wagner's eyes because Oedipus and Jocasta are duly rewarded by 'two lusty sons and two noble daughters.' What then are we supposed to make of the fact that the curse visited by the Gods on Oedipus carries over to those children? After all, it is not as if Wagner is unaware of this. True, he does get around it in a fashion by disabusing the Gods of their responsibilities and shifting the problem onto human society. Nonetheless, the children do not escape their family fate. On them '. . . henceforth, as on their parents, there weighed the irremovable curse of that Society.'[24]

The second factor – the question of intentionality – only muddies the waters further. We are told that Oedipus and Jocasta are not culpable because they didn't know. 'Oedipus and Jocasta knew not, in what social relation they stood to one another: they had acted unconsciously, according to the natural instinct of the purely human Individual'[25] Here, as in the last quote, he is playing the social card. But of course we know that it is not, chiefly, a 'social relationship' at all. It is one of blood. Nevertheless, we are, I assume, supposed to infer that their ignorance is the reason why those wonderful children came about. While this is true with respect to Jocasta and Oedipus it does not, of course, obviate the problem of a curse (central to the agenda of *The Ring* as it is to the Theban plays) or, for that matter, the violation of the taboo. They both remain facts irrespective of the argument from ignorance. But whatever he intends, Wagner has subverted his own pantheistic agenda. Now the argument from Nature, from 'natural instinct', is in trouble. If Nature spared the pair because they were ignorant, and if that is accepted as an axiom, then the biological explanation as to the healthy continuation of the species, dependent on exogamy, must be driven from the field. It is also difficult to see any kind of mechanism whereby Nature, unless it/She is transported to the level of an omniscient God, will ever be in a position to be cognisant of which incestuous actors are in the know and which are not and then to act or interfere accordingly.

All of this might sound to some degree like nit-picking. And in respect of the anomaly between *Opera and Drama* and the stage works it is. In the latter case we are simply confronted by the incontrovertible fact that knowledge is a necessary ingredient in the narratives. Characters struggle to discover their own identity, what their lineage is, what their real names are, and so forth. Ignorance is not bliss; but knowledge can be. *The Ring* is structured in part as a great riddle to which at the end Brünnhilde knows the answer; which is also to say – as she does repeatedly – that she knows 'all things.'

The imperfections, the shortcomings, then of Wagner's pantheistic agenda are themselves central to the problem he is tackling. He seems to be as in thrall to Oedipal desire as any (knowing post-Freudian) person today could be and yet he does not, horrified, run away from it. Rather he seems determined to have it realised theatrically and thereby to make full use of the freedoms intrinsic to the world of the imagination. Thus he allows, or indulges himself in, exactly those scenarios that rational thought rules beyond the pale. Intellectually, and possibly emotionally, he cannot free himself entirely from either bourgeois morality or Freud's posited universal and forbidden desire. It is not simply, therefore, that he knows he is playing with fire. He is also disturbed to find himself doing so; which may be why in his writings he isn't able to come clean on the problem. There is, however, one case – albeit also in the operas – when he gives it a very good go.

At the beginning of the second act of *Die Walküre* Fricka confronts her husband, the God Wotan. She is outraged that he has engineered the coupling of the Volsung twins, Siegmund and Sieglinde. It is clear that her complaints are not without reason, and this is quite aside from her pain at Wotan's infidelity. He is the twins' father. One assumes she does not make much of this largely because she is well used to his faithlessness and his promiscuous fathering of children by other women, both mortal and godly. Instead she puts her case stringently, albeit with understandable passion. Furthermore, it would seem her arguments are incontrovertible. In the end Wotan is forced to capitulate and abandon the Volsungs. But before this tragic climax is reached there is a long set-to of tremendous power. Like so many of the one-on-one confrontations in *The Ring* it well illustrates how the tetralogy can deliver grand scenes that deal with serious matters in a highly exciting and dramatic fashion. This often comes about because of the ambivalent and contradictory forces that are, productively, at work. In this case it is particularly clear how Christian and pagan elements struggle over the available oxygen in *The Ring*. This should not surprise us when we remember that it was written in a Christian culture and for a Christian audience. In that, it unavoidably implies constantly the faith system that it, ostensibly, precedes and which its characters can, theoretically, know nothing of. Fricka, for instance, sounds like a very proper, bourgeois and devout lady. It is as if she steps out of the myth (dragging an unwilling Wotan with her) and into the 'modern' world; a world of written contracts, wider marital obligations, and, above all, non-negotiable restrictions on sexual practice; namely exactly those restrictions that pagan Gods are notoriously untroubled by and consequently violate with panache.

Fricka demands: 'When did it ever happen that brothers and sisters were lovers?' Wotan's initial and complacent reply is: 'Today you have seen it happen.' Since surtitles have come into fashion, even in German theatres for German operas, this line now usually garners a knowing – or is it an embarrassed? – chuckle. One might ask why. Could it be an unconscious homage paid to Freud's often ridiculed but conceivably all too perspicacious speculations? Whatever the reason, Wotan goes on to point out that the incestuous act has taken place naturally. . . 'of itself.' There is, therefore, nothing to be said against it. And if Fricka were to grasp that it is a natural and an instinctual occurrence, she would also see that it is worthy of her blessing. This is a little rich and one is not surprised that she doesn't feel any inclination to go down that road. Nonetheless, we might note that when setting this scene Wagner was reading *The World as Will and Representation* for the first time and would have come across in the supplements to the fourth book the observation, already noted in chapter two, that 'in all sexual love, instinct holds the reins.'[26] However in Wagner's hands instinct is not so much a biological drive as an expression of wide bountiful nature herself.

Fricka, however, is having none of it, whether it comes from Wotan/ Wagner or Schopenhauer, and duly overwhelms the God with arguments drawn from precedence and custom (*Gewohnheit* again). She has been shamed and ridiculed, and Wotan is simply lying as to the freedom of action the supposedly natural sibling couple now enjoy. Rather they are unambiguous products of Wotan's will (in Siegmund 'I find only you'). Moreover, as a couple they are sinful, an abomination, her language (for instance *frevelnde*) often having connotations of blasphemy. All of this undermines the argument from nature. Of course, in this case no argument is made from ignorance simply because the whole of Siegmund and Sieglinde's long, and ultimately ecstatic scene in the first act is constructed from the incremental steps they take in the discovery of their lineage, their names, and, therefore, their destiny. As the sword is drawn from the tree and Siegmund (who comes, as he explains, with all too many epithets) is given his 'proper' name by Sieglinde, their bliss knows no bounds. Knowledge and desire are co-mingled. They are both, for the first time, open-eyed. There will be no gratuitous self-blinding in the manner of the Greek Oedipus here. Knowledge is joyfully won, perceived, and indulged. The last line of the act is Siegmund's triumphant cry: 'So let the Volsung blood increase.' And it duly does, producing an offspring as 'lusty' and 'noble' as any born to Jocasta and Oedipus.

Yet it is true that they are not free agents. The sword, as Fricka makes clear, has been driven into the tree where it has, anthropomorphically, been waiting for Siegmund. Their destiny is pre-written. Or at least it was until she interfered, violently subverting the narrative and then rewriting it. Nonetheless, all that is to come after the first interval. Experiencing the act itself – one of Wagner's longest and most successful, homogeneous lyrical arches – how can we avoid the conclusion that under the right circumstances *knowing* acts of incest are damn fine things? Why then in *Opera and Drama* can't he just simply say so?

Wagner does, however, pursue the matter further when he turns to one of the incestuously produced children of Oedipus and Jocasta: Antigone. But the dichotomy remains. What he wants to make of her is consistent with the conventional attitude to incest found in the essay, rather than its ecstatic celebration in the stage works. He takes the story from Sophocles' third Theban play, *Antigone*. After Eterocles and Polynices, the two sons of Oedipus (who are, of course, also their father's brothers) had failed to rule in harmony, Thebes falls into the hands of their paternal uncle Creon. Both brothers die in battle. Creon decrees that Eterocles should be buried with all appropriate honours, while Polynices is to be left to rot. Their sister Antigone cannot accept this and has Polynices properly buried, whereupon she is punished by Creon. Buried alive she hangs herself before Creon, who has a change of heart, can rescue her. Wagner sees the story as illustrating how 'the State now turns upon Society itself, to crush it; inasmuch as it wards from it the natural sustenance of its being, in the holiest and most instinctive social feelings.'[27] We should not forget that at this time (1851) Wagner, in exile in Zurich, was still in his radical pseudo-communist phase. All the great spiritual notions, usually wrapped up in the noun *love*, are still struggling to find some kind of expression in his arbitrary notion of a nominally socialist, anti-state, model of collective life.

Wagner insists that Antigone is pure human love personified. Furthermore, because of this she can free her brother (or at least his corpse) from the 'curse' that follows their parents' *Blutschande* or incest. Consequently her love annuls the state; brings it crashing down. So here again is the idea of a flourishing utopia that enables the maximum expression of love and, once again, it is presented to us in untheorised opposition to the practical, empirical world. 'Antigone knew nothing of politics; – *she loved*.' And she was '*fully conscious*' of this. 'She knew, what she was doing, – but she also knew that do it she must, that she had no choice but to act according to love's Necessity.'[28] In fact she is like Christ as revealed to us in *Jesus of Nazareth*. She will set love free; free, above all, of the bounds of convention. And by the same token she is also a true sister of that other product of incest: Siegfried. In the long letter to Röckel from 25/26 January 1854 Wagner writes passionately about his Ur-Christ; the boy we get to see on the stage is all instinct and innate, exuberant virtue. Siegfried is good, not because of his thoughtfulness – his thinking about the world is utterly shackled by his simplistic, empirical and immediate perceptions – but simply because he *is*. He is virtue incarnated. And how do we know this? Well, if the Wagner at the time of the Röckel letter is to be believed, it is because he 'never ceases to love.' What this has to do with his belligerent attitude to Gunther when he first meets him in *Götterdämmerung* ('fight with me or be my friend'), or his hostility to Wotan in act three of *Siegfried*, or his palpable relish when he tells the Gibichungs how he butchered Mime, or indeed killing dragons, we can put aside and return instead to his ideological Greek sister. Nevertheless, we should not forget Siegfried, for one has the feeling that when Wagner read Sophocles' *Antigone* he immediately sensed a causal link between her paradigmatic status as the embodiment of love and her incestuous origin.[29]

Wagner is not being eccentric when he makes much of the character of Antigone. She is a crucial figure in German literary history. Of particular interest is her importance to Goethe, not least because he does not automatically deck her out, as Wagner does, as an incontrovertible, paradigmatic ideal. For instance, there is no automatic assumption that her love for her brother is impeccable. Johann Peter Eckermann in 1827 suggested just such an elevated interpretation when talking to him, but Goethe pointed out that there must have been 'countless' cases of extreme sensual attraction been between brothers and sisters. Which is to say, that what was for the Wagner of the essays self-evidently improper and a block to nature's way (in contradistinction to the Wagner of the operas), and what Schopenhauer saw as violating the principle of the attraction of opposites, is airily dismissed by Goethe. He goes on to adopt a position that is, at least epistemologically, closer to Freud's, although he could hardly have intended that. He suggests that Sophocles was in the first instance inspired by the myths ('Sage') of the people where the tale of the thwarted burial of the brother was already to be found. That is, the creation and structure of his works are not the product of an 'idea', but rather of something that came to him from a tradition; one that already existed in the culture and out of which a compelling drama could be fashioned. We might infer that such a drama would be meaningful because it decoded, by implication, a matter that was important to the community and, moreover, quite possibly embedded in the collective psychology of the tribe. In other words, he had stumbled on Antigone in the same way Freud had stumbled on Oedipus, although he did not have Freud's near ready-made *Weltanschauung*, nor, one imagines, the desire to make out of incest something as comparably fundamental.[30] At which point we should consider what Britten made of Greek thought and philosophy.

This takes us to the heart of *Death in Venice*. It also means that the relatively narrow and intense philosophical bond between Wagner and Schopenhauer is replaced by something far more loose, many-sided, and potentially disruptive. For while Britten, and for that matter his librettist Myfanwy Piper, might not have engaged with the classical Greek world in the dedicated even scholarly manner of Wagner (probably), or Freud (certainly), or Thomas Mann (possibly), it transpires that what they produced is exceptionally profound and rich in connotations. To what degree this is a product of the lack of both a focused grand theory and an unmistakable, no matter how contradictory, Wagner-like ideological programme is again a matter of speculation. But I believe it to be the case. What exactly, then, were they taking on board when they joined the long line of German and British artists and intellectuals who succumbed to a fascination with Greek philosophy, literature, and life? This question is particularly pertinent because in their case the entry point would seem to have been specific. It was the general question of sexuality and, more particularly, the phenomenon of man/boy love.

We should, first, acknowledge how intellectually downgraded the standard heterosexual union emerges in Greek thought. In this respect it was of little use to Wagner, who as we noted in the first chapter, regarded the Greek attitude to love as 'foreign to Germans.' True, there is the striking example of Xenophon's account of Ischomachus' relationship with his wife: *The Economist* (*Oeconomicus*). But the title is significant. It is an account of the division of labour between husband and wife. Above all, it is concerned with the proper running of the household and the farming estate of which it is the centre. It can, however, be seen as an early step in a process that was, under the Roman emperor Marcus Aurelius, to put the notion of family, of the 'concordia' between husband and wife, and thereby 'the effortless harmony of the Roman order'[31]on the first place. But this is a long way from the Greek symposium where men, often married and attended by women who served them, danced for them, and might well have acted as prostitutes, discussed the nature of love, famously addressing the awkward phenomenon of the man/boy relationship in the context of the rival claims of ethereal and carnal love. Awkward, because it was seen to be a threat to social order and, in addition, it gave rise to problems within Greek philosophical Idealism.

Socrates, for instance, addresses the phenomenon of man/boy love in order to underline the distinction between the body and the soul. In fact he sees an antagonistic relationship within both pairings: that is, within the relationship between ethereal love and bodily sex on the one hand, and within the social and emotional relationship between the man and the boy on the other. Both are dangerously a-sychronic. And this will, in particular, become marked and disruptive if the man gives in to his carnal desires for the boy. While such desires are taken as read – which is a matter that many people subsequently, including Wagner, have found uncongenial – succumbing to them is likely to produce a disturbing (and humiliating) imbalance. An Athenian freeman caught in that bind ('for ever cringing and petitioning a kiss') is less likely to be a good citizen. On the other hand, in the heterosexual relationship 'the wife at any rate shares with her husband in their nuptial joys.'[32] Though why a man should be less inclined to be enslaved by his love for a woman than by his love for a youth is not entirely clear. Presumably we are to believe that the conventional marital relationship is likely to regulate that sort of thing, factoring out any anti-social elements and diminishing the probability that the Athenian freeman might debase himself. Whatever the case, the key point is that in the Socratic speculations the marital example is a meagre one – pleasant certainly, but philosophically unfruitful. The man/boy relationship on the other hand is, no doubt because it is the site of difficulties, full of intellectual possibilities and thus grounds for serious discussion.

As we approach the Socratic dialogue *Phaedrus* – the text that Thomas Mann, and hence Piper and Britten, tackled in *Death in Venice* – we might as well begin with Socrates' statement: 'How far the love of soul is better than the love of body.'[33] It does, of course, rather load the dice, but if we are going to discuss Socrates that is unavoidable. As a good Greek idealist he is utterly committed to the ontological supremacy, to say nothing of the axiomatic existence, of the spiritual over the earthly. Consequently any bodily sexual activity is going to be very considerably diminished. For instance, when it comes to free sexual indulgence he is inclined to talk of 'swinish affection.' Frankly one can't avoid the thought that for him sexual desire equates lust and is, as a result, easily catalogued as just plain base, even if it is not to be avoided by most people.[34]

Nonetheless, as Socrates is going to be the principal source of wisdom on this matter a, conceivably common sense, assumption should be dismissed immediately. However much he may condemn corporeally indulged man/ boy love, however much he may stress its negative social and moral aspects, he does not seem to have been sexually indifferent to boys. In Plato's *Charmides* he is portrayed as blatantly aroused when the beautiful and eponymous youth makes his climactic appearance,[35] and when he says in Xenophon's *Symposium* that 'For myself I cannot name the time at which I have not been in love with some one', the context makes it clear that he is talking about youths.[36] Put simply, Socrates controls himself because he thinks yielding to carnal desire in this matter would be wrong. For instance, he is even able to resist – carnally – the beautiful Alcibiades, though this does not mean he is indifferent. Britten had already come across this in Hölderlin; poems recommended to him by Prince Ludwig of Hesse. In the third of Britten's *Six Hölderlin Fragments* ('Socrates and Alcibiades') composed in 1958 the philosopher is asked: 'Why, holy Socrates, do you court/ This youth all the time?' It might be thought that Socrates thought the boy a god. What follows knits together materialist and idealist qualities that, as we will see, are essential to the Greek argument. 'He who has pondered the most profound thoughts, loves what is most alive' and 'And in the end, the wise will often/ Bend toward that which is beautiful.' Nonetheless, in Plato's *Symposium* we learn that a line must be drawn. Alcibiades arrives late, he is drunk, and makes a speech in praise of Socrates, during which he relates how he pursued him, reversing the normal seductive and power relationship of the man/boy model. 'So I invited him to sup with me, just as if he were a fair youth, and I a designing lover.'[37] He got so far as to sleep with Socrates on the same couch and under the same cloak, but despite all of his efforts there was no hanky-panky.

One will, in a moment, put aside the question of the (potentially) socially disruptive nature of the relationship as it is not strictly relevant to either the purely philosophic Socratic argument on the nature of love, or to the programme of the opera. But not yet. For instance, we should acknowledge that Aschenbach's fall is also a social one and his behaviour in pursuing the boy through the city would have given rise to gossip. No doubt that is a peripheral consideration when placed alongside his spiritual journey, but it is notable that Katia Mann, Thomas's wife, recalled in a German television partially dramatized, documentary (*Die Manns – Ein Jahrhundertroman*, Director Heinrich Breloer 2001) that her husband was duly fascinated when he saw the beautiful Polish boy in real life in 1911 while they were holidaying in Venice but didn't – thank God – actually follow him around. In any case, one wonders if Socrates isn't worried by what he sees as the social dangers of paedophilia simply because the practice is not only in the public sphere but also very widespread. It was normal for an as yet unmarried man in his twenties or thirties (the *erastes*) to function as a mentor, and to fall in love with a teenage youth (the *eromenos*) irrespective of whether it led to sex or not. Yet sex acts involving two males were a popular subject of illustration (common on vases for instance) and the whole question was scatologically dealt with and exploited in many of the comedies. It was out in the open; an everyday part of social life. Moreover, it could be acknowledged in an untroubled manner.

For instance, we know that at Xenophon's Symposium Lycon, the father of the *eromenos* (Autolycus), is present at the banquet and this indicates that the love of the *erastes* (Callias) is proper. Indeed Socrates uses the presence of Lycon to suggest that Callias' love has reached a higher (Platonic) phase. What binds Callias to Autolycus is: 'Love divine. This I infer as well from the fair and noble character of your friend, as from the fact that you invite his father to share your life and intercourse. Since no part of these is hidden from the father by the fair and noble lover.'[38] Paradoxically, in underlining a rare and virtuous, which is to say a practising non-sensual, man/boy friendship Socrates is drawing our attention to the, presumably more common, alternative. It might also remind us of Aschenbach's plan to address the Polish family, above all the mother, in order to warn them that the city is no longer safe. In doing so he would put himself in a less compromised position. Unfortunately – although that is to assume a lot – he flunks. But returning to the Greek example, we might ask what evidence is there that, as long as both the *eromenos* and the *erastes* continue to behave as free, self-respecting, Athenian citizens, a carnal relationship would impair social life? It is assumed, after all, that both will later marry and produce children. No matter. Of more interest are the abstract arguments devised to regulate actual behaviour.

Put simply, there appears to be a contradiction, or at the very least an abrasive relationship between opposites in the Socratic argument. The potentially corrupting – because it is potentially physical – man/boy pairing becomes, in what might be seen as a dialectical trick, the royal road to higher things; to a proper understanding of the soul. This is accomplished when the older lover, after acknowledging his carnal feelings, succeeds in spurning sensual desire. He manages this in as much as he discovers in his lust for the boy something loftier and non-carnal. However, it is fundamental to the argument that he can only get to the latter state via the good offices of the, potentially degenerate, former. The end result may well be a denial of his libido but it cannot come about unless there has been a struggle; a deep experiential engagement with the power of fleshly love. And this is not simply because the libidinous desire is improper and must be overcome and trashed in the cause of true piety, as though an encounter with the forces of darkness were a necessary rite of passage into the light. Rather, it is because the carnal state also teaches; it has to be a part of the equation. Moreover it can never be definitively factored out. In other words Greek thought, in this instance at least, is indeed truly dialectical. Nonetheless, in respect of the antagonistic relationship between sexual and spiritual values the homosexual pairing emerges as the key unit. Heterosexual love is not, it would seem, in a position to effect the same kind of, albeit contradictory, quantum leap.

At the beginning of *Phaedrus* Socrates is clear that the soul is immortal. This is no doubt reassuring, but it does not of itself banish sensual pleasure as a consideration or marginalize the body. And Socrates doesn't pretend otherwise. 'In every one of us there are two guiding and ruling principles which lead us whither they will; one is the natural desire of pleasure, the other is an acquired opinion which aspires after the best.' On the basis of this distinction between bodily indulgence and higher abstract thought, we are brought to understand that desire and passion lead us to the abyss. Furthermore, the higher principle, being an expression of reason, must be in its very nature sober. 'When opinion by the help of reason leads us to the best, the conquering principle is called temperance; but when desire, which is devoid of reason, rules in us and drags us to pleasure, that power of misrule is called excess.'[39] This pull of nominal opposites is explained by Socrates in an analogy. We are in the position of a charioteer whose winged chariot is pulled by two horses, one of which is noble, the other base. The former is linked to the Gods to whom we strive, the latter we have trouble controlling and it drags us down. It is worthwhile noting that we are talking about a winged chariot because Socrates is explaining to us the nature of the soul, which in this analogy is threefold: the charioteer and the two horses.[40] The chariot itself is the potential means of transport to the higher ethereal sphere. Zeus after all had a famous air-borne chariot with, we are told in Homer's Iliad (Book VIII 1–52), two 'bronze-hoofed horses . . . with flowing manes of gold.' But his horses were a 'willing pair.'

In respect of the threefold analogy of the soul, Socrates is drawing our attention to the very element (baseness) that, we might think, he would want to rigorously expel from serious, or long-term, consideration. Alternatively, we might conclude that baseness is addressed because it is, unfortunately, a fact of life and therefore cannot be got rid of simply because it is unwelcome. But neither is the case. Socrates' position is bolder and more demanding. The soul is stuck with the ignoble horse – it is to be mastered, it cannot be definitively banished – chiefly because Socrates has need of Eros, and Eros is in part sensual. This is because in the first instance it comes to us empirically, namely through the agency of sight in our quotidian lower world. We perceive it in the form of beauty, the quality 'most palpable to sight.' Which is to say we perceive it in the form of its 'earthly namesake': the beautiful youth.[41] When in the novella Aschenbach is confronted by the sight of Tadzio it is exactly this consideration which steers his philosophical thinking: '. . . beauty alone is both divine and visible'[42] and '. . . it is the sole aspect of the spiritual which we can perceive through our senses.'[43]

Of course, it is axiomatic to the language used, whether by Socrates, Mann or Piper, that in this ideological system beauty has to be invested with ethical values; values that we might not feel to be self-evident. Nonetheless, we note that the horse that wishes to drag us down is ugly: 'a crooked lumbering animal, put together anyhow,' while the other has 'a lofty neck and an aquiline nose,' and does not need the whip. Incidentally, the good horse is fair, the bad horse dark.[44] Even so, we cannot have the one without the other. And this becomes most pertinent when we are confronted by great beauty in the physical world. It is disorientating. For instance, Socrates was struck dumb by Charmides: 'When I saw him coming in, I confess that I was quite astonished at his beauty and stature; all the world seemed to be enamoured of him; amazement and confusion reigned when he entered; and a troop of lovers followed him.'[45] It is not insignificant that the goal of the dialogue with Charmides that follows is 'temperance' or sobriety. In other words, reason, which is also a manifestation – like beauty – of the soul, or the higher realm. But of course reason is not so overt, so upfront, and so stunning as the sight of corporeal beauty itself. Moreover, it is something for which one is going to have to work hard. Reason or temperance will require mental effort; not merely the ability to open one's eyes. In any case, we might suspect that temperance was not much on the minds of Charmides' 'troop of lovers' or, for that matter, on the minds of all the others present, who immediately struggled to get a place next to the beautiful youth.

This privileging of beauty might seem to us rather arbitrary (Socrates was famously ugly), but in the Greek *Weltanschauung* beauty was impeccable, a divine sign. In Plato's Symposium virtue and beauty are, without any apparent difficulty, coupled in the little duologue between Socrates and Agathon on the basis of another premise that is also, perhaps, not self-evident to us. But for the Greeks it seems it is. Socrates asks: 'Is not the good also the beautiful?' Agathon replies: 'Yes.' Socrates then makes the desired, but, in reversing the terms, logically unsound and certainly arbitrary inference: 'Then in wanting the beautiful, love wants also the good?' and the compliant Agathon duly capitulates: 'I cannot refute you . . . said Agathon.'[46] Of course this will work logically if it is assumed that the two terms are identical, but then it is a mere tautology and proves nothing. In any case this seems improbable. After all, Socrates himself was one and not the other. And Alcibiades likewise, although in his case it was beauty, as perceived by the eyes, that was present and goodness (particularly sobriety) that was missing.

The same point is made at greater length when Socrates tells of the schooling he received from the wise woman Diotima. It also pushes the argument forward. Again we are instructed that love 'may be described generally as the love of the everlasting possession of the good.' Thus is the corporeal transcended, 'the beauty of the mind is more honourable than the beauty of the outward form.' Indeed we even get beyond the beautiful youths themselves and, theoretically, 'see the true beauty – the divine beauty, I mean, pure and clear and unalloyed, not clogged with the pollutions of mortality and all the colours and vanities of human life.'[47] Socrates has learnt from Diotima and her analogy of the ladder how we can ascend to higher things. However for the storyteller, even when influenced by Socrates, the divine seduction of beauty comes with an inbuilt destructive anomaly that proves hard to resist. What the philosopher is able, it seems, to easily reconcile courtesy of abstract thought, the novelist's love of tension and a dynamic disruptive narrative may well pull apart. As Mann observes when Aschenbach is first stunned by the sight of Tadzio: 'For in almost every artist nature is inborn a wanton and treacherous proneness to side with the beauty that breaks hearts.'[48] And breaking hearts, rather than constructing timeless, bogus syllogisms, is what literature and art is often about. It is doubtful whether the glib equation between beauty and goodness could under these circumstances survive. Nor can the shift, noted in respect of Diotima's analogy as interpreted by Socrates, whereby beauty is divested of its physical attractions and seen as a purely spiritual commodity. The fact is, this point is reached through a meeting with the likes of Charmides and Alcibiades and not someone who is as physically ugly as the dark horse with which the charioteer must struggle.

In other words, no matter what the philosopher may desire he is still stuck, at least in the Socratic model, with the awkward and dramatic/narrative fact that the initial incontrovertible step remains the visual encounter with earthly beauty. It is indeed the moment when Aschenbach first sees Tadzio in the hotel and begins what he thinks are merely going to be his 'novelist's speculations.' In fact, however, it turns out to be a blinding, wholly disorientating, moment and it engenders both love and carnal desire. It is not going to be easy to stay in control, to keep a firm hand on the reins. And it is not clear where one will end up: Mount Olympus or in the abyss.

Above all, no matter how transcendent the final Socratic goal, circumventing the youth whose beauty manifests the impeccable higher realm is going to be difficult to pull off once and for all. Indeed, it is hard to regard him, even in the philosophical content, as merely a means to an ethereal end. It is, for instance, notable that we are assured that when naked Charmides is 'absolutely perfect' in appearance. This is the bodily perfection that, we must assume, will transport us to the ethereal. But first of all the charioteer feels 'the prickings and ticklings of desire.'[49] Moreover, the contemplation of this desirable perfection sets both horses in conflict as each strives to fulfil its different and probably opposed agenda. However, if handled well and properly appreciated, it is the noble horse that emerges the victor. Nonetheless, the metaphorical language that is employed in order that we might understand this comes over, at least to the reader of impure thoughts, as flagrantly carnal and phallocentric. We are told of the noble horse that its wing 'moistens and he warms' and as 'nourishment streams upon him. . . ' the '. . . wing begins to swell and grow from the root upwards.'[50] The end result of all this 'heat and perspiration' is that the chariot is up and away. It has taken wing and is free of the baseness that seems, however, to have provided a good deal of the psychic fuel necessary to overcome the lustful steed to which it is yet even now still fettered. Furthermore, should all this be managed, one has the feeling that it has been a very near run thing.

But it is the power of physically manifest Eros that is the hostage to fortune in Socrates' (and Plato's) idealized world view. The dangerous element is therefore not only essential because the beautiful youth manifests Eros. It is also necessary because only when thus manifested can the lover take a further step and recognize the power of Eros in its highest form, and thereby overcome his desire for that which is so palpably desirable. This does not seem a very practical proposition – or even a very logical one – but Socrates nevertheless sets the bar unbendingly high, not least because he is compelled to play with fire. 'Now he who is not newly initiated or who has become corrupted, does not easily rise out of this world to the sight of true beauty in the other; he looks only at her earthly namesake, and instead of being awed at the sight of her, he is given over to pleasure, and like a brutish beast he rushes on to enjoy and beget; he consorts with wantonness, and is not afraid or ashamed of pursuing pleasure in violation of nature.'[51] When examined in this framework, Eros has become part of the problem rather than the solution.[52]

Even so, this is to undersell the dialectical power of love. For 'the madness of love is the greatest of heaven's blessings.'[53] And that enables Socrates to play a little trick. 'I told a lie when I said that the beloved ought to accept the non-lover when he might have the lover, because the one is sane, and the other mad. It might be so if madness were simply an evil; but there is also a madness which is a divine gift, and the source of the chiefest blessings granted to men.'[54] The psychic dangers then of love – which in this context amounts to the high Socratic ideal love – are considerable. We might infer that it can, as in the case of Aschenbach, lead to a dissolution of the self, to the risible but revealing assumption through make-up and hair dye of a fake identity. Nonetheless, Socrates' argument forces us to conclude that tangible Eros needs to be in the world, even when it drives us mad. Aschenbach is acknowledging just this when in the opera he cries out: 'Ah, Tadzio. Eros, Ganymede. See I am past all fear, Blind to danger, Drunken, powerless, Sunk in the bliss of madness.' Furthermore, when we look both at Mann's novella and Britten's opera we must also consider whether Eros also is, or indeed needs to be, in the Word.

The Socratic analogy of the high and low (spiritual and earthly) horses harnessed, if not shackled, together sets up a binary pairing that can be pursued throughout a great deal of German thought. Wagner, for instance, would have surely been aware of the passage from Goethe's Faust. In Part I (Scene: Outside the Gate of the Town) Faust talks of the 'two souls' that dwell in his breast and that cause him anguish. They are siblings and '. . . each is fain to leave its brother/ The one, fast clinging, to the world adheres/ With clutching organs, in love's sturdy lust;/ The other strongly lifts itself from dust/ To yonder high, ancestral spheres.' It is, however, a ubiquitous theme and suggests the deeper question of the struggle between empirical and transcendental thinking in German philosophy. That, however, can be put aside. Of more relevance to *Death in Venice*, and in particular to Piper's libretto, is the manner in which Nietzsche employed the same, apparently fundamental, binary pairing courtesy of the Apollonian and Dionysian models in his The Birth of Tragedy.

Nietzsche's terminology, however, is rather like Schopenhauer's and Wagner's. It tends to shift a bit. Nonetheless Dionysus, or his 'votary', is associated with the satyr and the dance and: 'It is not difficult to imagine the awed surprise with which the Apollonian Greek must have looked on him. And that surprise would be further increased as the latter realized, with a shudder, that all this was not so alien to him after all, that his Apollonian consciousness was but a thin veil hiding from him the whole Dionysian realm.'[55] And no matter how confused, or subtle, Nietzsche's various shifts and intellectual manoeuvres in the The Birth of Tragedy become, this particular synthesis between the earthy and the spiritual is at all times not so very far from the Socratic position. Above all, Nietzsche's account does not work in terms of unbridgeable binary opposites, although it begins with a binary pairing. Just as the two horses in Socrates' analogy of the soul are indissolubly interdependent so that what is most telling, finally, is their shared role rather than – as perhaps Socrates might have initially intended – their mutually combative discrete personalities, so Nietzsche's Apollonian and Dionysian realms are really part of an integrated, if unstable, whole.

This is a matter of particular importance in *Death in Venice* the opera. There one is, at least prima facie, struck by the discrete and opposed character inherent to the epistemology of the same binary unit. One might say that the two horses (the analogy is never used in the opera, although in the novella there is an association between Tadzio and the personification of the sun, Helios: the 'naked god with cheeks aflame [who drives] his four fire-breathing steeds through heaven's spaces'[56]) are always at odds and there is never any overt suggestion of a synthesis, whether stable, harmonious or otherwise. But Apollo and Dionysus are participatory characters, usually only heard unless the producer decides otherwise. While Aschenbach sleeps, they engage in a struggle for his – we must assume – soul. Dionysus urges him to 'receive the stranger God' and his votaries appear and dance, celebrating at the climax an orgiastic sacrifice. The dream is taken directly from the novella where Aschenbach also hears a voice calling on him to 'receive the stranger God.' Mann then describes in detail the bacchanal that follows, how it descends into a sick and wild ritual of 'bestial degradation.' It leaves the waking dreamer in 'the demon's grip.'[57] Nietzsche is not mentioned in either case and in Mann there is only one reference each to the two Gods. In the opera, however, their struggle for influence is critically important. Apollo calls upon Aschenbach to 'Reject the abyss,' while Dionysus admonishes him not to 'refuse the mysteries.' More notable still, there is, it seems, a victor. Apollo, presumably vanquished, leaves the field with the repeated refrain 'I go, I go now', leaving Dionysus in implied command. We should also note that Dionysus is sung by the baritone who sings all of the seven (inimical?) characters; namely the agents who manoeuvre Aschenbach to the point where he falls. In this straightforward disposition of ideological forces Aschenbach can also be said to have lost. Piper, for instance, remarked to Britten: 'There is no doubt in my mind that Aschenbach was a devotee of Apollo.'[58]

In the end, however, matters did not, I believe, turn out to be so straightforward, whatever the original inclinations of the major creative artists involved might have been. And this must also include Pears who drove Piper to distraction with his various suggestions. Having a counter-tenor as Apollo was, for instance, his idea. In any case, at this point we might quote just one passage from the opera. In act one, scene five Aschenbach is contemplating the sea which he regards as 'a form of perfection' when Tadzio comes onto the beach. His response? 'Ah, here comes Eros – his very self.' The Polish boy duly shows his hostility to the Russian family and Aschenbach is pleased. But why? Because: 'There is a dark side to perfection. I like that.' And so, if we are to come to terms with the deep dialectical struggle at work here, should we. Furthermore, the Aschenbach of the novella is well aware that narrative does not allow of timeless beauty in the manner of the philosophical dialogue. Charmides may well have been perfect, but he is not going anywhere outside of the discourse on beauty. Tadzio, however, has imperfect teeth. He is, Aschenbach speculates, probably 'chlorotic' and will not live to grow old. 'He did not try to account for the pleasure the idea gave him.'[59]

Surely Pears, whose thinking about sexuality was subtle and not disposed to either propaganda or black and white distinctions, had some inkling of the deep ambivalences involved. He wrote to Sidney Nolan: 'Ben is writing an evil opera and it's killing him'[60] It would be wrong, I think, to conclude that the work was evil simply because it was a killer. Any major composition at this time, no matter how benign, would have had the same effect. *Death in Venice* is indeed evil . . . inherently. But then again it is also inherently good. And quite possibly for the same reason. Pears – I choose arbitrarily to believe – knew this. While he was making his début in *Death in Venice* at the Metropolitan Opera in November 1974 he wrote a love letter to Britten marked by exceptional depth of feeling and gratitude. In it he thanked him for this 'great Aschenbach.'[61]

Mention has been made more than once of Ganymede. It was a story of some interest to both Socrates and Thomas Mann and that is how it earned its cursory mention in the opera. Ganymede is, however, a striking example of the theme with which we have been dealing. A shepherd lad of incomparable beauty (in tales of this type the beauty always has to be incomparable despite, as we have seen, there being a plethora of available comparisons), one assumes him to have been the right age for an *eromenos*. For instance, Garry Wills points out that the language used to describe him means that he is older than a boy and, in the Greek mind, fit for sex.[62] And this is the way he is usually portrayed in European art, with the notable exception of Rembrandt's hugely theatrical picture. This shows Ganymede as an ugly, pudgy toddler pissing with terror as he is dragged up to the heavens. It is perhaps rather disturbing that this picture is called the *Rape of Ganymede*, though no doubt we should banish – assuming we can – any sexual connotations and think solely of something along the lines of an abduction. However, such things are always considerably more easily said than done. In any case, Ganymede's distress, or good fortune, is the result of becoming the object of Zeus' love . . . or lust. The God duly spirits him aloft. In this instance, as in several others, Zeus forgoes the chariot and resorts to metamorphosis. He turns himself into an eagle, so we might say that Ganymede too is winged up to the heavens, or at least to the mythological Greek equivalent found on Mount Olympus. Safely ensconced there he becomes Zeus' cup-bearer and is granted immortality. Later he attains proper heavenly significance while remaining a physical entity. He becomes a moon; a satellite of Zeus/Jupiter.

The problem with this is that while the ethereal option is thoroughly indulged, along with all the corresponding spatial and metaphorical authority, the motivation is, in Socratic terms, flagrantly base. And Socrates was well aware of the problem. In, above all, Xenophon's *Symposium* he attempts to clear up any misunderstanding, even going so far as to provide some etymological proof for his interpretation. 'As I maintain, it was not for his body's sake, but for his soul's, that Ganymede was translated to Olympus, as the story goes, by Zeus. And to this his very name bears witness, for is it not written in Homer? And he gladdens (*ganutai*) to hear his voice. This the poet says, meaning "he is pleased to listen to his words."' Ganymede: 'bears a name compounded of the two words, "joy" and "counsel," and is honoured among the gods, not as one "whose body," but "whose mind" "gives pleasure." '[63] One has the feeling that the philosopher is protesting too much. No matter. Taken on its own terms, the Word, as idea and praxis, would appear to be the authority on which Socrates bases his – we might think – arbitrary interpretation. It is also the basis on which Zeus loved, non-carnally, the beautiful youth. One might also observe that Socrates' explanation, unknowingly as it were, loosens the etymological link between Ganymede and its Latin derivative *catamitus*. But that is of itself hardly going to expunge the suspicion that this beautiful boy – *pace* Socrates – belongs in a conceptual world that is, in part, evoked by the term catamite.

In fact the Ganymede story is a potent expression of the forces at work here not because it resolves the dialectical opposites in the manner the Platonists want, but because it keeps them troublingly in play. In Thomas Mann's *Death in Venice* the older, creative man (certainly 'educated' enough to, theoretically, suffer from the desire for sexual 'debasement' suggested by Freud in his account from 1912 and introduced here in chapter two) is confronted by all the dissolution that love can bring. On seeing Tadzio for the first time in the hotel foyer – the boy is at the *eromenos* apposite age of 'about fourteen' – Aschenbach is as struck as Socrates when he first saw Charmides. He 'noticed with astonishment the lad's perfect beauty,' and was appropriately reminded of the finest sculptures from the high period of Greek classical art.[64] But the older man, initially, is able to keep his wits about him. He certainly does not imagine that he is destined to be put in the position of the most enamoured and debased of *erastes*. He merely observes and indulges in what he imagines to be professional, detached (*fachmännisch* in the original) speculation. In fact Aschenbach reverses the Socratic process in that he must fall, although he goes down Diotima's ladder (the analogy employed in Plato's *Symposium*) gradually. But his fall is nevertheless complete and revelatory; arguably more revelatory than the reverse business that gets Socrates and his diligent pupils up and out of the empirical pigsty of everyday sexual lust. In any case, Aschenbach will learn much too much for his own good. That is, if his 'good' is defined in terms of his ability to survive, socially and psychically, in the world of high European civilization. For when his degradation is complete we are left with the impression that he has attained a rare understanding; an understanding of the nexus brewed from the imprecise ingredients of virtue and beauty and love and sex. It is a brew that would be too much to stomach at any drinking party to which Socrates had been invited (although it could be said that he had suggested the recipe), and it may even be too much for civilization. Can we really survive knowledge of this sort; or is not the readiness to greet death the prerequisite for the revelation? And are we pushing the (neo-)Platonic argument maybe further than it will go if we attempt to prise the Socratic account – even if we do take it to be unproblematic – out of its heathen context and enshrine it within later Christian thinking?

But it is to Phaedrus and Ganymede that the Aschenbach of the novella turns in order to get a grip on the disorientating phenomenon with which he is confronted. Looking at Tadzio on the beach, he recalls how Socrates told Phaedrus 'of the shuddering and unwonted heat that come upon him whose heart is open, when his eye beholds an image of eternal beauty' and 'of the impious and corrupt' who cannot appreciate beauty's higher nature. 'So beauty, then, is the beauty-lover's way to the spirit but only the way, only the means, my little Phaedrus.' Then, taking some comfort in the Socratic argument, Aschenbach feels again the creative impulse and the sudden desire to write. 'Eros,' he speculates, may love idleness, but in this instance it has driven him to the word.[65] In short, Eros is (also) doing its Freudian duty in guiding the libido to a sublimated creative outlet. At this point Aschenbach's thoughts turn to Ganymede. Aschenbach, like Zeus, will 'snatch up this beauty into the realms of the mind, as once the eagle bore the Trojan shepherd aloft. Never had the pride of the word been so sweet to him, never had he known so well that *Eros is in the word*.' What he then, inspired by Tadzio, produces is, allegedly, so lofty, so poignant with feeling, that it would shortly 'be the wonder and admiration of the multitude.' However: 'When Aschenbach put aside his work and left the beach he felt exhausted, he felt broken – conscience reproached him, as it were after a debauch.'[66] At which point we might ask ourselves whether there isn't something in the feverish language Mann uses ('shuddering and unwonted heat' etc) that is reminiscent of the manner in which Socrates describes how the wing of the good horse reaches its tumescent apotheosis. Certainly the dialectical opposites have not been neatly disentangled and the bad definitively expelled. In short, the debauched Aschenbach has fallen into the trap. And from now on the only way is down . . . or is that up?

In the opera all of this reaches its ambivalent and wholly successful climax in Aschenbach's final substantial solo: 'Chaos, chaos and sickness. O Aschenbach . . . famous as a master . . . all folly, all pretence. O perilous sweetness, the wisdom poets crave, Socrates knew, Socrates told us. Does beauty lead to wisdom, Phaedrus? Yes, but through the senses . . . But this beauty Phaedrus, discovered through the senses . . . leads to passion . . . and passion to the abyss.' It is a piece written to exploit the part of Pears's voice that Britten found so bewitching. He spent some time on it. It is, he wrote, 'all-important' and it 'needs deep thought.'[67] How right he was.

The celebration of interrelated opposites, of ambiguities, that is given absolute cognitive priority here is clearly not the simplest line to take. It flies in the face of what we might choose to see, at first sight, as the self-evident meaning of much that is foregrounded in the opera; a straightforward story of a decadent collapse which robs the central character of all his virtuous and creative qualities. That, however, is to take a superficial line. Contemplative thinkers and creative artists (whether composers or writers) are prone to end up with something that they neither wholly intended nor even perhaps suspected when they first set to work or gave their imaginations room to exercise. And while there is always the danger of a descent into incoherence (although exactly that is also an appropriate consequence of a narrative centred on the leading character's psychic disintegration), the rigorous pursuit of both a dangerous idea or a seductive desire can, as Aschenbach above all learns, lead to discoveries and epiphanies that far exceed what one had hitherto believed or felt.

This is very much the overt agenda of Mann's novella, although how it developed in the writing I cannot know. I do, however, choose to believe that he went much further than he had initially thought he would. Nonetheless, Mann is explicit, and extremely brave in working through a narrative designed to reveal things to do with sexuality and creativity, baseness and ethereal strivings, that many at the time – including his wife's uncle – found outrageous. The book is unambiguously a narrative of discovery; one that is, it transpires, inexorably focused on a telos which, initially, the hero hardly took account of: death. And that is to say it is a death wrapped in unanticipated connotations and far-reaching consequences. Moreover it must be – or, better said, the narrative that leads to it must be – experienced, felt, in order to be understood. Only then can its unparalleled mix of degradation and elevation, of collapse and redemption, become actual. In finding a creative and imaginative narrative into which he can place Socrates' unconvincing but intriguing speculations, Mann is able in fiction to unlock exactly that bewitching and destructive nexus that cannot be controlled stringently in a pure intellectual context. He avoids the rationalisations which Socrates employs to skate over his own dilemmas. Above all, he rejects the Manichean tendency that would radically part the evil flesh from the divine soul. Instead he exploits what one might see as Socrates' failure in this respect; or rather Socrates' implicit acknowledgement that rigorous dualism is untenable despite his fixation on an uncompromisingly idealist final telos. Mann's genius and bravery are freed by a genre that accepts and encourages contradiction. And it is this that Britten took – how knowingly took I cannot say – from the novella. But he does give to the novella a greater aesthetic term of reference that takes it aurally into those areas that Mann/Aschenbach can only hint at. It is surely interesting that Thomas Mann told his son Golo that if someone were to write the music he imagined for Adrian Leverkühn it should be Britten.[68] Leverkühn is the composer and implicit title character of Mann's *Doktor Faustus*. He makes a pact with the devil, creates great works, and descends into the abyss along with Hitler's Germany.

But of course one does not have to accept all this special pleading. A more direct, wholly unambiguous approach to the opera is quite possible. 'The death, spiritual as much as physical . . . its ravages . . . offers no redemptive gleam within or outside the dramatic context.' Furthermore: 'The abyss is man's destiny whether he treads the Apollonian or the Dionysian way . . .' Therefore Britten's opera is 'merciless.'[69] This has a no-nonsense feel about it. It is prepared to look cold reality in the face and not to flinch. The opera is about the inexorable and unambiguous power of death composed by a man who knew that he was not long for this world. Biographically, this does rather downplay the fact that Britten, and everyone else, hoped that the coming heart operation would save him. But more importantly it sells the opera short. It confuses intellectual courage with simplification. Donald Mitchell, who was not only a perceptive critic but also a co-worker on the opera, takes a sober yet sensible approach. He writes of Britten being conscious of the need 'to keep in balance the opposed forces of Apollo and Dionysus, order and chaos, form and feeling'; a quite possibly complacent opinion to which we will return in the final chapter.[70] Still, it seems fair enough. It is also necessary if you want to survive. However, one has the, conceivably anarchic, feeling that the final opera reaches its unparalleled heights because the balance has been violated; great risks have been taken. Hence death is the inevitable outcome.

We can pursue this a little further if only in the, conceivably dubious, cause of keeping the waters muddy. As a strategy this does, however, enjoy the benefit of being consistent. After all, this chapter proclaims the axiom that it is in the mud that the radiant truth sits, certain that it has come down where it wants to be or, at the very least, where it has to be on occasions. Or, to put it another way, that – as Auden suggested in The Sea and the Mirror – Caliban and Ariel are bonded by their interdependent differences. And here we should note that one sentence already quoted from the novella ('Eros is in the word') and linked to the Ganymede legend, was put directly into the opera libretto by Piper. This too encourages me to suspect that she was more than merely aware of the fundamental ambiguities at work in Mann's masterpiece.

Aschenbach's grand declaration, while watching the 'Games of Apollo' on the beach, that 'Eros is in the word' takes on the status of an absolute first principle. It is not simply that Eros and the word are coupled, as Eros might otherwise be coupled with something else, let us say the (Schopenhauerian) genitals. Rather it is that the signifier 'word' as used here accrues to itself powerful even unprecedented ontological meaning. The Mann/Piper declaration (and it is worthwhile noting that Britten makes so much of it in a genre where the word is normally seen to occupy the second place) amounts to a good deal more than saying that Eros is in the world. Although, as we have seen, that has to be the case for Socrates.

Perhaps what is most striking here is that the 'word,' in this its most far reaching expression, can even, somewhat ironically, spring the boundary that divides Greek Eros from Christian Agape. The irony is that Agape is St Paul's chosen term for love and/or charity and it is Greek; the language in which Paul wrote. Therefore while we are compelled to see Eros as both sacred and profane, Agape must remain uncontaminated. After all, according to the First Epistle of John 4: 8, 'God is Agape', and God has to be impeccable. Consequently it is not surprising that various Christian theologians have insisted on a stringent separation between sacred and sensual love. Anders Nygren has said that 'Between Vulgar Eros and Christian Agape there is no relation at all.'[71] Whether either Britten or Mann thought Eros vulgar might be questioned, but this is no doubt the reason why, to take one example, the Coptic texts discovered last century, which suggested a carnal relationship between God incarnate and Mary Magdalene, caused such a kerfuffle. Wagner, above all at the time he was at work on Parsifal, would have found them meat and drink, once – that is – he had been able to overcome his surprise. Hadn't he first thought of the idea at the time he was writing *Jesus of Nazareth*? Whatever the case, ambiguous Eros is not to be straightjacketed.

We might remember that the Gospel of St John (surely the most literary and poetic of the gospels) announces itself with: 'In the beginning was the Word . . . and the word was God.' And perhaps using St John and 'Logos' (John's Greek term put into English as 'word') some kind of mix between Eros and Agape can be engineered. After all, John also tells us: 'And the Word was made flesh.' (John 1: 14) Logos, meanwhile, implies reason, the quality most attributed to Socrates and one that he celebrates under the rubric of sobriety. Nor should we forget that 'word' as a signifier can stand for Greek civilisation itself. 'Barbarians,' by definition, didn't speak Greek. Indeed it seems that if we look at the etymology of the Greek word, the first barbarians they met must have made, at least to Hellenic ears, a babbling sound, rather like the *Gelabber* Wagner professes to hear in the Jewish language. Nonetheless, in the end – at least for the purposes of this discussion – the unresolved relationship between Eros and Agape, together with any attempt to overcome the (Manichean) dualism of sinful flesh and divine spirit and/or mind, is best seen as an innate problem of Christian thinking. It is one, however, that has been productively troublesome. Wagner seems to have coped with it readily enough; in that his colonisation and sexualisation of conventional religion seems to have been a natural, if at times problematic, route that simply had to be taken. But it troubled Britten greatly, as it did Thomas Mann, and it duly takes us back to the theme already introduced in the second chapter.

The engagement with classical Greek thought that has been underlined here emphasises the dangers of Eros, and therefore it must, at the very least, raise the question of the place and meaning of Agape. It reminds us also of the problem that many creative homosexual artists have had with their sexuality and the bogus, but conceivably brilliant, solutions they have devised to get around it and to sublimate their erotic nature. In this it also draws our attention to the revealing character of that endeavour; namely, of the manner in which art, to its eternal credit, swindles. While Britten's attitude to sexuality has already been touched on, something might now be said about Thomas Mann's. He was, after all, Britten's absent but creative co-equal in the birth of the last opera.

We know from his diaries (and can infer from much else) that Mann was very conscious of his homosexuality. Furthermore, he was also troubled by self-loathing because of this 'abnormality.' Following a youthful and committed love affair with the painter Paul Ehrenberg ('I have lived and loved'), he seems to have repressed that side of his sexuality so severely that it was solely a psychic and imaginative part of his life.[72] Nonetheless the power of his feelings ought to be acknowledged for they seem to have been exceptionally disturbing. When his first son Klaus (pet name Eissi) was at the *eromenos* age of fourteen, Mann confesses in his diary to being 'enraptured' with him. He thinks him 'terribly handsome in his swimming trunks' and tells himself that it is 'quite natural that I should fall in love with my son.' His conclusion is that a return to the homosexuality (passive or otherwise) that had preceded his marriage to Katia Pringsheim is unavoidable. 'It seems I am once and for all done with women?' The question mark is interesting, for matters, as is invariably the case with Mann, are ambivalent. He is not nearly as at ease as his 'quite natural' claim would suggest. In fact, his reaction reminds one of Aschenbach's growing confusion when looking at Tadzio: 'Eissi was lying tanned and shirtless on his bed, reading; I was disconcerted.'[73]

The sublimated power of all this for Mann's extraordinarily productive and profound literary output is something suitable for speculation . . . and perhaps little else. Though one does note how exceptionally potent it is because it combines pederasty *and* incest. And although it will not be pursued here, it is fair to remark that homosexuality and incest (and suicide) were common ingredients in the extended Mann family, which may be one of the reasons why the paterfamilias took such care to present to the world a picture of solid bourgeois success and respectability. The double life that this necessitated may not have been psychically satisfying, but it was stunningly productive. After all, as he said: 'The secret and virtually silent adventures of life are the greatest.'[74] Do not most great artists, at the very least, have to face up to this? Whatever their strategies and no matter how elaborate their creative language, they are all in the end naked; ambivalent certainly, but exposed.

And indeed, nothing may be more productive than the bad fit between love and sex, especially when placed in the philosophical and religious context. That is, there would appear to be a host of tensions at work, ranging from the artist's wholly personal psychic struggle through to his creative and intellectual labours. And while it may seem an anachronistic point – the product of assumptions and prejudices that today we have allegedly overcome – this struggle might have been especially telling in the case of homosexuals. Nor should this be seen as merely a problem foisted on guiltless individuals by social narrow-mindedness and past ignorance: naturally matters are more difficult for gay men simply because they are so often socially excluded and abused and so on. Instead it would be better to consider the Freudian premise that every individual's sexual life is never wholly and unproblematically worked out. Still, that might too easily lead to the glib conclusion that gay artists (in this case Britten in particular and the men pertinent to his life) are simply the victims of psychic struggles that are universally shared, something which many gay men would regard as the denial of their own lived, sexually specific experiences. On the other hand, it could be suggested that in being gay such men have a selfish interest in giving those struggles a meaning and a character that places them as artists outside the shared sexuality of the species. Consequently they would have the option of putting themselves in a special category of insightful victims to whom, as a result, extra privileged qualities might accrue.

Whatever the case and whatever one chooses to assume, the homosexual artists we have been looking at seem to have had a hard time dealing intellectually and morally with their sexuality. Certainly a harder time than Wagner, who despite all the little affairs and grandiose suffering as would-be lovers let him down, gives every arrogant impression of being utterly secure in his own self-identity.

Mann may have had deep problems and have consequently repressed his sexuality, but W. H. Auden, his one time son-in-law (he married Erika

Mann to get her out of Nazi Germany) despite being famous today for his uninhibited, though private, acknowledgement and celebration of homosexuality (read *A Day for a Lay*), seems to have been particularly tormented. This is ironic since he had played an early role in Britten's acceptance of his sexuality. Nonetheless, later in life Auden stated: 'I've come to the conclusion that it's wrong to be queer, but that's a long story . . . all homosexual acts are acts of envy . . . [and] . . . the more you are involved with someone the more trouble arises, and affection shouldn't result in that.'[75] It is not self-evident why this last point would not apply equally to heterosexuals, but it is clear that Auden regards homosexual relationships as in some way inherently wrong. It is also clear that this problem only got worse as he returned to, and struggled with, Christianity. He claimed that: 'Few, if any, homosexuals can honestly boast that their sex-life has been happy.'[76] Well, to what degree is the opposite true of heterosexuals? Auden also confesses that there are days when being a homosexual without a place 'I can call home' and a person 'with whom I shall be one flesh, seems more than I can bear . . .'[77] One notes the potency of Christian language in this, but asks nonetheless whether today – when gay marriage is possible in both the UK and the USA, the two societies of which Auden had most experience – the assumptions on which it is based still hold. There is clearly something deep and, paradoxically, metaphysical in his use of the term 'flesh.' But in appealing implicitly to Genesis and the creation of Eve and to the repeated biblical evocations of a man and wife as 'one flesh', is he really just signalling a well-known and largely poetic flourish of Christian ideology, or does he have in mind, as I suspect, something much more fundamental and ontological? It appears Auden believes there has to be a lack in the homosexual life, in the gay sexual experience when measured against the heterosexual alternative; that to be gay is to have in some way gone awry. Presumably we are to infer that being of one flesh is a metaphysical option open to heterosexuals but not to homosexuals. Auden's sincerity is unmistakable, but it is unlikely that the gay community, certainly these days, would be inclined to agree. Nor am I convinced that thoughtful, even Christian, heterosexuals would be any more inclined to assert the radiantly positive alternative option implicit in Auden's unhappy assumptions. Perhaps the problem Freud attributed to the husband, inhibited from indulging his full libido with someone he was obliged to respect (and why did he not allow the same difficulty to the wife?), might even apply among homosexuals. In other words Auden may be stumbling over a problem that has to do with sexuality in general, rather than dealing with the supposed intrinsic riches or debilitating effects of any particular option.

At one time Auden resorted to psychoanalysis. He had this in common with his fellow artist Michael Tippett, also troubled by his homosexuality. One might also mention E. M. Forster, the librettist of *Billy Budd*. He recorded his struggles with sexuality in the Foreword to *Maurice*. He seems to have thought that after *A Passage to India* his homosexuality simply made it impossible to write further without being bogus. As a mature artist he couldn't deal with the matter. Perhaps there is an irony here in that Britten, who it seems as a young man had to be convinced by his brilliant friends that he was 'queer', appears to have attained a stable, successful and creative emotional life. Auden, who suffered greatly when he discovered that Chester Kallman had been unfaithful, is both instructive and misleading in this context: '. . . sexual fidelity is more important in a homosexual arrangement than in any other. In other relationships there are a variety of ties. But here, fidelity is the only bond.'[78] Again one doubts this today, if one hadn't doubted it before. But then again, it could be a fundamental ontological truth that no social environment can alter. And yet it seems a wretched and hopelessly inadequate axiom when applied to Britten and Pears. Whether there is a further irony in that the relative solidity of their relationship facilitated Britten's engagement with, and understanding of, the deeper dilemmas embedded in Mann's *Death in Venice*, is at least a proposition we can entertain. Whatever the case may be, I certainly don't think he avoided the full, contradictory and torn import of Mann's novella. Nor, however, can one be certain that he engaged with it from an untroubled position; a position of strength as it were. But, to employ an otiose cliché, aren't all self-respecting artists, when you get down to it, supposed to be vulnerable and torn?

I wonder whether much of the foregoing argument with respect to both Wagner and Britten does not embody, potentially, a popular intellectual solecism. *Parsifal* and *Death in Venice* were the last operas of both men, and there is a tendency to treat all last works as inevitable end points, as though the narrative disposition – an explanatory trope very strong in the conceptual arguments of this book, although not in its structure – demands an unambiguous telos. It is, moreover, a feature of conventional biographies about creative artists that they reproduce this trope. The last work is the greatest, it is a culmination of a life's endeavours, and so forth. It is as if the artist began the climactic work knowing that it was to be so. While this can of course be the case, it is hardly likely to be the rule. Knowledge of that sort is usually *ex post facto*. There is, however, some evidence that both *Parsifal* and *Death in Venice* were regarded by their creators as final works. True, Wagner did contemplate other things (Lenardo based on a character from Goethe's *Wilhelm Meister* for instance[79]) and Britten had at one time thought very seriously about operas based on *King Lear* and *Anna Karenina*. But during the work on their last operas the two composers seem to have become very aware that this was indeed to be their ultimate statement in the form. Wagner, in fact, became increasingly definite on the subject, telling Cosima repeatedly that after *Parsifal* he would write only symphonies, albeit in a new form.[80]

In Britten's case everything was in doubt because the heart operation was postponed in order that he should complete *Death in Venice*. In other words, the work was judged by him to be so important that he was prepared to take a considerable risk to get it finished. None of this means, of course, that either opera has to be a summing up, a resolution of the grand problems with which the artist had struggled . . . and so forth. Nevertheless, with respect to Britten, the notion of a final work would underline the degree to which he was prepared in *Death in Venice* to come clean – or at least to come as clean as he could – on the question of creativity and (homo)sexuality.[81] There are also grounds for seeing *Parsifal* as an appropriate endpoint. It is as though Wagner had painted himself, philosophically, into a corner and the opera, along with his writings at the time, illustrate this. It is not surprising that he should have thought that the future for him lay in non stage works, in so-called absolute music. To appreciate this we need to put the opera back into the framework of Wagner's wilful interpretation of Schopenhauer and to hold on to the importance of both narration and telos.

In act one of *Parsifal,* Gurnemanz, the oldest and most authoritative figure among the knightly monks, famously observes that in the Domain of the Grail 'time here becomes space' (*zum Raum wird hier die Zeit*). It is an odd and cryptic theoretical flourish. There is no philosophical underpinning to the observation and no dramatic context in which its meaning can take shape, let alone become for the punter transparent. The opera qua opera does not seem to be able to do anything for the observation. *Parsifal* remains, no matter how static in places, a dramatic construct and duly makes full use of the aesthetic language appropriate to that. Above all, and as we have had cause to note, it swindles brilliantly, mixing discourses and playing fast and loose with its key sexual and religious symbols, employing them in narratives that exploit their ambivalences, wilfully according to each the significance and power associated with the symbols and narratives from which it is normally excluded. Given that it is, consequently, a work which can be said to turn sin into a sacrament and to invade religion in order to sanctify an a-religious and incestuous alternative – one in which the mother may be possessed and, moreover, as a representative of the mother of God – one can hardly expect a discourse more appropriate to a university seminar room. In fact one wonders just what Wagner could have done to make *zum Raum wird hier die Zeit* theatrically and intellectually immediate and explicable. One suspects that any move in that direction would somehow subvert not just the form of the opera as an aesthetic construct but also expose the fact that *Parsifal* – more than most stage works and to its credit – is not upfront as to its actual agenda. Nonetheless, time becoming space is an important flourish, however hollow or pretentious in itself. It is not there solely to pull the wool over our eyes or to impress us with the deep and incomprehensible intellectual nature of an opera that we might otherwise be shamelessly enjoying.

Essentially Gurnemanz's claim is an upturning of Schopenhauer's understanding of the nature and perception of music, which '. . . is perceived . . . in and through time alone, with absolute exclusion of space . . .'[82] It is as if Wagner is not satisfied with the special epistemological status of music as he finds it in Schopenhauer, for whom it is, uniquely, a means of encountering the indivisible will-in-itself. Furthermore, it is a copy of the whole and not trapped in the various phenomenal expressions of the will. Therefore it deals in 'essence', while the other arts deal in the 'shadow', and so forth.[83] Wagner, it seems, would like to go further. In outbidding Schopenhauer on the special epistemology of music, he hopes to clamber up onto a theatrical and philosophical level higher than might otherwise have been thought possible, even given the lofty place of music in Schopenhauer's philosophy.

If music has access to the will as no other aesthetic activity does, then this must be for Wagner access to the highest state of the will as he imagines it. And this is, paradoxically, the will-less state, the state of utter enraptured renunciation that Wagner finds during his last years embodied in the 'person' of the Saviour on the Cross. And for this fusion between music, the will, and the will-less Saviour to happen, time must be transcended. This must be so because we know, courtesy of Schopenhauer, that true knowledge born of resignation and contemplation rather than striving is timeless knowledge of the world. 'Timeless' in that it 'is subject to no change, and is therefore known with equal truth for all time.' Furthermore, Wagner is not going to have any trouble agreeing with Schopenhauer that while Art in general is privileged, it is Music, above all in 'the work of genius', that '. . . repeats the eternal ideas apprehended through pure contemplation . . .'[84] As a result, Wagner now rejects – at the very least implicitly – narration. It is revealed as hamstrung and debilitating. It will not get us to the Saviour and is as irrelevant (in that they are not narratively related or staged) as all the adventures and all the endeavours that, we are to believe, have taken place between the second and third acts of *Parsifal*. During these absent years the title hero has struggled to find the correct path back to the Grail, as he says: 'Countless perils, battles and conflicts/ Forced me from the path.' But that narrative is off the stage. Instead, in the largely static final act we are simply shown the arrival of one of the two ersatz saviours, Parsifal, who has returned for the express purpose of redeeming the other: Amfortas.

Parsifal thereby fulfils the agenda that was, implicitly, ascribed to him as the holy fool in the first act. He has become 'wise through compassion.' And compassion as an emotion is not very productive narratively. In other words, the gulf between Parsifal and Siegfried remains unbridgeable. Doing has been replaced by empathy and understanding. Consequently time has been replaced by space. In this way the Wagner hero has, ostensibly, attained the high Schopenhauerian state whereby the ego has been overcome, and the problem of individuation and the interpersonal struggles that it generates, expelled from experience – or at least from stage experience. In propaganda terms, Wagner wants us to believe that his hero now belongs among the panoply of Schopenhauer's will-less elect. His blood-brothers are St Francis, the Buddha, and Christ. After all, it is individuation that, lamentably, causes the will to objectify itself in a plurality of alienated forms and to create a world populated by competing individual egos. a process which is exclusively explained within a purely temporal framework. But by creating such an, ultimately, ego-free hero as Parsifal, Wagner is able to take the Schopenhauerian terms to do with time and space and invert them. He has triumphed over the principle that asserts: 'Our self-consciousness has not space as a form, only time; therefore our thinking does not, like our perceiving, take place in three dimensions, but merely in one, that is, in a line.'[85] In *Parsifal* this is not only inapplicable; it states plainly the opposite of what is in fact the case. Wagner has once again remained – as he would see it – loyal to his chosen mentor, while employing him to serve his own, quite possibly opposed, ends. But once the ego and individuation have been banished, and once time no longer allows for events, neither character-based theatre nor narratively-dependent drama are relevant. Rather, they have become impossible. Wagner has risen to the point where the playhouse can no longer meet the agenda he has set for himself. Redemption, on this level, makes the music drama redundant.

Five

Redemption

Two theoretical considerations need to be tackled if this discussion on the respective nature of redemption in the work and thought of Richard Wagner and Benjamin Britten is to be concluded in a manner with which I, at least, can live. One has, on occasions, been explicit in the preceding pages. The other, while certainly implicit, has never been dealt with directly. The first concerns the general nature of narrative and the specific importance of a telos. The second drags into the spotlight the problematic character of all discourse. It suggests that any attempt to create meaning, to tell stories, to communicate in any kind of medium, can never be wholly self-contained or free from contradictions. Silences that speak loudly, together with implied alternative and disruptive narratives are always part of the mix. Further, in order to appreciate the genius of the creative artist we need to pay due respect to the manner in which he has seductively disguised those contradictions, silences, and implications; how he has manipulated and tricked us – and, on occasions, quite possibly himself. Both of these considerations have far reaching theoretical consequences, and each in its different way opens a can of worms. It is not the intention here, however, to address them on their own theoretically difficult and often arcane terrain, but solely in the context of Britten and Wagner.

First, then, the question of narrative which can be said to have, hitherto, played an odd role in this essay. For instance, although much has been made of the final operas of each composer the essay has not been structured as a chronological progress through their respective work as though that would be the most revealing and elucidating approach. Nonetheless, narrative has been an important conceptual consideration. This has been up to now particularly clear with respect to Wagner. In the previous chapter it was argued that in his last work he, at the very least, evokes – whether intentionally or otherwise – the idea of a non-narrative form and that this subverts his creative undertaking as far as that undertaking is based on the drama. However, the question of narrative goes deeper.

Rather than seeing storytelling as an arbitrary matter that concerns merely the choice of a particular genre or form together with its attendant narrative strategies, I regard it as being epistemologically important. I maintain that narrative has in and of itself a unique epistemological status. I have written about this elsewhere[1] and I do not want to go into a detailed argument now. Suffice to say that the notion of telos, of a goal, is treated as not only an inevitable and critically important component of the narrative undertaking, but, more importantly, as a site where meaning and moral significance are most present. In other words, the Kantian position with respect to a teleology and a telos as found in the *Critique on Judgement*, and outlined briefly in the previous chapter, is pertinent. Nonetheless, when this is placed within the narrative framework and then considered in respect of stage works, the resulting form also assumes an odd and imbalanced character. This is simply because the telos is brief. True, a final chorus or a final death scene may well be a fitting climax, aesthetically and thematically, to the evening's experience, but in temporal terms it is always meagre. The great pleasures of the theatrical entertainment are likely to have been found in the long stretches of the drama that took us to the climax, otherwise we are simply pleased when it finally starts to come to an end and we know that soon we can go home. But if the work is successful we will feel, and have some understanding of, how the preceding narrative has vindicated and enhanced the endpoint. Furthermore, the climactic actions of the drama will have a retrospective effect, in turn enhancing what we have already experienced. In short, the climax is likely to possess unequalled authority. A firm, unambiguous telos suggests a powerful, proven argument; a story that has got to a point where everything is settled. A case has been made, an ideology has quite possibly been put before the punter, a cathartic experience has been engineered, a didactic message may have been declared, and – if the artist is both confident and thoughtful enough – an implied programme is there to be inferred. This, of course, is Wagner.

However, the conceptual danger with this is inbuilt into the notion of telos itself. A telos tends to be singular, and in being singular it is prone to simplify. Hence in respect of polemical discourses it can readily underpin propaganda. In general stage works, denied the scope and room for argumentative manoeuvre appropriate to – let us say – the novel, tend to foreground the potential singularity of a telos. And this is arguably yet more manifest in the opera house. Playing with multiple narratives and plural outcomes is hard enough in spoken drama, but in an opera, where there is not going to be anything like the same textual generosity or opportunities, the tendency to drag everything to the one authoritative close is hard to circumvent. Comic operas, for instance, are invariably in hock to a joyous and very collective last ensemble in which all the loose ends are neatly, or brusquely, tied up. Such an ensemble is in every sense appropriately called the 'finale.' Tragic operas, meanwhile, resolve – or try to resolve – all narrative tensions with the death, at the very least, of the privileged hero and/or heroine and thereby draw a would-be unambiguous line under the preceding story. And no matter how absurd the various plots, or indeed in how cursory a manner the telos is engineered, apparent clarity and authority are usually the desired aim in both cases.

Wagner's stage works constitute particularly striking examples of the power of a telos to confer meaning on the preceding narrative. Above all, they engineer an often remarkable homogeneity between the narrative bulk of the evening and its lofty, if brief, conclusion. With Wagner we can seldom talk about a cursory relationship between narrative and telos. Consequently the endpoint that has to be reached is not only exceptionally confident, it is also exceptionally meaningful. We might, by way of an aside, consider this in the context of a crucial consideration prominent in his theoretical work. It is, however, an example that can only have an implied relevance for, and a place within, his music dramas. If Wagner had been a classic nationalist and racist, he would have instructed us by virtue of a teleology that led inexorably to the great final victory of the Teutonic peoples. Many of his countrymen, often inspired by him, did just that. But, despite his unequalled celebration of both high German values and legendary German heroism in a time replete with economic growth and military victories, he is more interesting. He suspects that 'we' are all going to hell in a handcart. The racially inferior types will win in the end. Did he not tell King Ludwig on 22 November 1881 that: 'We

Germans especially will be destroyed by them'? One notes immediately how consequential that 'especially' is; the privileged race must preserve its status even in defeat. So it seems that the utopian goal which is very present as a necessary afterlife in the agenda of the stage dramas, is contradicted by the black pessimism of the theoretical work that supposedly reflects actual reality outside of the playhouse. It is ironic, but apposite, that Hitler was of Wagner's opinion when he came to write his Testament; but then again he did so surrounded by the overwhelming evidence of own wilfully staged *Götterdämmerung*. Inference as to the immediate disaster was hardly necessary. The key difference being that whereas Wagner saw the Jews as triumphant, Hitler – who had done so much to avert that particular danger; a danger that had tormented him remorselessly – told his lieutenants in his last days that the Slavs were the coming people; he had underestimated them. However in both cases a telos is absolutely indispensable to the racist *Weltanschauung*.

If in Wagner the relationship between the narrative and the telos is especially intense – unlike, say, in Handel opera, where the ending, or final short chorus, often has the feel of being arbitrarily, even indifferently, tacked on – the nature of the theatrical climax can be said to be enhanced in propaganda terms. Being a temporal objective to which the narrative has laboured – consciously as it were – it ceases to be a state of final being and becomes instead a goal, an objective. And because Wagnerian redemption is something that has to be worked towards and, moreover, often at exceptional length – at least when compared to most stage works – it is both intensely dependent on and thoroughly expressive of the narrative guts of the work. And by narrative guts is also meant the often one-on-one polemical, even philosophical, set-tos which are such a striking feature of a Wagner opera. In some cases there is even the feeling that the telos has been present (both in storytelling and musical terms) from the beginning – *Tristan und Isolde* being the most obvious example. In other – rare – cases the intellectual difficulties and aesthetic short-comings of the work are expressed in the bad fit between the narrative and the telos. This is very much the case with *Götterdämmerung* which suffers under Wagner's increasingly sophisticated development during the long period of the textual gestation and musical composition of *The Ring*. The telos is regularly re-conceived in order to shoehorn it into a greater narrative that is gradually losing coherence and rationality.

Even so, there is a contradiction here. It is not only the pre-telos period – that is to say almost all of the playing time of the piece – that is steered by narrative. For although Wagnerian redemption is wholly goal-orientated, when reached that goal is not the end of things. It is not merely – or indeed perhaps essentially – a fixed state of being about which there is nothing more to be said. Which is to say, it is not a more lofty version of the happy-ever-after scenario. That is, naturally, the preserve of marriage, which in both kitsch and high narrative art functions as the end of the fairytale in that the tale is wholly dispensed with and only the fairy – or fairies – are left. Rather, Wagnerian telos implies a further narrative that simply continues in a better world. Ironically, this only underlines the indispensable and liberatory nature of death; ironic because death in the hands of other creative theatrical artists is usually the sign of an absolute end. Even more than pairing off the right lovers at the altar, it customarily draws a definitive, uncrossable line under the precedings. In Wagner, however, it can be seen as giving a fresh narrative impulse that makes the existence of a post final curtain story indisputable. It is a line that can and must be crossed. And while we are not allowed to experience how this post-death world works itself out, we do know that it comes with the territory. Above all, the opera would be ideologically gutted without it. In fact it reminds one of the Marxist notion of socialism. That will be a state that conforms to the paradigm of a classless society where everyone receives what he needs and gives what he best can; that is to say a society that has transcended all previous antagonisms, chiefly those of capitalist class exploitation. It must, therefore, be susceptible to narrative description. It's just that aside from underlining its harmonious and creative character, Marx and Engels really can't tell us very much about that narrative. Nor could Wagner in his Communist period, but for the assurance that his libido would be liberated from petty bourgeois restrictions.

No doubt a utopian telos is not merely a nice thought. It is also likely to turn out to be a useful, even for some theorists a necessary, notion when it comes to tackling in conceptual terms the relationship between historical narrative and future storytelling. But difficulties crop up when there is an attempt to describe the utopian ideal – any utopian ideal – in nuts and bolts terms. Dystopian societies, on the other hand, seem to positively encourage the imaginative act. They flourish, for instance, in violent fantasy films of the *Mad Max* type. Indeed they seem now to constitute a new cinematic genre. Perhaps the notion of a utopia is best left as a wishy-washy hypothesis or pushed, as is often the case, into the realm of science fiction. It may well be assumed to exist on a faraway planet in a distant galaxy; something which makes it much more believable. And in truth, in the world of Wagner opera we really don't know what Senta and the Dutchman, Tristan and Isolde, Siegfried and Brünnhilde will get up to after the curtain has fallen for the last time and the portals of a, possibly socialist, but certainly utopian Valhalla have been thrown open. But we do know that they have a future.

There is one further irony that should be mentioned here. *Parsifal* is similar in thematic material, form, and language to all the other redemption operas; which is to say all the operas after *Rienzi*, excluding the comic *Die Meistersinger.* And yet it forgoes death for the major players, but for the ruthless manner in which Kundry is tossed aside. In doing so it rather exposes just how arbitrary and unmeaningful death in the Wagner world really is. It is a theatrical gesture; a formal and familiar trope, but it is bogus in character. Ironically, the Wagnerian *Weltanschauung* celebrates death in an unusually extravagant manner not to make clear its unendurable and absolute theatrical force, but to reveal its awesome promises. This, of course, is one of the reasons why ecstatic Wagnerian death is such an opiate and an aphrodisiac for the punters, who simply can't get enough of it. Nonetheless, its absence in *Parsifal* is a mere technicality. There is no reason to make any distinction between pagan post-death Valhalla and the redeemed Christian (or, if one wants, ersatz Buddhist) life enjoyed in Monsalvat. In both ideal worlds life continues, despite our ignorance of its daily goings on. Although it should be admitted that were we informed as to those goings on, it is likely that the business would cease to be ideal . . . in any sense. The nature of narrative and the dramatic tension that fuels it would see to that.

As has been pointed out more than once, the Wagnerian package as to telos and the afterlife, is not part of Britten's agenda. At best, he leaves us in doubt. Which is also to say that he can face up to death in, ideologically, a raw and unvarnished manner, as a good deal of the instrumental and orchestral music makes clear. He is not likely to reduce redemption to a sop. And if consolation is employed it does not come with absolute authority. Despite being usually Christian in nature, it is seldom expressed in language similar to that employed in the funeral service (drawn from 1 Corinthians chap. 15) that promises the 'sure and certain expectation of the resurrection to a better life.' Wagner's higher couples of course have no need of any such assurance. They experience the miracle at the point when they enjoy, consciously, their faux expirations.

But this gives Britten's notion of redemption a character that looks paradoxical in the Wagnerian context. Redemption in the Britten *Weltanschauung* is both more universal and more particular. There is, for instance, no division between morally higher and lower characters in the sense that a racial or an ideological test can be applied to discern who is eligible for redemption and who is not. Of course this does not mean that Britten's characters are equally admirable or deplorable, but *merely* that they are all – equally – human. Therefore in their different ways they are, without exception, candidates for salvation or, presumably, perdition. We might remember how Claggart (arguably the wickedest character in Britten's fecund panoply) suffers. Does anyone really suffer more? Furthermore, it is a suffering born of his crude black and white view of the world. But that does not mean that we cannot imagine a world (and perhaps an afterlife) in which he, too, could be numbered among the redeemed. It might in fact be an interesting exercise to take, wilfully, the emphasis off the suffering Vere, who in the Epilogue declares himself saved by Billy, and think of the same proposition with respect to the black-hearted master-at-arms. The agonies with which he has, presumably, always lived surely exceed those of any of his fellows.

But the greater complexity of the matter in Britten is to be found, arguably, in its richest form in those men and women who might be thought of as the equivalents of Wagner's higher characters; equivalents in that they are not foreign to lofty visionary experience. One sees immediately that they are not nearly so impeccable as their Wagnerian cousins and, moreover, they do not err simply because they enjoy an excess of virtuous exuberance or because they are so naïve as to be led, like Wagner's privileged but artless boys, by the nose. It is the ambivalent nature of Grimes, Lucretia, Vere, the Governess in *The Turn of the Screw*, the Madwoman in *Curlew River*, Aschenbach, Phaedra that makes of redemption something highly problematic and much more rooted in the complex character of the human animal and, moreover, much more dependent upon the civilisations, the plain immediate stage communities, that those human animals have managed to cobble together. I am not even sure that as stage or musical constructs they really escape to somewhere else. Not even those like Lucretia and Phaedra who choose suicide and die before our eyes. And this produces the paradoxical state whereby death as an aesthetic phenomenon in Britten has real meaning outside the theatrical discourse. It continues to have presence and purchase as a problematic concept. Put pretentiously, it is death in itself. Do we, for instance, take Phaedra literally when she declares at the end of the cantata that 'death will give me freedom'? It is more likely that death will just give her death. Freedom here being nothing more than the negation of – that is, the end of – suffering. It is in Wagner that death brings 'real' theatrical freedom . . . or salvation.

And what of those non-human-beings in Britten? Are his ghosts the equivalents of Wagner's Nibelungen and giants and Walküres, and those linguistically articulate birds and dragons? Surely not. Britten's ghosts are not at all excluded from the morality and the humanity of the world of those they torment. Peter Quint and Miss Jessel are in a dreadful state. The Wingrave family is haunted by both its history and the present rigid and inhuman tenets that that history has rooted immovably in Paramore. These people may well be horrifying, but more than that they are pitiful. However the ghosts who torment the vicar in the Hardy song 'The Choirmaster's Funeral' from *Winter Words* are magnificent, not only in their impeccable moral character – the lesson they teach the amazed, and we might think terrified, clergyman is as noble as any that might be taught – but also in their less than impeccable Christian nature. True, they look 'Like the saints in the church glass', but they are impish devils nevertheless. Consequently the vicar's waking nightmare makes for a happy picture. It has, albeit only momentarily, the concrete kick and presence that theoretical speculation on either a world after death, or indeed a world after the revolution, so often, and so tragically, lacks.

We might therefore conclude that in the matter of redemption Britten has, perhaps unknowingly, fulfilled the terms expressed by a principle that his one time mentor, W. H. Auden, promulgated when struggling during his attempted re-engagement with the near lost Christian faith of his youth. 'Eternity is the decision *now*, action now, one's neighbours *here*.'[2] Britten, it might be noted, not only said late in life to Sidney Nolan 'Auden is in all my operas,'[3] he wept when he heard of his death,[4] as Auden did when he received his last letter to Britten by return post and torn to pieces.[5] Neither man really escaped the other, and both surely regretted the rupture, although it may have been necessary if Britten, the junior partner, was to fulfil his own independent artistic destiny. In any case we should when thinking of the nature and meaning of redemption in Britten's work remember a verse from one of Auden's most famous poems: the ballad *As I Walked Out One Evening*. It was written many years before the break with the composer and it states a deep, although in some ways pessimistic, imperative command. 'O stand, stand at the window/ As the tears scald and start;/ You shall love your crooked neighbour/ With your crooked heart.' Crooked neighbours are not loved in Wagner. Like Mime, they are mocked and then slain.

We can stay with Britten as we tackle the second theoretical consideration mentioned at the beginning of this chapter: the problematic nature of all (artistic) discourse, the degree to which it is subverted by its own narratives and symbols. Perhaps, however, full disclosure is necessary here. Many of the ideas associated with the approach I am taking were once placed under the rubric of post-structuralism and were greatly influenced by French linguistic and psychological theory. That theoretical school has rather slipped off the radar in recent years, no doubt undone by the anarchic core secreted within it. That led, above all, to the glib conclusion that all discourse, which is also to say all creative work, could be treated as equally valid and worthwhile in that each piece was, unconditionally, vulnerable to a process whereby it was flooded by limitless, seemingly alien, signification. This apparently 'foreign' material was, however, taken to be – if the critic were honest and stringent enough – unavoidably implied by the language and semiotics of the piece itself. But this all led to the notion that every text could be legitimately manipulated (or deconstructed) to mean whatever the consumer wanted. Making distinctions then became a wholly arbitrary and wilful act, in which any notion of authoritative value judgements was exposed as illegitimate and, most certainly, politically incorrect. Well, this was arguably the case when the theory was taken to its (logical) extreme. I don't entirely share this judgement, but that is not important now. What must be confessed, however, is that I am influenced by a good deal of post-structuralist theory. This is particularly so when it is not pursued to 'logical extremes' but, rather, employed as a set of techniques and strategies that can be applied in analysis, even when that analysis is, as here, driven by overt pre-given values. The best example with which to appreciate this is *Billy Budd*, but the comments that follow could be seen as applicable in theoretical terms to all of the works discussed in this essay.

Billy Budd shifts between three different planes. It has, for instance, an unmistakable social term of reference. This is determined, in effect, by the incarcerated world of the men on the ship. It is ruled over by a captain who possesses the power of life and death; a leader portrayed as an erudite, benevolent, but ultimately agonised tyrant. It is a world, therefore, that embodies of necessity a compromised notion of justice and a barely contained praxis of cruelty. There is also the sexual plane. It is heavily implicit but, by being gay, it cannot be addressed head on. There is, however, no relationship in the opera that has any heterosexual force whatsoever. Therefore desire and Eros have only an unspoken, except perhaps for Claggart's solo, male focused outlet. And lastly there is the spiritual plane centred on Billy. He innately – in a manner inseparable from both his narrative and symbolic roles – enhances the life of the crew and redeems, at the very least, Captain Vere. Billy, whose actions are never calculated, can be said to accomplish this simply because of who he is. But on none of these planes is the thematic material worked out in anything like an upfront or rigorous manner. Instead, in all essentials they are governed by ambivalences, contradictions, and silences. And, furthermore, the three planes shift and spill into each other, not in order to make matters clear, but to deepen, and quite possibly enrich, the confusion.

Vere is socially torn. He knows how much the officers owe the men, but he flunks at that moment when he could have saved Billy. Consequently he betrays the crew for whom Billy was also a blessing. Moreover he knows this and, in the Epilogue, admits it. He also rationalises the authority he holds. But the basis on which he does so is flagrantly ambiguous. We are to believe that when it comes to mutiny the men may have had, at a push, some justified grievances at Spithead. In other words the men do have some rights, though they are accorded them by their betters. They are hardly rights they can be said to enjoy on the basis of their own worth as men. However Spithead is forgotten when we remember 'The Nore, the Nore.' That was anarchy and revolution. In the novella two matters relevant in this context are mentioned. They are not in the opera. *The Indomitable* was at the Nore;

Vere was given the command after the mutiny was suppressed. Furthermore, he is also worried that should he show clemency in Billy's case he will actually encourage a fresh mutiny. In the opera, however, it is his failure to save Billy that brings the crew to the brink of rebellion. Meanwhile, the role sexuality has played in all this, in Vere's guilt, in Billy's status on the ship (in Melville he embodies the phenomenon of the 'Handsome Sailor'), in Claggart's passionate loathing, is there to be inferred. It certainly can't be established. But it can hardly be ignored either. And lastly the spiritual dimension, which most directly evokes the notion of redemption, is present constantly, but is paradoxically most explicitly pertinent in a scene which, in fact, does not occur on the stage. Never has the notion of the 'gap' as it is employed in post-structuralist theory – the unstable space that always separates that which is said from that to which it refers – been made more extant and, paradoxically, unmissable.

This is the 'scene' that follows the drumhead court martial. Vere goes into the anteroom to inform Billy of the sentence. Yet before we look at this, the degree to which the traditional values of what is, in effect, the literary criticism taught post F. R. Leavis in the universities should be addressed. It still influences standards. That is, to admire the opera is to admire its integrated character, its near seamless construction ('structurally the opera is among Britten's greatest of achievements'[6]), its aesthetic harmony, its status as a flawless whole and so on. By the same token to lament the absence of the same qualities is to criticise the opera on the most fundamental level. In other words, the traditional aesthetic and critical values in play are not those I employ here.

With respect to the missing scene we see nothing that could allow us to make any positive judgements of the sort mentioned in the last paragraph. Instead thrity-four discrete chords that, I am told, harmonise the notes of the F major triad are played . . . while nothing happens. In short, we will never know what went on in the room during this solemn musical interlude. Melville, despite what some commentators seem to think (largely because of the remark 'Beyond the communication of the sentence what took place at this interview was never known'), does in fact speculate. However, as the speculation is jejune (perhaps the captain embraced Billy) and as it is kept deliberately out of the opera, we can forget it. Which is to say, we have no option but to accept the unseen 'scene' in the terms in which we encounter it in the theatre and then try and come to some conclusion as to what it is all about. Of course, one might take a bald common sense line and simply state that Vere was blessed as a result of the fateful encounter with Billy and that music, because it takes us into places where words cannot go, is ideally the means to express this, and so forth. Even so, the nature of that blessing must remain a mystery to us. And this is hardly incidental. After all, given Vere's emotional and torn state in the Epilogue, the effect of the blessing can hardly be said to have been unambiguous.

The conundrum of the missing scene together with the (ersatz) chords has elicited a great many instructive, if not always enlightening, responses from critics. Claire Seymour, who calls the passage the 'interview chords' lists, in 2004, several commentators, in particular Donald Mitchell, Philip Brett, Clifford Hindley, who have stressed their great significance and she duly notes each interpretation.[7] But this only underlines how the thirty-four free floating signifiers can be readily defined to suit everyone's disposition. Going back to a time closer to the première, we note that Patricia Howard says that the chords express 'by sonority alone the extremely complex range of reactions and emotions taking place behind the closed door.'[8] No doubt. But we are surely entitled to ask just what these reactions and emotions actually are. Furthermore, it is interesting that attempts to find some kind of context in the rest of the opera's score into which the chords can be folded, or from which they can attain (extra) musical meaning by association, also seem to fail. The consensus is that they lie 'outside the motivic scheme.'[9] Above all, writers always load their comments with pure speculative observations when tackling this 'scene.' They can't avoid foregrounding how thin the cognitive ice here is and how nervously they navigate it. Consider but one sentence by Erwin Stein. 'The changing colours *seem to* convey rapid changes of emotion, ranging, *one might conjecture*, from surprise to fright – from terror to resignation; and an even higher stage of mind *is perhaps suggested* by the last chords. . .'[10]

Clearly, we have simply not been given enough in order to engage meaningfully with both what is (allegedly) happening somewhere on the stage and with what we can hear coming out of the orchestra pit. There is nothing – or not enough – to be going on with. Put in the context of traditional literary criticism we could say that the objective correlative (to use T. S. Eliot's term) is not up to expressing what the drama at this point appears to want to express. We can draw a comparison here with the two most visionary moments in Britten's other operas: Grimes's 'The Great Bear and Pleiades' and Aschenbach's 'Socrates' aria. While other people are present in both cases (in the pub, on the beach), each solo is exactly that. The rapt singer is, in some profound sense, alone and words combine with music to give us a good deal to think about. Furthermore, the comparison with the *Billy Budd* scene is particularly and pungently striking in that the latter involves an encounter. This would suggest that there simply must be more; more, that is, that we could be going on with. After all, something interactive did take place. The matter can hardly be reduced to a single statement, let alone a private vision. Therefore the strategy whereby all this is kept from us seems excessively wilful.

One last possible, and relevant, contradiction might be mentioned here, not least because it is a contradiction into which these remarks are also inclined to slip. It is odd that Britten should be criticised, at least by some, for foregoing text in *Billy Budd* and then for resorting to spoken dialogue, with the music sidelined, at the climax of *Gloriana.* One could hardly blame the composer if he thought that he was damned if he did and damned if he didn't.

Nonetheless, the problem of the censored scene also reminds us of the importance of narrative. It is in that framework that the matter becomes most interesting and the power of the gap most obvious. Because the event is a necessary – indeed arguably the most indispensable – step in the story, we know we are being shortchanged once we realise that we will have no access to it, apart from the music. This is underlined by the fact that in *Billy Budd* the narrative line is unusually strong. The framing device of a Prologue and an Epilogue, as devised by the librettists, means everything is thrown into flashback. But this also means that the narrative is given, it carries authority, not least because we are, in effect, learning it from the most informed participant in the tragedy itself. He is telling us of – and he is quite explicit about this – the events that happened all those years ago 'in the faraway summer of 1797' on board *The Indomitable.* And given that the man who tells us this is the only man we see in the Prologue and the Epilogue and given that he was present during the scene that has been banished from the stage, we are surely right to feel that the wool is being pulled deliberately over our eyes. The question then remains, is it being pulled over our eyes because we are being, legitimately, invited to think of things more profound than mere text and music together can express, or because the whole business is essentially a fudge and the thematic material of the opera can, when all is said and done, be neither acknowledged fully nor honestly dealt with on its own, albeit manifold and unstable, terms?

Further, the problem with the missing scene is often made, unwittingly, clear by the audience. If they don't know the opera and therefore don't know that the thirty-four chords are draped in an aura of great, although indefinable, significance, they seem to assume that the critical scene is about to be played. That is, their priorities are wholly narrative in character and, no doubt assuming the music is there to cover the set change, they tend to cough, chatter, look in the programme book, and so forth. Customarily, when the stage is closed to them many punters in the opera house immediately downgrade what they hear. They start to treat it as though it were little more than background muzak. As a general rule, if during an intermezzo between scenes the curtain is lowered there is an immediate increase in audience noise. This reaction, while unendurable for the informed punter, is not wholly improper; at least not according to Auden who took a dim view of orchestral music in opera if it sidelined the singers.[11]

Billy Budd also foregrounds, unknowingly, a further and crucial element of the later post-structuralist agenda: the fundamentally problematic and unstable nature of language and semiotics. If texts cannot connect utterly with what they intend to signify, the authority of what they are taken to mean is always vulnerable to sabotage. In fact texts tend to imply such a plurality of significations (usually other texts or discourses) that they evoke things they, or better said their authors, might otherwise seek to suppress. This of course assumes that the theorist will, unlike Roland Barthes, permit a fellow as antediluvian as an author into the equation. However, more of that later.

Throughout Britten's work this sense of excessive and disruptive meaning is most obvious with respect to sexuality. It is a subject simultaneously implied and denied. But *Billy Budd* has in addition a particular and unusual relationship to spoken or sung text. It seeks, and in this case knowingly, to dramatize the ambivalent nature of language when language is placed in a specific dramatic context. Billy is not only illiterate, he suffers, as we have already noted, from an ultimately fatal disability. He stammers. In a sense this shields him from the task of coming to terms with, and articulating, the grand themes that swirl around him. For even when using sung text – and he likes to sing – he underlines his identity as the foreign and mysterious angelic body (the 'foundling') in that his language is simple, direct and naïve. This is clearest in his beautiful solo 'Billy in the Darbies.' His stammer should be taken therefore as the perverse sign of his special character. He too is, Parsifal-like, a type of holy fool.

Nonetheless, Billy has entered language in a manner that only exemplifies the Lacanian principle that that entry can never be complete; that it is always under the threat of dissolution and chaos. Like the psyche itself it might in the end just disintegrate. And in a sense this last possibility, which a tongue-tied Billy is *forced* to endure when confronted by Claggart, is what the crew actually choose; that is to say consciously choose or, at the very least, adopt under duress because they have at this point no alternative that they can stomach. At the climax they reject syntax and discourse. In the grunting chorus – the moment when they are close to striking for freedom and smashing the tyranny that stands above them on the quarterdeck – they make plain that they have no entry into the ideas and values that their articulate and patrician master, who likes to read the Greek classics and plainly thinks he cares for his men, enjoys as a matter of self-evident right. It is one of those moments when the libretto and music of *Billy Budd* say probably a good deal more (specifically in this case more politically) than any of its creators really wanted to say. One thinks, for instance, of Forster's hatred of causes. Nonetheless, if we were to consider this while keeping in mind the missing scene as an antipode, we might conclude that the clarity of both the drama and the music, together with the perverse clarity of the bestial 'text' as the men come close to putting off their officers, do indeed flood the opera with more meaning than it can satisfactorily process at this point in the narrative. On the other hand, the missing scene is so nebulous, musically, as to actively invite a plethora, indeed an unrestricted number, of speculative meanings. It comes close to the paradoxical point whereby an excess of signification means that nothing can be of any particular significance. In effect, it sluices meaning as a useful, precise, and thereby explanatory commodity from out of the opera, leaving it in an arbitrary and indefinable state.

All of this is best expressed by one of *Billy Budd's* key metaphors: the mist. It reminds us, although I hardly think the composer and his librettists would have intended this, of just how nebulous in aesthetic and polemical terms the whole undertaking is. The mist is not, by the way, given any particular significance in Melville. In the opera, however, it is, as a phenomenon and a metaphor, rather laid on with a trowel. From the moment in the first scene of act two (in the revised version of 1960) when Vere remarks 'I don't like the look of the mist Mister Redburn,' it starts to colonise the imagery of the opera. From a bland beginning it accumulates a mountain of extra signification: 'The mist creeps in to blind us' and so forth. At the end, Vere might choose to claim that the mists have cleared, but this is a delusion. Instead we see that he remains as ambivalent a figure as he ever was. After all, he knows that there has to be 'some fault in the angelic song.' Nothing is unambiguous. All of this is, further, underlined by the narrative structure. One has the feeling that the failed pursuit of the French ship – like Kundry's kiss in *Parsifal* it stands at the centre point of the story – is the fulcrum on which the action turns, that Claggart wouldn't have got away with his 'so foggy a tale' (as Vere calls it) had the enemy been engaged and beaten. As Billy says: 'We'd have caught that Frenchie on a clear day. Oh that cursed mist!'

In general, however, one should not assume that the mist is merely a strategy of evasion; another device whereby the shifting language (textual and musical) fudges the thematic material, deferring questions that are too awkward to address directly. It certainly does this, not least because it underlines the 'confusion' that Vere sees everywhere, within and without. But it also enhances matters and, paradoxically, it does this too because it fudges. After Billy has struck Claggart dead, Vere suddenly declares 'The mists have cleared.' Yet what he sees is terrifying. But what is it? It is not simply that the boy must (to put the matter crudely) die. He also seems to have some inkling of who Billy (now the 'fated boy') is; or at least he has some feeling for who he might be. How fascinating then that he should at this point repeat Claggart's text and music 'Beauty, handsomeness, goodness'; that the implied sexuality that invests the shared relationship of the opera's leading triad of men (this is the only scene when they are alone together) should suddenly burst through here. What, indeed, has Vere sensed? And, in all fairness to the opera's creators, we should ask ourselves two further questions; albeit ones that we cannot answer definitively. Namely, that whatever it is that is going on in Vere's mind here, is it something that could be put satisfactorily into words? And if not, should we not perhaps be grateful that the matter has in all its contradictions and silences been pulled, perhaps unintentionally, into the spotlight?

This is not a consideration that should be examined solely in the context of Britten, although it does underline the importance of doubt and the lack in textual matters of an overriding, unbending and authoritative voice in his work. It is, however, on principle no less applicable to Wagner . . . as indeed it is, in pure theoretical terms, to the work of anyone else. In the context of Wagner opera the question of the ambivalences, gaps, and contradictions of both his written work and the operas can be seen clearest when we look at the role of women. Here Wagner gets himself into something of a pickle in that he combines what we might see as a classic phallocentric mindset with an aesthetic theory that highlights the privileged figure that he is otherwise inclined to downgrade. But Wagner always had problems with women.

One thing Wagner cannot do is simply cut the Gordian knot and indulge his unbridled phallocentrism to the full; not least because his phallocentrism is not, in fact, unbridled. Women are not only essential to him as a conventional, albeit exceptionally egotistical, heterosexual male. More importantly, they are vital for both his aesthetic praxis and his ideological agenda. Perhaps if he had been, exclusively, a sexist philosopher he could have adopted the position of Nietzsche (who famously encouraged men not to forget the whip in their dealings with women) or Schopenhauer. After all, any assumptions as to the Sage of Frankfurt's innate intellectual stringency would be all too readily exploded by his committed, passionate even, misogyny. Indeed his short essay *On Women* is often just plain nasty. He is, however, in the happy position of discovering that it is no intellectual stretch to get a handle on them. You only have to look at their shape to see that women are not built for thinking. Remember those flat-headed women of southern Germany mentioned in chapter two. Of course Wagner is also prone to this sort thing. As he tells Mathilde Wesendonck, he had learnt from the Buddha that 'women are far too subject to their sexual identity and hence to whim and caprice . . . to be able to achieve the . . . deep contemplativeness necessary for the individual to renounce his natural inclinations and achieve redemption.'[12] But this is a remark of greater consequence then anything found in Schopenhauer's essay in as much as it reminds us of the more elaborate argument tackled, with near palpable difficulty, in *Opera and Drama*. There the woman has to go through the sexual encounter in order to acquire the soul that will, in turn, make her fit for redemption. Above all, such is the place and function of the 'eternal womanly [or feminine]' in Wagner's *Weltanschauung* that he once again cannot follow his mentor as faithfully as all his admiring protestations would suggest, although at times he may have wanted to. For instance, in the *On Women* essay Schopenhauer, always an unsentimental observer of anthropological matters, points out that polygamy is really quite normal and life in general would be much better if it were still practised. Were that the case: 'the lady, that monster of European civilisation and Christian–Teutonic stupidity, with her ridiculous claim to respect and veneration, will no longer exist; there will still be women, but no unhappy women, of whom Europe is at present full. The Mormons' standpoint is right.'[13] We have already noted how, in particular in his last incomplete essay (*On the Womanly in the Human Race*), Wagner's racist agenda makes this, otherwise sexually desirable proposition, awkward. But the notion that the woman was not, albeit under particular circumstances determined by the composer, fit to be 'venerated' would have been impossible for Wagner to swallow.

The basic, and rather crude, contradiction is clear enough. The Wagner we know from his letters, Cosima's *Diaries* and the various biographical incidents, is an exuberant, self-indulgently tormented, domineering, self-obsessed genius who regards women, when all is said and done, as his devoted helpmates; helpmates who accede to his authority in all matters. Of course it could be said that he saw everybody in the same light, but, in being a heterosexual male, young women would have to fulfil a role that will always make them special. And given that, for whatever reason, Wagner comes to see sex as the site of deepest meaning across the board, such women must perforce be invested with an identity and status that is going to be in certain respects unsurpassable. In its most upfront ideological, as well as actual, expression this is the role fulfilled by Cosima and, moreover, in an exemplary fashion . . . at least for propaganda purposes. That their marriage was not, however, exemplary or ideal only underlines the difficulties that the arrogant male gets into when he attempts to marry his libido and his ego to wilful theories concerning the rightful place of women as revealed to him by human history and human nature. In the end there has to be in Wagner's case a bad fit, even an abrasive relationship, between the personal on the one hand and the theoretical essays and the aesthetic undertaking on the other.

In some senses this dilemma is inbuilt into the nature of opera itself. Once the castrati period is past, the greater power, flexibility and tonal colour of the female voice, especially the soprano voice, assumes the dominant place. She duly becomes the star, commanding massive fees and able to make demands of the men who write for her. Romantic and artistic relationships between composers and their prima donnas become proverbial. Young Wagner, for instance, had a close relationship with a singer who inspired him: Wilhelmine Schröder-Devrient. In general, a form then evolves, above all in Italy, in which the key radiant figure on the stage stands there in implied contradiction to her social and legal status when off it. Furthermore, a concomitant aesthetic genre likewise evolves that exploits the dramatic tensions in this. For instance, despite what we are told, it is a fallacy that the opera is not over until the fat lady sings. It isn't over until she dies. Death and, for a period, mad scenes become the trade mark of Italian opera. Heroines as stage figures are certainly allowed to dominate, to exercise power in the narrative, though they do this almost exclusively through their sexual and emotional nature rather than through their intellect. They are also permitted as artists to colonise the genre and influence the whole apparatus of opera making and opera production. And appropriately enough they become for the public objects of worship as a result. But on the stage they are not allowed to live. Consequently, devising novel deaths for sopranos becomes part of the librettist's trade. In the end the female stars – the Divas – are like brilliant butterflies that live momentarily in the spotlight only for their very characters to be torn from them as they dazzle us with roulades and cabalettas, often in manner largely free of text. They usually lose their senses as a reward for getting all the best tunes and a near monopoly of all the showy bits. In a way they are like the crew of *The Indomitable* and dispense with textual language at the climax, but in their case it is to ascend into what is unambiguously a higher aesthetic discourse. Madness is emotion pure. Who needs words? Think of Lucia di Lammermoor's disciplined vocal game with the flute when she is, supposedly, utterly dolally. These puppet goddesses are celebrated for their command of pure sound (bel canto) in its most extraordinary and, quite possibly, unnatural form. No doubt for the prima donnas on the stage this is exactly the price they insist on paying. But as an expression of the place of women, both sociologically and dramatically, it is a wretched business.

Wagner, however, dismisses this job lot by the simple device of investing the woman with a unique moral, and one might say philosophical, significance. This is certainly dependent in part on her sexual allure, but that is hardly going to turn out to be the whole story. The reason is paradoxical. It is because the importance of the sexual congress for the, often unschooled, male is emphasised massively. This is made clear in as much as the sexual agenda spills over into knowledge; knowledge that the female possesses. Consequently both – sex and knowledge – duly attain interdependent and enhanced meaning. And this is the crucial step that allows, compels even, Wagner to take the feminine into new territory on the opera stage.

Of course, as he well knows, this is part of his cultural Teutonic inheritance. Goethe's immortal feminine, as the site of higher moral and spiritual knowledge, is a birthright he embraces fervently, even though he once argued that Faust flunked the great redemptive, Gretchen-based, task; something he made clear to Mathilde Wesendonck in a letter on 3 April 1858. It followed an argument on the previous evening.[14] The same heritage is even there on the musical stage in embryonic form in the work, above all, of Carl Maria von Weber, whose operas belong to the generation immediately preceding Wagner's. But no one will make anything like as much out of it as he will. After all, knowledge, and certainly not sublime knowledge as to redemption and the noumenal world, is not something we associate with the tragic heroines of Italian opera. They are invariably victims, undone by unscrupulous baritones and jealous contraltos, or by consumption, or by the arbitrary if imaginative vicissitudes of fate.

But this is not, as we have seen, an unproblematic endeavour for Wagner. The active, youthful hero still remains the doer and as such is the dominant narrative figure in the music dramas. And no matter how ideologically necessary, how brilliantly engineered dramatically and how sensationally scored, the meeting with the woman is, ultimately, male-centred. He takes, she gives . . . even if she does, as a necessary reward, win her soul courtesy of 'fecundation' as a result. It is as if, but for magnificent Brünnhilde and death-obsessed Isolde, Wagner is forcing on his operatic agenda the values he finds in the life around him, in German history, and in his racially-disposed anthropological speculations. But it is also inbuilt into the dramatic world Wagner quarries for his material. That is not Faust-like (he never managed to complete a youthful Faust Symphony; it survives as an overture), but the phallocentric, action rich, hero-dependent world of German and Nordic history and myth. Even Parsifal, which has been characterised here as fundamentally pacific in terms of its deeper ideology, can't avoid the consequences of Wagner's passion for the heroic past. The hero may well break his bow and arrows in the first act after it becomes clear to him that killing the swan was a cruel, even a blasphemous, act, but there are all those 'battles and conflicts' essential to his learning process that he mentions in the third. Most striking and discordant, however, in an opera that will celebrate the lamb of God and a life of Schopenhauerian renunciation, are the accounts of his offstage approach to the magic garden and the citadel in the second act. The excited Flower Maidens describe how he butchers their knightly lovers. When he appears his 'sword still drips with blood!'

Of course women can play a strong, even queenly, role in these tales but they are more likely to be driven by jealousy and revenge than Wagnerian higher values. At times one feels that Wagner is trapped, albeit willingly, in narratives that are often difficult to manipulate in order to realise the special Gretchen-like status of the woman. It might be added that Goethe and his stage alter ego were also caught in a similar bind. One often feels that the high, womanly-centred, meaning of the whole thing, proclaimed mightily in the final lines of the second part of Faust ('she' leads us onwards and upwards), has only a feeble, even an incidental, place in the rich varied story itself.

Certainly, despite the exceptions, there is no overlooking Wagner's difficulty in finding a narrative place for the woman commensurate with her higher meaning. As he explains at some length in *Opera and Drama*, she must submit. She is, when all is said and done, destined for the second highest (in narrative terms) step on the evolutionary and aesthetic ladder, although she may well be incomparably sublime when it comes to spiritual values. In the following extract, for instance, it is the man who is, when all is said and done, the profiteer, although the engagement needs 'the 'eternal womanly' of Tone-art' – which is to say music – in order to do the intellectual business. 'Through the redeeming love-kiss of that Melody the poet is now inducted into the deep, unending mysteries of Woman's nature: . . . From out of the lonely, fearsome reaches of her mother-home the woman had been self-driven, to wait the nearing of the beloved; now, with his bride, he sinks him down, and learns the hidden wonders of the deep.'[15] Furthermore, when she has submitted and when everything, in respect of both spiritual worth and deeper knowledge, has been taken from her she can, at least in the final opera, be simply cast aside.

Wagner is caught in a further bind of his own making. As a composer he paints himself into a corner when, as in the last quotation, he defines the drama as male and the music as female. The matter becomes even more serious when he is forced to concede, most explicitly in the Beethoven essay (1870), that music takes precedence over text. Music, as it were, says more. It has not only greater expressive power, it is also closer to essential truth. All this he had read – although he knew it all along – in Schopenhauer. So in this instance, at least, he is not inclined to quibble with, let alone manipulate, the master. Clearly music pure – the language he shares with Bach and Beethoven and to which he pays homage – is just that much more suited to an encounter with the spiritual or noumenal world. But the end result of this is perforce a further ideological underpinning of the privileged figure, although with respect to both his dramatic agenda and his theoretical labours he is starting to find her increasingly recalcitrant. We might as well put aside the private difficulties that came with the territory when one had Cosima for a wife, except to acknowledge that what she had to put up with would have greatly exceeded his own everyday burdens.

As a result of these antagonistic forces Wagner ends up hanging firmly onto the 'eternal feminine' while endeavouring to make her fulfil the particular aesthetic and ideological programme he has worked out for her. It is not surprising, therefore, that she becomes the site where the struggle to be rational, to stay in command of the material, is most obvious. She will always end up 'saying', at least by implication, more than she should, if only for the perverse reason that Wagner wants her to say so much, including much that is unsayable. Perhaps it is no wonder that at the end he has Kundry shut up. Yet in turning her into the central figure of a dumb show he is compelled, how appropriately, to reveal her massive significance as the agent of both knowledge and redemption. But we should consider 'her' role (or roles) throughout the drama as a whole, because given that she was a split figure in Wagner's mind before he even got down to writing the libretto for *Parsifal*, we can best appreciate how adroitly he has taken advantage of his own difficulties in the matter.

Looked at over the three acts we can see how the opera identifies three separate frameworks for Kundry. She is, in effect, placed in a pagan, then a Jewish, and finally a Christian milieu. And, like the triad of thematic material (social, sexual, spiritual) that makes up *Billy Budd*, these three racial and religious categories are not discrete and self-contained. Instead they spill over into each other opportunistically.

Initially we meet Kundry as the wild pagan woman, a figure who has recourse to necromancy, who flies around the world in search of potions and balms that might ameliorate Amfortas's suffering. In fact she is, as we learn in the second act, a type of Nordic Walküre. At least that is implied by one of the names Klingsor gives her: *Gundryggia*. But from the beginning she is also dressed in morally attractive garb. We know, for instance, that she never lies, and her body language, especially when Amfortas is mentioned, expresses her tormented and sensitive nature. In the second act the pagan Kundry is still present, not least because this is the act where necromancy, as opposed to Christian ritual, has the field to itself. Furthermore, when we read Wagner's description of her as she is dragged on to the stage for her critical preordained rendezvous with Parsifal ('there appears a youthful woman of great beauty – Kundry, in a completely different form – lying on a bed of flowers, clad in a revealing, fanciful garment.'), we see that she is the very personification of eroticism. She evokes the clichéd ideal of the heathen oriental seductress, forbidden and thus desired; a figure of much fascination to European intellectuals, particularly painters, of the period. But the Jewish element is already there. Klingsor has summoned her up from 'the blackness below' by tormenting her with her titles 'Shedevil of old! Rose of Hell! Herodias you were – and what besides? Gundryggia there, Kundry here! . . . Your master calls: arise!'

Herodias, we should note, married her brother-in-law and was as a result regarded in some quarters as incestuous. At the very least John the Baptist and, we might also infer, the author or authors of Leviticus regard her as guilty of something very similar. In Leviticus we are told that such a marriage is 'an unclean thing' and will be childless (chapter 20 verse 21 & chapter 18 verse 16); a punishment that recalls the rationalisations Wagner got himself into when discussing the healthy progeny of the incestuous (mother/son) union of Jocasta and Oedipus. All this puts Kundry by implication in an intimate relationship with John the Baptist, which is to say she also takes a step in the direction of Christ. And when she tells Parsifal of the reason for the curse under which she suffers (the mockery of Christ on the Via Dolorosa) her ambivalent Jewish/Christian status is made yet deeper and more intense. The process is completed in the third act when she assumes the New Testament duties performed by, as is generally but arbitrarily assumed, Mary Magdalene; duties, that carry over the incestuous subtext (in act two she was for a critical moment Parsifal's mother and duly rewarded him with that 'redeeming love-kiss') into the heart of Christian iconography. But these are also, it must be emphasised yet again, the defining characteristics of the Wagner female when raised to the level of a paradigm. Kundry has abased herself. She has, in effect, blessed the redeemer, and been rewarded by his blessing. And she 'serves.' At which point she is silent. What more could be made of her – or indeed made out of her?

The miracle here is that she has been put to so many uses without the whole ideology of the opera unravelling. Rather, the shifts have been so subtle and seductive that Kundry can be said to have woven the opera's many threads into the unproblematic whole that enraptures us in the theatre by virtue of both its drama and its elevated religious/spiritual, message. Like Christ's robe it is seamless. But if we look closely at the weave we find the alternative narrative of incest and phallocentrism adroitly interlaced in exactly that higher Christian discourse.

We can further appreciate this general point – the woman as the site of Wagner's contradictory plethora of meanings – if we leave that opera where the seamless compositional (and arguably thematic) material is most striking and consider the opposite. Namely the redemption opera where the divided nature of the woman and what she signifies is not only initially assumed but conspicuously, even punctiliously, maintained.

In *Tannhäuser* the disposition of the feminine qualities is especially clear because the two key elements (sexual and spiritual) are, it seems, rigorously and irreconcilably divided between the two female figures: Venus and Elisabeth. In this early work Wagner does not – presumably it is beyond him at this time – resort to a composite figure. But when we look a little closer the matter turns out to be, at least in ideological terms, far from black and white in that the initial disposition of ideological forces, far from simplifying matters, steers the composer into ever choppier waters.

Given the simplistic model he has set up, Wagner is compelled to fudge the redemptive message. Virtuous and virginal Elisabeth dies having not gone through the all-meaningful rite of sexual passage. Her innocence, which is also to say in this context her ignorance, is left unsullied. She is neither the privileged site of sex nor knowledge. Aside from her sacrifice, there is nothing to be learnt from her. All she ever had was her purity and she even needed to make an effort to hold onto that. As she confesses in her third act prayer to the (real) Virgin, she has had impure thoughts. 'If ever a sinful desire/ or earthly longing rose within me,/ I strove with *untold anguish* to stifle it in my heart!' (My emphasis.) She may have been only human but her determination to remain impeccable is well-nigh heroic: 'O take me from this earth!/ Let me enter, pure and spotless,/ into thy blessed kingdom!' After all, it was her unblemished state that gave her the authority to save Tannhäuser from the outraged knights in the Wartburg at the end of act two. 'Cast aside your cruel swords,/ and give ear to a spotless virgin's words.' It should be remembered that Tannhäuser has just besmirched what is, allegedly, the highest moral good: spiritual or non-corporeal love. Becoming overexcited he had shamelessly praised sensuality and the Venusberg.

Furthermore, if we are to pay proper attention to the mixed messages that Wagner is, intentionally or otherwise, sending out, we need to acknowledge that in the singing contest that instigates the affront it is sinful Tannhäuser who is employing the new music typical of Wagner's redemption dramas while the other knights remain trapped in the fake minstrelsy of the middle ages. In short, Tannhäuser is the heroic Wagnerian radical, an early version of another hero who also enters a singing competition: Walther von Stolzing. But the knights on the Wartburg are like the Nuremberg town clerk Beckmesser. They cannot open their mouths without making clear how pedantic and anachronistic they are in all matters aesthetic. In other words, both central figures in *Tannhäuser* imply the opposite of what they overtly represent. Immaculate Elisabeth is, in the Wagnerian scheme of things, crippled in her higher function precisely because she is explicitly placed outside the world of sexual experience, while her would-be lover Tannhäuser cannot fulfil his role as the active male agent of redemption precisely because his sexuality is, in this case, characterised as debauched. He is a contaminated figure; one who has arguably already learnt too much, or experienced too much, courtesy of sex. Worse still, following the affront in the second act he is railroaded into a another narrative. He is to become a penitent and must now seek religious atonement by making a pilgrimage to Rome. In other words he is no longer active in the customary Wagnerian manner. Both with respect to sex and to heroic deeds he has been, in effect, narratively castrated.

At the very end redemption is engineered by the rather childlike storybook miracle of the Pope's staff sprouting leaves. True, this can be seen as Elisabeth's final gift in that she has also prayed for Tannhäuser's salvation and will do so in heaven. (Wolfram tells him 'Your angel pleads for you at God's throne, and her prayer is heard! Heinrich, you are saved!') But in being a wholly idealist notion locked within religious iconography, it cannot amount to the salvation that Wagner usually seeks to dramatize. By the way, we might note that Tannhäuser shares his Christian name (he is the only redemptive Wagner hero with one) with that other lost soul of German art, also saved by the sacrifice of a good woman: Faust. Well, that is what he tells Gretchen, anyway. In any case, after her prayer Elisabeth leaves the stage alone. She will not allow Wolfram to accompany her. She is, in effect, all symbol; scarcely a character of the sort we find in the normal line-up of Wagnerian forces. And indeed she has few one-on-one encounters. There is, surprisingly, only a single scene when she is alone with the nominal hero and that can hardly be said to take the form of a love duet. Instead it, too, is wrapped up in religious sentiments: 'Blessed be this hour,' and so forth. Eros, let alone plain eroticism, just doesn't get a look in outside the Venusberg. So while *Tannhäuser* is an aesthetic and dramatic construct that certainly plays with the form of the redemptive music drama, it cannot realise it. No wonder Wagner said to Cosima three weeks before he died: 'I still owe the world a *Tannhäuser*.'[16]

It is, in particular, striking that Elisabeth and Tannhäuser have nothing to do with each other in the third act. She is left imprisoned in her ideological chastity belt and leaves the stage before he appears. When he arrives after his rejection in Rome, he is tormented and doomed. The first step in his salvation is when Wolfram calls on the symbolic power of Elisabeth. It is necessary merely to utter her name to set sensual love, which has suddenly reappeared in the form of Venus, to flight. The magic word alone prevents Tannhäuser from backsliding and throwing himself once again into the realm of the pre-Christian Goddess. Then Elisabeth's bier is carried on and Tannhäuser dies. He does, however, witness the lame miracle of the Pope's staff and is in the happy position of knowing, at the very moment of death, that the portals of heaven are open to him. The verdant staff has been paraded on to the stage by the returning pilgrims.

In general the *Tannhäuser* construct is so hobbled by the composer's determination to stay loyal to the initial and simplistic distribution of its ideological forces that the independent deaths of the two principals can come across as clumsily engineered, even risible. Neither the ideas involved nor the narrative that they ostensibly drive really rise to the level of that found in the normal Wagnerian constellation and there is, consequently, no good reason for either of the privileged pair to expire. In truth there is no great Wagnerian death in play here because both characters cannot escape the suffocating world of religious piety. By the time we get to the end we need a spot of debauchery to freshen things up. But poor Venus is scarcely allowed a look in, which may be why producers sometimes push her wilfully into those scenes from which she is banished. Yet this only tends to foreground the problem. No matter. Whatever the case, it remains unlikely that we can satisfactorily convince ourselves that the hero has earned the high Wagnerian end that would have been his aesthetic birthright in any of the other redemption operas. And of course this is not despite his final unblemished religious status (the pilgrimage to Rome and so forth), but because of it. Spiritual values have been allowed in this drama to triumph ideologically and unconditionally. As a result they are exposed as inadequate when seen in the light of the mixed spiritual and sensual denouements of the other music dramas. Certainly, when Tannhäuser does pass over it is hard to believe that there will be anything sensually satisfying waiting for him on the other side in the Christian Valhalla. Elisabeth is hardly likely to become a full, sensual woman simply because she has died. One feels that she will always be ferociously spotless.

There are further ambivalences in *Tannhäuser* that are, while seemingly incidental, telling. Consider the innocent Spring song of the shepherd boy at the opening of the third scene of act one. Tannhäuser has escaped the Venusberg and everything around him is now fresh and unsullied. The simplistic black and white division of values is being insistently underlined. But in fact the song is ambivalent. The old German Goddess (Frau Holda) to whom the irreproachable shepherd boy sings was later to change her identity when Germany was Christianised. She evolved into a Venus figure, employing her sensuality and magic to lure men into wickedness and degeneracy. In other words she is exactly that which is, superficially, least appropriate to this moment in the narrative and its attendant mood. And yet Wagner draws our attention to all of this in his own introduction to the work.[17]

A more striking example of mixed signals concerns the morally impeccable Wolfram. He is Tannhäuser's best friend but is also profoundly devoted to Elisabeth. Furthermore, he is always going on about stars. They seem to have a special metaphorical significance for him. And then in the last act he has the most beautiful and lyrical solo in the opera: his aria to the evening star. The language he uses is appropriately enough pure and elevated. Is he, we might ask, enraptured by the sight of the heavenly body or by Elisabeth? 'I always gladly greeted thee:/ from a heart that never betrayed its faith/ greet her when she passes,/ when she soars above this mortal vale/ to become a blessed angel in heaven!' But then we might ask ourselves a further question: what or who is the evening star? Surely it is Venus.

I am always fascinated in these matters by questions that, usually, can't be answered. Namely, how aware of these contradictions was Wagner? How much did he see and then suppress? What, for instance, did he really think when the Dresden medical students started to make jokes about the mount of Venus? Was his disgust merely a smokescreen for public consumption, or an act of self-delusion? In this context, one last example seems to me particularly apposite, especially with respect to the specific question of the marriage between sensuality and religion.

On 25 April 1882 Richard and Cosima Wagner are in Venice standing in front of Titian's *Assunta* in the Belle Arti, and Wagner's language, as reported in Cosima's *Diary*, makes full use of all the ambivalence that is contained in the signifier 'Mary'; something we might remember in respect of all the Marys found at the foot of Cross. Wagner is enraptured with how the head of the 'virgin' glows and he confesses that music has nothing comparable. Most notably, the image reminds him of his own notion of the sex drive which, we are told, is in this picture free from all desire. It is the will enraptured and redeemed (*entzückt und erlöst*). This is an astounding statement. Is this how he really thought about sex as an actual bodily praxis, or is it merely a piece of propaganda; a grand rationalisation? One can't help but wonder what Cosima thought about it all, especially when one remembers some of her *Diary* entries concerning Richard's inability to control his libido. And indeed we might remember Freud's explanation of the difficulties the 'educated' male has in achieving full sexual satisfaction with his respectable spouse. Certainly the Schopenhauerian gloss Wagner puts on his rationalisation (the Will enraptured and redeemed) comes over as one lofty gesture too many. But the truly telling element is the easy move – easy, that is, for Wagner – from the contemplation of the ascending virgin to an allegedly elevated notion of sexual desire (*Geschlechtstrieb*). It is interesting that three years before this Cosima, who for both public consumption and for the instruction of her children (for whom, it should not be forgotten, the *Diaries* were written) did not deviate from the master's authority or question his opinions, had already compared the Titian *Assumption* to that most intoxicating brew of sexuality, transcendentalism, and ascent into the higher realm: Isolde's Liebestod . . . called by Wagner a *Verklärung* or transfiguration. It seems that Richard and she were much moved by the comparison, and duly ended up in each other's arms.[18] Surely a fitting resolution if there ever was one.

This discussion of gaps and silences and suppressed but disruptive narratives is not irrelevant with respect to another theme. It was dealt with in chapter three, although the reader was warned then that it would resurface. It is the problem of the unpalatable ingredients in the Wagner stew and how this has led the Wagner loyalists, who not only want to remain true but keep their good consciences, to deny the existence of the indigestible elements – at least in the music dramas. Of related relevance, but arguably of more interest, is the general question of the epistemological status of the unpalatable ingredients themselves. Assuming that they are there and, further, assuming that they are in one form or another to be found in Wagner's operas, what does that mean for the punter? To what extent do the operas have to be morally clean to be enjoyed or, better put, to what extent do their unpleasant aspects demean the works, even, conceivably, making them impermissible?

One person of no little significance in the world of Wagner opera who is clearly troubled by this is Daniel Barenboim. Bemused, he asks with palpable sincerity: 'How was Wagner able to write music of such nobility and also to write his monstrous anti-Semitic pamphlet?'[19] He means *Jewishness in Music.* But this is to miss the point entirely. The truth is much more disturbing. In being dumbfounded by the moral discrepancy, Barenboim lays before us by implication a split man, expressed in two discrete psychological identities. But there is only one, and Wagner is no more contradictory than most major creative artists or, for that matter, you or I. Of course vice (and Barenboim really has a good deal more to worry about than merely one pamphlet when it comes to Wagner's anti-Semitism) and virtue exist side by side in the human psyche. Well, in fact they are hardly likely to be discrete qualities. They will colonise each other and, moreover, poison and enrich each other. How it all turns out is going to be, before the fact, something of a mystery. What, one wonders, would have happened to the mix of deplorable and creditable qualities in Hitler's psyche had he been accepted into the Vienna Academy of Fine Arts or been given the opportunity to study architecture.

There may be another irony here. After all, Wagner is that composer most celebrated for the homogeneity of his work. Moreover this is, with respect to both content and form, a knowing and a deep struggle on his part. And for many of his admirers it is exactly his apparent success in pulling off the desired homogeneity in his music dramas that most marks him out; something which no doubt underpins their discomfort when they are subsequently forced to confront the unpleasant stuff. Their dilemma then lies in the need to perform a type of limited surgery in order, paradoxically, to preserve the much-celebrated and perfect whole. They want to save what Barenboim sees as 'noble' (the music) – although making judgements of that sort about music is rather dodgy – and to outlaw what is 'monstrous' (the anti-Semitism).

I must confess that while it may seem impossibly irreverent – immoral even – I have never in this matter shared either the fears of the flat-earthers or the disgust of those determined to wipe their hands clean and have nothing more to do with Wagner at all. Put complacently, I really don't see the problem. We should, however, consider another clear statement of it. A good example, although it is now an old one, can be found in Hans Rudolf Vaget's critical review of Paul Lawrence Rose's *Wagner: Race and Revolution.* As Rose had exposed the deep anti-Semitic basis of Wagner's writings and music Vaget, who at the time was having none of it, concluded that if Rose were right, Wagner's music dramas 'would have no place in any cultural practice that we consider acceptable, and we could not, in good conscience, go on listening to the music of Wagner as though it were music like any other.'[20] Why on earth not?

Before pursuing this we might consider the proposition that the problem could be circumvented, or at the very least turned into something less troublesome, if we dispensed altogether with the author (or composer), and instead just stuck to the text (or the music drama). This would mean freeing ourselves of the fan mentality. For it is not insignificant that both Wagner and Britten have fans. It would also mean that arguments as to the negative (or positive) characteristics and behaviour of both men would then be simply beside the point. In other words, we could adopt Roland Barthes' position and factor the creative artist out of the equation, claiming that, in effect, he just doesn't exist and, moreover, never has. Certainly this would at a stroke sweep the problem of biography off the table. The trouble is, however, that an author-free text, far from being less ambiguous, is even more a mesh of contradictions simply because authorial authority is no longer present to rule certain things in and certain things out of court. That would hardly worry stringent post-structuralists of course, but it wouldn't help the Wagner apologists either. For instance, any incontestably positive text, at least when judged on the basis of traditional aesthetic practices, could be readily turned into something negative when it fell into the hands of any self-respecting radical critic. Merely to produce a sunny morally impeccable tale is to imply the opposite. Alternative narratives would have to be, on principle, inscribed somewhere within the radiantly untroublesome and uplifting 'original.'

In other words, the popular assumption that in great art (as opposed to just nice art) the evil things are there to enlighten us as to the profundities of what is glibly called the human condition, and not to seduce us into wickedness, may not be tenable. Indeed it may not be tenable even within the traditional framework of literary criticism. Would *The Merchant of Venice* be a lesser thing if it were accepted that the author's portrayal of Shylock is both simultaneously anti-Semitic and humanist and, moreover, that the irresolvable stage struggle between these two competing positions enhances the play? And how should we respond if we feel that a text is, in a blatant manner, dealing with things of which we disapprove and, furthermore, is doing so in a way that is designed to entertain us, profoundly or otherwise? Of course we could just bin it. But what would it mean if we were to feel titillated or excited by stuff that we were convinced was morally indefensible, at least when the matter was reduced to either/or values? This would, in particular, be a problem if we were also of the opinion that the text was conspicuously engaging with important and difficult matters and, moreover, in a serious way. That is, despite the, quite possibly superficial, titillation or the morally indefensible opinions of the author, the work could not simply be rated as trash. We might, for instance, find a novel about slavery written by a convinced slave owner enlightening, and, depending on the author's aesthetic skills, engrossing and a pleasure. At the very least, this sort of thing problematizes the relationship between the creator and the consumer. In short, there is no avoiding the myriad difficulties embedded in aesthetics.

So to get rid of the biographical (in this case Wagner and Britten) would not get us anywhere with respect to their compositions, unless, that is, we had a rigid agenda that we were determined to impose upon the work, or were hell bent on unlimited room for play even to the point of maximum incoherence. This was one of the reasons why in the Preface the option of addressing the works only was rejected.

An additional incentive to keep the biographical is more subjective, although I imagine it is fairly widely shared. Ditching the author just makes the work that much less interesting. In particular, it tends to weaken its potency as a document that has a historical term of reference – that is, its own place – underpinned by the personal circumstances of its composition.

Furthermore, there is no reason why adopting an author friendly position should in any way lessen the meaningful role of textual ambiguities. In fact one might argue that in knowing what the author wanted – or claimed he wanted – those ambiguities are themselves enriched largely because the text is likely to prove at certain points overtly recalcitrant. We can see how the author struggles with his material. So, here we stick with Wagner and Britten as personalities. And now we can return to Vaget's dilemma.

Vaget's position, which is by no means unique to him, implies a notion of aesthetics and discourse which is rejected by the assumptions of the immediately preceding paragraphs. Quite frankly, I think it rests on a fallacy which itself is, shakily, underpinned by the special power – one might say paradigmatic power – of the Holocaust. But more of that in a moment. Put simply, and remaining within the biographical framework, we have to accept that bad people are capable of doing great and wonderful things and that good people are quite likely to be uncreative and may even turn out to be insufferable bores. However, this matter cannot be reduced to a mere technical question as to how bad those people are or how wonderful the things they do or create. Of more interest is the awkward, and for the Wagnerian flat-earthers impossible, proposition that the great works of art exist neither independently of nor in spite of the deplorable characteristics of the artist . . . but because of them. That is, it is not that we are all in the gutter although some of us are looking at the stars. Rather it is that some people are splashing around in the gutter; playing with the disgusting stuff to be found there. And, further, that the geniuses among them might well make something splendid out of just such untreated raw material.

In other words, the biographical element is also productive because its morally disturbing (as well as its uplifting) content duly gets into the discourse. Art, in short, is not to be judged as successful with regard to both content and tone in that it meets the prevailing standards with regard to, let us say, a book of recipes or a collection of sermons. Its 'goodness' as art cannot be evaluated by the norms appropriate to such discourses, although such discourses would no doubt profit from the artistic or literary skills of the authors in question; assuming, that is, that those skills were not allowed to shatter or undermine the formal boundaries appropriate to such books. But creative work appeals to the whole panoply of our desires and thoughts – whether conscious or otherwise, whether celebrated or repressed. In addition it can open us up to things of which we might not have thought or have been terrified of thinking. And in doing all this it fascinates, it entertains, it gives pleasure, and it appals. And one of the reasons it does these things is that it actively encourages that which would be normally

– and certainly in cook books and sermons – regarded as forbidden. And this is something that Thomas Mann, Benjamin Britten and the fictional Gustav von Aschenbach, to their collective profit, discover.

In short, there is no reason why a morally good piece of fiction should be more enlightening or more aesthetically successful than a morally bad one. Indeed, at the risk of indulging in a contradiction in that the hard and fast principle now in play will be qualified by it, I am inclined to entertain the proposition that the opposite is more likely to be the case. Writing profound works of fiction that are morally good can be quite a challenge. They easily descend into homilies. I often feel that Tolstoy struggles, although usually successfully, with this problem. It is true that, on the other hand, morally bad books can likewise descend into mere shockers, but at least they don't bore from the get go. But why not let the author imaginatively indulge his distasteful appetites as well. I am much more likely to be interested in that – and even to learn from it – than I am likely to be captivated by a creative artist wedded to piety. This is not to say that one has anything against virtue rewarded. It's just that one doesn't want to see that happen until quite a lot of dreadful things have also happened in the interim. Why else the reward?

All of the above enjoys the advantage of being straightforward. As a result one should not be surprised if it sounds too neat by half. And I admit that this is troubling. Certainly there has been a great deal of effort spent over the centuries, stretching for instance from the classical Greeks to Kant, to couple aesthetic pleasure with morally uplifting content and effect. And given that I have had recourse to both Kant and the Greeks this anomaly has to be, at the very least, acknowledged here.

It has already been underlined that Kant makes out of aesthetics a unique presence that resolves the deepest contradictions between empirical experience and transcendental knowledge. Above all, it is the 'beautiful' that allows him to reach the universal ('For where any one is conscious that his delight in an object is with him independent of interest, it is inevitable that he should look on the object as one containing a ground of delight for all men.'[21]) and thereby to make moral judgements whose terms of reference are absolute. Furthermore, in its most elevated form the beautiful is – self-evidently – free of arbitrary values. 'Every one must allow that a judgement on the beautiful which is tinged with the slightest interest, is very partial and not a pure judgement of taste.'[22] Whereupon it becomes clear that aesthetics and goodness have to be profound and uncontaminated sibling commodities. This inspires Kant to a neat oxymoron '. . . the judgement of taste, with its attendant consciousness of detachment from all interest, must involve a claim to validity for all men . . . there must be coupled with it a claim to subjective universality.' Consequently, when we consider the 'sublime', which unlike the beautiful is a cognitive faculty intrinsic to ourselves, we can marry aesthetics with normative values. 'As a matter of fact, a feeling for the sublime in nature is hardly thinkable unless in association with an attitude of mind resembling the moral.'[23]

Perhaps one might see all this as a somewhat more lofty and intellectually challenging version of the apocryphal exchange between Walter Pater and a student. On being asked 'Why should we be good?' the great aesthete replied: 'Because it is so beautiful.' Presumably the same causal tautology in the reverse would be pulled out of the hat if the question were put: why should we try to create beautiful things?

Of more relevance, at least in the context of *Death in Venice*, is the Greek position. There it is an axiom – a near self-evident state of affairs – that the beautiful and the good (along with balance and proportion) are interdependent. In Plato's *Philebus* Socrates explains that '. . . the power of the good has retired into the region of the beautiful; for measure and symmetry are beauty and virtue all the world over' and '. . . if we are not able to hunt the good with one idea only, with three we may catch our prey; Beauty, Symmetry, Truth.'[24] This should be born in mind when we turn shortly to Donald Mitchell's comments on balance and proportion, particularly as found in Britten's last opera, largely because I do not share his opinion. But if I have stressed the anarchic 'abyss' in connection with Plato/Socrates' *Phaedrus* it is not solely due to wilfulness. It is above all because Mann, Piper, and Britten have chosen to exploit exactly that. They claim that this is what 'Socrates told us.' Furthermore, it would be unfair to argue that in taking this line they are merely serving their own – and utterly honourable – selfish and prejudicial interests as creative artists. They are also, as has already been suggested, exploiting a deep anomaly embedded in Socratic thinking.

In general, then, we cannot escape the happy conclusion that art sets us problems; rich and welcome problems. It would be a lesser thing if it didn't.

Therefore the fan mentality, the adoration of the devotee, is likely to misrepresent the whole business and produce out of the artist a shallow chimera. Creative artists need to be protected from their fans; none more so than Wagner.

But what, for instance, if we discovered that the great painter was actually a, quite possibly practising, paedophile, or that the author of dazzling novels got his sexual kicks out of car crashes and, moreover, that both the paedophilia and the sadomasochism are there in the pictures and the novels? And what if we find ourselves, when either looking or reading, suddenly intrigued or even aroused by both? Would not that enrich the experience, albeit on occasions in a disturbing, and thereby fruitful, manner? Let me finish this digression then with a personal example whose conclusion may not be universally shared. John Ford's *The Searchers* would make my – and many other people's – list of the ten greatest films of all time. Yet despite what Ford was later to say about the mistreatment of American Indians, it is peddling a racist message.

In this context the chief conundrum that the case of Wagner exemplifies is that the good and the bad are so exceptionally interdependent. As has been argued at length, the foregrounding of love, the celebration of nobility, the indulgence of heroic suffering and so forth are dependent upon racism. Anti-Semitism drives and creatively animates the Wagnerian virtues. Furthermore – and most disturbingly – this can only be ignored by complete indifference or wilful blindness. The loveless Jew may not be the blood-brother of the loving Aryan hero (according to Wagner that would be genetically and racially impossible), but he is his aesthetic and intellectual twin nonetheless.

If, as I hope, the reader who is not a Wagnerite has been struck by the blindingly obvious, even banal, nature of the preceding paragraphs – as opposed to finding them loaded with shocking implications – he might now ask, in no doubt a justifiably exasperated manner, what on earth is the actual problem that the flat-earthers have with Wagner? Why do they have to defend him in a manner that makes them, if not him, look ridiculous? It has, in fact, got nothing to do with the perfectly reasonable assumption that Wagner was in many ways a bad man. That assumption is, on a deep level, no more relevant than the mistaken argument that Britten's compositions are admirable because he was, as I choose to believe, in many ways a good man. Nor is it merely the more obvious, and misguided, question as to how one composer managed to overcome his badness and the other his goodness in order to create masterpieces that are commensurate with the profound mixture of overt and suppressed evil and virtue innate to human beings and their collective lives. Rather, we have to acknowledge that Wagner gets it in the neck – deliberately from his critics and unintentionally from his fans – not because he was bad as such, but because his badness violates a taboo; moreover a particular taboo that since the Second World War has enjoyed an unequalled, near paradigmatic, status. It has, consequently, been able to exercise an unequal power in Western culture.

Put simply, we are not nearly as disturbed by artists who were paedophiles or sadomasochists as we are by artists who were, or are, anti-Semites. Following the Holocaust, anti-Semitism has attained, in Western culture (at least) the status of an absolute vice. It is the signifier of an evil so potent, so impervious to qualification, that it can be used as the yardstick with which to measure all others. It is the one sin that is never, under any circumstances whatever, excusable. Therefore it is, in principle, that element that we do not wish to see accorded any ambivalent value or function whatsoever in the dangerous and otherwise promiscuous cornucopia that is the rightful prerogative of art. It must be employed simply as itself – that is, as the sign of an Absolute – or it must be suppressed and avoided like the plague.

Now this is, admittedly, an extreme account of the situation, but it is still close enough to the general state of things as to be valid. The topic is quite simply toxic, and not just in Germany and Israel. Nonetheless, it is striking how hobbled contemporary German society still is with respect to criticising the policies of the state of Israel and how readily the Israeli establishment and sections of its popular media are to categorise any criticism of those policies as an expression of anti-Semitism. Ironically, this has become even clearer because the situation is changing. As the absolute is ever more compromised by historiography, as it begins to lose its status as an exclusively moral object of study, the determination on the part of those with a vested interest, of whatever sort, in the paradigmatic taboo to hold on to it gets yet more hysterical. It is not surprising then that Wagner as the most remarkable and quite possibly influential German anti-Semite of the pre-Nazi period has become a lightning rod in all matters to do with the subject. And consequently it is also understandable that so many of the Wagner apologists go to such lengths to assure their readers that they are not themselves anti-Semites.

On the other hand, those who conclude that Wagner and his operas must be beyond the pale are only paying due homage to the same taboo; a taboo that they are determined, for a variety of possible reasons, not to forgo. But in doing so they trivialise art; they reduce Wagner to a bogeyman, and – most perversely of all – they likewise reduce deep historical and aesthetic problems to slogans. A taboo is not the best strategy to deal with either anti-Semitism or history; but it can be a successful means of getting your way in matters of, supposedly voluntary, censorship. Consequently, both extreme groups in the dispute – flat-earthers and unbending denigrators – dismantle and reassemble Wagner so that he can be presented to their camp followers as a two-dimensional cartoon figure.

Although it is an aside, one should underline how Eurocentric the business can be and how this bolsters the arguments of those most in hock to the taboo. In Germany in the 1980s there was an acerbic and at times bad-tempered debate among historians (and many other commentators) as to the status of the Third Reich and the Holocaust. The so-called Historians' Debate was interesting, at least in part, because it was the Left that was passionate about holding onto the unsurpassable nature of Nazi crimes. As a result they were in real danger of taking up an ahistorical position; a danger that was not in all cases avoided. Left intellectuals needed the moral (evil) absolute by which the present virtues (such as they were) of the Federal Republic could be measured. The debate itself, however, became messy in that the Right, for its part, was keen to relativise Nazi crimes by measuring the Holocaust against the Gulag. Consequently it often degenerated into an argument as to body counts and methods of extermination. But what if one were to break out of that arbitrary historical framework and to consider instead the transatlantic slave trade of the seventeenth through to the nineteenth centuries? Body counts there would certainly exceed either the Holocaust or the Gulag. But that crime, although in many ways a European crime, does not have the same purchase or the same epistemological function as anti-Semitism. The reasons for this are certainly interesting but not particularly relevant here. One, however, because of its theatrical nature I would like to mention.

The Holocaust is often reduced, and powerfully so, to the privileged signifier 'Auschwitz.' Auschwitz is certainly a specific place where specific crimes were committed. But it is more than that. It has become the signifier that embodies of itself – in a potently concentrated form – the collective horror of the Shoah. In short, it exercises an aesthetic power. It has proved itself aesthetically useful, attractive even, as a climactic site of monstrous and redemptive acts. Moreover its history, like that of the Holocaust, is short and by that fact alone dramatically effective. Consequently 'Auschwitz' is readily dramatized in books and films and opera. Narratives of the Holocaust employ it regularly, often, not surprisingly, as a dystopian telos. In the context of astonishing barbarism and depravity, it reminds us, however perversely, not only of the power of art – the storyteller's art – in general, but also of the demands of the theatrical, one might say, operatic undertaking.

None of the above considerations should deflect us from acknowledging the folly of the Wagner fans in trying to keep a discussion of these matters outside the firewall they attempt to throw around the master's operas. That strategy is just as foolish as trying to get him off the hook by pointing the finger at other major European artists who were also anti-Semites. It appears Dostoevsky is generally regarded as a handy candidate in this context. But this is done – and it seems to me a rather peculiar strategy – in order to complain that these fellows are not subject to the same vilification that is heaped on poor Wagner. But would it make any difference if they were? And, assuming that they are not, how is that grounds for cutting Wagner some slack? The reasons for this are certainly cultural and historical – which is to say that they are in part arbitrary – but they don't get Wagner off the hook. But, then again, the argument being made here is that he shouldn't be let off the hook. He is far more interesting, intellectually intriguing, and musically seductive left twisting in the wind.

Still, one does on occasions sympathise with the flat-earthers. Once there is a bogeyman any amount of mud can be slung at him indiscriminately and with a hypocritically good conscience. So it is always nice when something positive comes to light, or when Wagner can be cleared of a particular charge. Even so, the desire to find something exculpatory can easily lead to a degree of wilful self-delusion.

In a brace of articles in *The Wagner Journal*, Derek Hughes argues that Cosima's *Diary* entries from 11 and 14 August 1881 have been misunderstood, above all by Paul Lawrence Rose. Apparently Wagner was not applauding the manner in which Jews had been treated harshly in the Russia pogroms of that year, but rather the treatment meted out to the anti-Jewish demonstrators. Furthermore, Hughes sees this as indicative of a failure of Wagner's critics to research the 'hinterland.' Assuming that Hughes is right – and I do think he is dealing in a wilful assumption rather than a proof – there is always a danger of trying to construct something too big for the foundation that has been laid. After all, what is actually being established here? There may conceivably have been a lack of background research with respect to interpretations of the *Diary* entries, but given that Hughes, along with everyone else, duly observes that Wagner 'held and frequently expressed deeply deplorable views about the Jews', one wonders how significant all this is.

Furthermore, the articles in the German press that Hughes uses to 'prove' that the reports of violence from Russia, above all from Kiev, concerned Cossack attacks on the anti-Jewish demonstrators, do not of themselves mean that the rabidly anti-Semitic Wagner would not have taken the opportunity to express support for attacks on Jews anyway. In fact Hughes points out that the anti-Jewish demonstrators (the Jews were being blamed for the assassination of Tsar Alexander II) are said to have also attacked Christian property. One might infer from this that violent behaviour and its motivation is not straightforward. And is not the history of pogroms in Russia – above all pogroms perpetrated by Cossacks – long and cruel? As far as I can see – and I claim no expertise – those of 1881 fit the pattern. Of course it is possible that the German press had reported specific and *exceptional* Jewish friendly acts on the part of the Cossacks and that Wagner was positively impressed by it. And this is the kernel of Hughes's argument.[25] But it could also be that the Cossacks were simply determined to put a stop to the destruction of (non-Jewish) property and, above all, to assert public order. In that case Wagner's approval would imply that gentile property was to be ranked above Jewish safety. It is reported that at least forty Jews lost their lives in the 1881 pogrom in the Kiev region. Let us hope that this indeed is what had shocked Wagner.

Hughes's argument is, however, particularly weak when one looks at the 14 August *Diary* entry. I would suggest that the only sensible interpretation of this is that Wagner is speaking approvingly of baiting (*Hetzen*) the Jews. He also sees this as an expression of Christian feeling, of which he of course – and especially in 1881 – has to regard in its highest form as wholly laudable.

As he says, Arthur de Gobineau was right; the Russians are still (*noch*) Christian, something of which, I think we may assume, he thoroughly approved. Gobineau was an extreme racist – and religious – theorist who had, despite differences of emphasis, a considerable influence on Wagner. He had been staying at Wahnfried in the period immediately before the *Diary* entries Hughes mentions.

We can get a better idea of the problem if we follow Hughes a step further. He says: 'Of course Wagner did not applaud violence against Jews'[26] As we are talking about 1881 anything that underlines Wagner's pacific – and new – *Weltanschauung* is not going to be gainsaid in this essay. Further, it is true that Wagner was in general no fan of violent public disturbances. The bourgeoisie seldom are. It upsets the horses and makes social life difficult. What may be laudable in Russia (no matter who was beating whom) would be intolerable in Bayreuth. Yet casual remarks (what is sometimes called in Germany table talk, often it seems with Luther's casual anti-Semitic observations in mind) can turn out to be double-headed snakes. People are likely to say all sort of things off the cuff. The human psyche is nothing if not messy and contradictory. For instance, four months after the reports on the Russian pogroms, Cosima records Richard suggesting that all the Jews be collected in a theatre which would then be burnt down during a performance of Lessing's *Nathan the Wise*.[27] Nor should we forget that this is the man who ten years before had gloated over the actual French defeat (*A Capitulation*) and wanted to see – with, it seems to me, some sincerity – Paris burn.[28] Now, Cosima treats the Jews/Lessing remark as a vehement joke. Clearly it was. But it is pretty tough stuff nevertheless, even putting aside any speculations on the subconscious role of humour. And that Richard, a discerning and passionate reader of his country's literature, should have chosen that particular humanist classic only makes the matter more deliberately nasty. Moreover, it remains so even if we are able to forget all those millions of Jewish corpses that were to be incinerated sixty years later. In fact we could put this to the test by considering the remark in the context of any other racial group who had endured a history of discrimination but had escaped planned genocide. Many indigenous peoples during the period of western imperialism might be considered. Would such a joke at their expense be any less offensive, or any more witty, had it been made by a colonial master? And then when one remembers that one month before this Wagner had written to King Ludwig in all seriousness (this is not table talk) that 'the Jewish race is the born enemy of pure humanity and all that is noble in man', one starts to wonder what is incidental and what is substantive.[29] Artists, along with what they create, are all too likely to violate the boundaries within which we attempt to constrain them.[30]

We can at this point return to the formal explanation of the chief difference between Wagner and Britten that was laid out in the first paragraph of the first chapter. There Wagner was stamped as didactic and focused; Britten as intellectually less polemical and more eclectic. It has been the principal aim of this book to pursue this distinction with respect to the, likewise differing and on occasions similar, uses to which both men put the notion of redemption. As we are now nearly at the end of this essay, we might consider whether, with respect to redemption, anything approaching a grand conclusion can be engineered and, in addition, whether anything fundamental can be said with respect to the respective merits of both composers when examined in that context.

No doubt it would be nice to declare a preference. I am reluctant to do so because I think such a declaration would be glib and not reflect my gut feelings. On one level, however, it is easy. Britten's notion of redemption is more attractive. It is free of any suggestion of a racial or national precondition and, consequently, it is axiomatically more universal and inclusive in character, which is another way of saying that it is less an instrument of propaganda. All that of course makes it both politically and morally more acceptable than what is found in Wagner. It does not however make it *ipso facto* more profound or aesthetically powerful. The question of profundity, in particular, is rather odd simply because the Wagner construct is clearly expressive of a lot of mumbo jumbo in respect not only of its Germanic special pleading but also with regard to both its wilful theology and, albeit ambivalent, phallocentric nature. The problem being that none of these considerations means that it lacks depth. There is nothing preventing the treatment of a theme from being simultaneously both superficially silly and seriously profound.

The fact that to believe (as I do) that there is no extant narrative that actually tells one, let alone reveals, what redemption can mean in definitive terms, and also to believe (as I do) that any narrative attempt to both dramatize the notion and to carry it into an afterlife will end up producing something utterly arbitrary and utterly fanciful, does not mean that the project has to be shallow. It is, for instance, glib to point out that in common-sense terms Wagner is just plain daft. Certainly there is a tendency on the part of many opera lovers who are not devoted fans of the master to laugh or shake their heads at all those dragons and mermaids and ladies riding through the heavens and whatnot . . . and then to gasp Barenboim-like: Ah, but just listen to that 'noble' music! That is certainly not a satisfactory position. Wagner's plots and even his nationalist and racial ideology do not make his operas foolish. If the opera-goer sees them as such it is likely to be because he is a vulgar empiricist who holds fast to the most crass option to hand. For beneath all the overt and seemingly risible stuff, although in part interwoven with it, is a real, if tendentious, encounter with redemption. It is a moral struggle. It may be overtly framed in anachronistic forms and poisoned by tribal values, but it is no less instructive and valid because of it. In fact, both the risible elements and the unacceptable racial theories are the chosen means – chosen of course by Wagner – that allow him to get at the more fundamental themes he seeks and, moreover, on a level that is anything but superficial.

Wagner confronts us with the deepest questions as to the non-quotidian (one might almost say a-quotidian) spiritual core of existence, of our quintessential nature, and of our striving to be true to that nature. That he believes that love, as he presents it, is both the core quality of existence and the dynamic force that animates our striving when we are at our best, is his choice. You don't have to share his anthropological views in general to find this attractive. And of course, all this is realised – or at least tackled – courtesy of music of the most inspired sort, employed in what is still a unique and seductive and accumulative manner. Above all, Wagner is always engaged with deep and genuine moral issues, even when (possibly most remarkably when) we are legitimately disturbed by the values in play. And he is so because he is in hock to love on all levels: sexual and spiritual, individual and tribal. It is through his wilful notion of love that redemption is realised. Furthermore, like a true great artist he is naked in the manner in which he pursues this – no matter how sophisticated that manner is – and thus he sets himself up for mockery. Nothing honours him perhaps as much as his ostensible foolishnesses and his demonstrable bravery.

It is usually a feature of great artists with a programme that they deepen their material along a fairly narrow track. If that artist is also motivated by a theory that the artwork itself should be exceptionally integrated and homogeneous, and moreover if he is in a position to accomplish that, then the deepening is likely to become ever more marked and effective. Which is to say that despite the apparently sprawling nature of his expansive music dramas, Wagner is ploughing a narrow furrow. And he is doing so while exercising uncompromising control over all the elements in the undertaking. Such an artist will always be to an exceptional extent at the mercy of the follies inbuilt into both his system and his *Weltanschauung*, neither of which are ever going to solve the intellectual and aesthetic problems to the absolute degree that he desires. The genius as megalomaniac will become very readily the victim of his own courage and determination, not least expressed by his conviction that in all essential matters he is not to be exposed as wrong. As a result, the struggle to deal with the problems that each new work generates along with the grander task to make everything work to an absolute degree, mean that more than most artists he is condemned to overt failure. Every megalomaniacal project is destined to collapse in its own terms if only because it sets up an absolute and impeccable model as to both an intellectual and an aesthetic programme that cannot in praxis exist. But this means that one does not simply acknowledge that Wagner's greatness comes with flaws. Rather it is to foreground that those are the flaws on which the greatness in part depends.

Britten, as has been pointed out many times, does not have a didactic programme; let alone a megalomaniacal one. It could be argued that, as a result, his work is richer or, at least, that the aesthetic terrain of his compositions is greater. But that should not be taken to mean that he is shallower than Wagner; that because he is not bound to plough the same furrow constantly he cannot go as deep into matters. However, if he is in his own way equally profound – or conceivably more so – it will be the result of the differences between them. That is, they are not trying to skin the same cat, albeit in different ways. They are both dealing in different animals, and this is so, at least to some extent, when it comes to redemption.

On the one hand one is struck by how differently the notion of telos functions in Britten's work. It is plural and inconsistent. With Wagner it strives to be singular and undeviating. With Britten we really do not know the final nature of redemption. It is worked for and attained in terms that are both reassuring and tragic. At the end of *Peter Grimes* there is little to console us with respect to the destiny of the nominal hero. Nor is there any welcome message to be inferred as to the goodness of human society in general. At the end of *Billy Budd* we are also saddened by the death of the hero (a much more unambiguous figure than in the first opera), but this time we have in addition some sense – albeit expressed in highly contradictory terms – of salvation; of virtue rewarded. With *Death in Venice* we are confronted by a much more powerful and ambiguous art work. The notion of salvation has been dragged down from the mystery of the stars, where it belongs in *Peter Grimes*, and from out the rosy dawn and the sea birds into which it is folded in *Billy Budd*, and put in the immediate here and now in the form of a silent but beautiful boy dancer. It has also been coloured and, for some commentators, diseased by a descent into knowledge and a willingness to give itself up to a profound ambivalence mixed from goodness and evil. One might say that in Aschenbach's descent redemption is contaminated. And therefore one might also say that it is, consequently, a profounder thing. By putting redemption into the world, even though the hero dies, Thomas Mann and Britten have been compelled to corrupt it, if only because that is the way it will work, must work, if knowledge and Eros (which are also Wagner's key ingredients) are to be in the phenomenal world. One can only, and not only by definition, escape into what is ethereal or sublime or noumenal (all terminology suggested by Wagner and even, on occasions, by Britten) by turning one's back on what it means to be human in the here and now. Britten's great achievement is, finally, to have found through a deep encounter with Mann's novella a means of rejecting that scenario and realising something much more dangerous and challenging. Therefore, if we accept that there are in fact deep spiritual values in play, as opposed to mere conventional religious sentiments, they are there in the figure of ridiculous Aschenbach, a great artist who has allowed himself, driven by Eros and a hunger for knowledge, to capitulate and who now expires in the fetid air with the make-up and the hair dye running down his cheeks.

The last paragraph selected three Britten operas arbitrarily to make a subjective, even a polemical, point. It could be argued that the most striking thing about strategies of this sort is what they omit, although it is surely not insignificant that these three works are Britten's largest undertakings in the genre. However, what is also clearly implied in the last paragraph is a progression, not just chronological, but, more importantly, with respect to the profundity with which redemption is handled. I happen to believe that this progressive deepening is unambiguously the case. But this must also mean that one ends up with a final contradiction. With Britten redemption survives and is realised on its deepest level, by having its sublime character, as it is usually understood, violated. That is as it should be. After all, one can hardly suggest that Aschenbach's destiny is something to be recommended in general. In the opera house, however, it will do very nicely.

This can be pushed a little further. The telos being celebrated here, and it would also apply to the *Third String Quartet* and *Phaedra*, is extreme and disruptive. There is a suggestion of the music becoming sparse, fragmentary, a sense even of disintegration. The quartet, in particular, is a long way from the seamless whole that is *Parsifal*. This should serve as a corrective to any attempt to play the golden mean card in a nonchalant and unconditional manner. That is, I don't doubt that Britten is sincere when he underlines how important balance is, yet I do not think that that condemns him unwisely to a middle of the road stance. He is bolder. After all, principled and uncompromising pacifism does not make one inclined to see both sides of the argument in order to adopt a fourth-form position packaged as an act of mature compromise; things not being either black or white but just varying shades of grey and stuff like that.

We should consider again Auden's letter to Britten from 31 January 1942 where he claims that 'Goodness and Beauty . . . are the result of a perfect balance between Order and Chaos.'[31] This is an attractive notion – and legitimately so. However it should not be allowed to escape the framework of purely aesthetic and formal considerations. It is not an ideological statement as to ethics or polemics. It may be a position that steers artistic practice, but it does not constitute a *Weltanschauung* or a discourse. Donald Mitchell, however, points out that, also in 1942, Britten had written to his brother-in-law: 'A carefully chosen discipline is the only possible course.'[32] From this Mitchell concludes that extremes are to be avoided. Using *Death in Venice* as an apparently ideal example, he talks of Britten seeing the need 'to keep in balance the opposed forces of Apollo and Dionysus, order and chaos, form and feeling.'[33] He argues that at the end of the opera the artist/protagonist has disintegrated but the work is whole. This, it seems, is evidence that Britten has, indeed, managed to keep the opposed forces in harmony and thereby avoided chaos.

Well, all of that is fair enough if you want to survive. But one has the feeling that the final opera reaches its unparalleled heights because the balance has been tipped, and radically so: that great risks have been taken. Moreover, one can always say that the work has survived as a whole. How could that be otherwise? What does such a statement amount to? King Lear may die but the play's the thing, perhaps? That's perfectly true too, but the play is a pretty shocking and misanthropic thing nonetheless; hardly an example I should have thought of an artwork in which the ideological polarities of chaos and order, let alone goodness and beauty (vis-à-vis evil and sin) are held in either harmony or balance. At the very least, as in *Death in Venice*, they wrestle with each other. Furthermore, Aschenbach's death cannot, any more than Lear's can, be reduced to an incidental consideration, as though it were but a timely schoolmasterly reminder of the dangers of going off the rails. That is, it's the sort of thing that happens to a chap if he stops doing his homework diligently and gives up rugger. And this is not merely, or even essentially, because Aschenbach is the 'protagonist' of the drama, the character on whom most of the action focuses. Rather it is because he is the figure who has to make the key ideological and emotional stage choices. Moreover, given his ecstatic paean to Phaedrus, it is hard to believe that we are being told courtesy of the composer's aesthetic language that the protagonist has chosen unwisely; that he has gone awry, presumably because he has ditched his earlier healthy and common sense appreciation of moderation. Rather he is an artist who learns in the course of the opera what it is to take risks. In other words he is so kernel to the opera that if he goes under he must, again like Lear, to some extent take the complete aesthetic structure with him. Rather than being harmonious and in balance, what is left on the stage now seems bland and inferior; gutted of its heart and soul. Unless that is, Tadzio can still be found somewhere and is able once again to do the fatal bewitching business.

It should be remembered that the piece Aschenbach writes on the beach under Tadzio's inspiration will be 'the wonder . . . of the multitude.' That it also makes him feel that he is debauched, that he has taken part in an 'orgy' does not mean that it is bad art, only that he has chosen an utterly new route and one, more to the point, that is dangerous. Nonetheless, to go down that route – especially if one has sight of the consequences and is prepared to embrace them ('Do what you will with me!') – takes a measure of artistic courage; courage that Britten clearly showed in the choice of material for his last opera. It would be no doubt easier for the artist to stay comfortably alive and to write as he always has. Don't forget that, at least in the novella, Aschenbach was already the 'creator of that powerful narrative The Abject, which taught a whole grateful generation that a man can still be capable of moral resolution even after he has plumbed the depths of knowledge.'[34] Well the Aschenbach who tells us in the opera that he is 'Famous as master writer . . . Self-discipline my strength, Routine the order of my days, Imagination servant of my will', is in for a shock. There is a great deal more knowledge to be encountered than he had hitherto dreamt of in his philosophy. And when he does find this out, his disciplined moral resolve is going to take a thrashing. That he responds so daringly to the blows – although he remains the victim of chance (the failed attempt to flee the city and so forth) and he is being manipulated by mysterious forces – takes him to a goal to which the middle path could never have taken him, no matter how soberly and diligently pursued.

All three major protagonists in the respective final operas of Wagner and Britten (Parsifal, Kundry, Aschenbach) are in thrall to Eros and to knowledge. If Parsifal becomes sublimely wise it is because he preserves, within the ideology of the opera, both his purity and, one sometimes thinks, his innocence – and that despite the second act rendezvous with Kundry. Even so, he has faced sin and felt all that rushing hot blood. It is, therefore, not surprising that Wagner finds it necessary to remove any residual ambivalence that we (or he) might feel. At the very end he has the ethereal voices declare that redemption has come to the redeemer (*Erlösung dem Erlöser*). This, for many commentators' gnomic expression, is perhaps best understood in the context of Wagner's (Schopenhauerian) comments on Christ in the late essays. There he underlines the first redeemer's immaculate nature. He axiomatically cannot sin. This is the status that the new redeemer now attains and it is made manifest by the dove that descends in the final bars. Parsifal will not, at least in an ambivalent or disorientating manner, encounter sin ever again, which is one of the most striking reasons why there is, in both ideological and dramatic terms, nowhere else to go that wouldn't be regressive.

But if Parsifal is a perceiving rather than a thinking man (one who absorbs knowledge empirically through a stage kiss and offstage adventures but does not process or intellectually play with it), Aschenbach is the embodiment of speculation and self-reflection. He does not rise above the ambivalent world but, knowingly, gives himself over to it. He becomes terribly wise because he is ready to – has consciously chosen to – succumb. It is therefore not inappropriate that Parsifal (unlike his fellow Wagner heroes) survives, radiant with knowledge, at least in propaganda terms, while Aschenbach expires, wholly spent.

Kundry, too, succumbs. But she, to an exceptional degree, is entangled in a web of irreconcilable forces that are, in their own way, as contradictory and as dangerous as the sublime and awful abyss into which Aschenbach has looked. She is the opera's active knowledge-giver and therefore knows only too well that knowledge can be terrible. She has always felt its torments. Consequently if the climatic ideology of *Parsifal* is not to collapse in on itself she must be expelled from the final constellation. Cleverly, if shamelessly, her way out, which she Isolde-like seems to choose in a state of ecstasy, is also sold to us as an immaculate end, all duty done. It is, we are to believe, an impeccable redemptive state duly attained. Well, it's hard to see Aschenbach's death as a sign of an impeccable redemptive state also duly attained. And yet I choose to believe that when all is said and done neither Kundry is as pure nor Aschenbach as fallen as we are being invited by many commentators to believe.

It was suggested in the preface that common sense made of redemption 'an unblemished ideal.' That, however, is hardly the point at which we have arrived. Both Britten knowingly and Wagner implicitly teach us that redemption is neither a simple nor an unambiguous business. Nor is it wholly radiant. Being suffused by knowledge and experience, redemption does not release us from the burden of being merely human. It is not an escape. Rather it confronts us with what is, one way or another, debased and all too human. To make the best of that will need struggle and courage in the here and now. Flight, even to the stars, is a deluded cop-out.

Endnotes

One: An Overview

1 LfL 2: 1338–9.
2 See Keller 'The Musical Character' in Mitchell and Keller eds (1972) and LfL 6: 310.
3 LfL 2: 1154.
4 LfL 1: 230.
5 CD: 26 April 1870.
6 See, for instance, Köhler (1996) 85–6 & Spencer (2007).
7 CD: 6 July & 20 November 1870.
8 Letters: 23 October 1877; see also Rieger (2011) 174.
9 LfL 3: 603–4.
10 LfL 2: 1015–16.
11 Sutcliffe (2012).
12 LfL 5: 444.
13 LfL 1: 547.
14 Sutcliffe (2012).
15 LfL 2: 654.
16 See, for instance, Powell (2013) 109.
17 LfL 1: 443.
18 Powell (2013) 120.
19 LfL 1: 449.
20 LfL 5: xxxi footnote.
21 See Magee (2000) 260.
22 Whittall (2015) 46.
23 Mann, William (1984) 12.
24 See Powell (2013) 133.
25 LfL 3: 88.
26 *The Art–Work of the Future* (1849) PW I: 113.
27 LfL 3: 280.
28 *The Wibelungen: World History as Told in Saga* (1848) PW VII: 275 & 289.
29 Bridcut (2006) 7–8.
30 Mann PDF (2001) 4.
31 Elliott (2006) 28.
32 Kildea (2013) 205.
33 LfL 6: 735 & Elliott (2006) 106.
34 Elliot (2006) 127.
35 Carpenter (1992) 536.

Two: Love and Sex

1 LfL 3: 618.
2 LfL 3: 620.
3 LfL 6: 234.
4 LfL 3: 221–2.
5 https://www.youtube.com/watch?v=440Pv6iSwcY
6 See Brett (2006) 66.
7 See also Harper (2013) 104.
8 Brown (1988) 99.
9 Freud (1912) 6.
10 Freud (1930) 34.
11 See Brett (2006) 91.
12 Ibid., 108.
13 See Millington (2006) 113.
14 Freud (1912) 6.
15 see *The Guardian* UK 2 October 2001.
16 Letters: 13 September 1834.
17 Letters: 26/27 October 1835.
18 Letters: 2 October 1835.
19 Letters: 21 August 1835 (Apel) & 4 November 1835 (Minna).
20 Letters: 2 October 1835.
21 CD: 11 November 1870.
22 CD: 26 May 1869.
23 LfL 5: 517.
24 LfL 5: 520.
25 LfL 1: 467–8.
26 See Elliot (2006) 3.
27 LfL 4: 555–6.

28 LfL 5: 223.
29 See Bridcut (2006) chapter 6.
30 Powell (2013) 160.
31 Bridcut (2006) 86–7.
32 Kildea (2013) 144–5.
33 LfL 4: 68.
34 LfL 4: 224.
35 LfL 6: 322–3.
36 Kildea (2013) 134–5.
37 LfL 3: 557.
38 Mitchell and Keller eds (1972) 350–1.
39 See, for instance, Powell (2013) 17.
40 LfL 4: 121.
41 LfL 6: xxx1.
42 Wagner (1983) 729.
43 CD: 24 November 1869.
44 CD: 16 May 1870.
45 Millington (2012) 210.
46 Ibid., 204.
47 *A Communication to My Friends* (1851) PW I: 347.
48 Ibid., 340–1.
49 Letters: 13 May 1846.
50 Letters: 26/27 June 1850.
51 CD: 29 March 1869.
52 Letters: *c.*20 December 1858.
53 Letters: early August 1860.
54 Letters: 7 September 1865.
55 Nietzsche (1911) 307.
56 Wille (1982) 34.
57 Wagner (1975) 64.
58 CD: 8 March 1870 (my emphasis).
59 See Borchmeyer (1991) 40f.
60 LfL 6: 481–2.
61 LfL 3: 308.
62 See Kildea (2013) 181–2.
63 Moffat (2010) 317.
64 LfL 3: 633–634.
65 LfL 6: 244.
66 Mann PDF (2001) 28.
67 Ibid., 5.
68 Ibid., 4.
69 LfL 6: 669.
70 LfL 5: xlii.
71 LfL 1: 321.
72 LfL 6: 219.
73 LfL 5: 196.
74 See Seymour (2004) 77 & 87.
75 LfL 1: 277.
76 LfL 5: 632–3.
77 LfL 5: 651.
78 LfL 6: 735.
79 LfL 5: 130–1.
80 LfL 5: 381.
81 See Seymour (2004) 206–7.
82 Kildea (2013) 401.
83 LfL 6: 550.
84 Kildea (2013) 206.
85 Robinson (202) 157.
86 Ibid., 159.
87 Abel (1996) 61.
88 See Seymour (2004) 331.
89 *Opera and Drama* (1851) PW II: 111.
90 Ibid.
91 Ibid., 114.
92 Ibid., 209.
93 Ibid., 235–6.
94 As I find Ellis here impossibly abstruse (and Wagner not much better) this is my own (free) translation. Given that I have aimed for clarity it must to some extent be a simplification. Here is Ellis's version: 'This charm is the influence of the 'eternal womanly,' which draws the man-ly Understanding out of its egoism,—and this again is only possible through the Womanly attracting that thing in it which is kindred to itself: but That in which the Understanding is akin to the Feeling is *the purely-human*, that which makes-out the essence of the human *species* as such. In this Purely-human are nurtured both the Manly and the Womanly, which only by *their union through Love become first the Human Being*.' PW II: 236.

And here is the original:

Dieser Reiz ist die Einwirkung des 'ewig Weiblichen', die den egoistischen männlichen Verstand aus sich herauslockt, und selbst nur dadurch möglich ist, daß das Weibliche das sich Verwandte in ihm anregt: das, wodurch der Verstand dem Gefühle aber verwandt ist, ist das Reinmenschliche, das, was das Wesen der menschlichen Gattung, als solcher, ausmacht. An diesem Reinmenschlichen nährt sich das Männliche wie das Weibliche, das durch die Liebe verbunden erst Mensch ist. Richard Wagner: Werke, Schriften und Briefe, The Digital Bibliothek Directmedia • Berlin (2004) CD Rom p 1759. See also Wagner Leipzig (1911–14) Vol 4 p 102.
95 Schopenhauer (1958) I: 275.
96 Ibid., I: 330.
97 Ibid., II: 566.
98 Ibid., II: 528.
99 Ibid., II: 532.
100 Ibid.
101 Ibid., II: 199.

102 Ibid., II: 507.
103 Ibid., I: 356 & II: 502, 504.
104 Ibid., I: 380.
105 Ibid., I: 278.
106 Wagner (1983) 510–11.
107 Letters: 25/26 January 1854.
108 Wagner (1911–14) Vol 12: 289. The letter is not in the Spencer/Millington collection.
109 Schopenhauer (1958) II: 552.
110 Ibid., II: 514.
111 Ibid., I: 378.
112 Ibid., I: 379.
113 Ibid., I: 128, 155.
114 Ibid., I: 170 & §31 *passim*.
115 Wagner (1911–14) Vol 12: 289.
116 See Kildea (2013) 38–9.
117 Ibid., 25.
118 Ibid., 532.
119 There is a great deal of literature. For instance: 'Benjamin Britten syphilis 'extremely unlikely', says cardiologist' *Guardian* 22 January 2013, an article by Hywel Davies in *New Statesman* 14 June 2013, and *Classical Music* 28 October 2014.
120 Wagner (1983) 301.
121 See Kildea (2013) 376–7.
122 Ibid., 338–9.
123 Ibid., 17.
124 LfL 3: 7.
125 Ibid., 4: 97–8.
126 See Banville (2013).
127 Ibid.
128 See, for instance, Kildea (2013) 45 & 458, but also *passim*.

Three: People and Nation

1 Fichte (1922) 147–8.
2 Ibid.
3 *The Wibelungen: World History as Told in Saga* (1948/9) PW VII: 259.
4 Ibid., 292–295.
5 See Köhler (1997) 310.
6 *The Wibelungen: World History as Told in Saga* (1948/9) PW VII: 293–4.
7 Ibid., 289.
8 Ibid., 263.
9 Ibid., 293.
10 *The Fatherland's Association Speech* (1848) PW VIII: 144.
11 *The Wibelungen: World History as Told in Saga* (1948/9) PW VII: 266–7.
12 *Know Thyself* (1881) PW VI: 272.
13 *A Communication to My Friends* (1851) PW I: 376.
14 Herder (1971) Vol II: 36.
15 Letters: 30 January 1844.
16 *Beethoven* (1870) PW V: 70.
17 Ibid., 68 & 73.
18 Ibid., 104.
19 Herder (1971) Vol I1: 156 & see also Vol I: 296.
20 Ibid., Vol II 154.
21 *What is German?* (1865) PW IV: 163.
22 Fichte (1922) 54.
23 *Opera and Drama* (1851) PW II: 357–8.
24 CD: 4 November 1872.
25 CD: 26 December 1873.
26 Brett (1983) 149.
27 CD: 26 September 1870.
28 *Jewishness in Music* (1869 Introduction) PW III: 119.
29 *Religion and Art* (1880) PW VI: 237.
30 See Kildea (2013) 385.
31 Ibid., 172.
32 Ibid., 466.
33 Kirsch (2005) 41–2.
34 Kildea (2013) 349.
35 Ibid., 131.
36 Ibid., 561.
37 *Opera and Drama* (1851) PW II: 181–2.
38 *Time* 16 February 1948.
39 See Kildea (2013) 3 & LfL 2: 1132.
40 Carpenter (1992) 419–20.
41 Brett (1983) 149.
42 Schopenhauer (1958) II: 448.
43 See Brett (1983) 52–3.
44 Ibid., 149.
45 Schopenhauer (1958) I: 257 & *passim*.
46 See Brett (1983) 97.
47 Ibid., 79.
48 See Carpenter (1992) 199.
49 Williams (1999) 145.
50 Ibid., 148.
51 Ibid., 147–9.
52 Rupprecht (2013) 7.
53 Brett (2006) 14.
54 Ibid., 49.
55 Ibid., 11.
56 Mann PDF (2001) 16.
57 Ibid., 42.
58 Ibid., 18.
59 Mann (1985) 180–1.
60 *The Art-Work of the Future* (1849) PW I: 71.
61 *Opera and Drama* (1851) PW II: 162.

62 Ibid., 162–3.
63 *The Art-Work of the Future* (1849) PW I: 74.
64 Ibid., 77.
65 Ibid., 71.
66 Ibid., 94.
67 *Opera and Drama* (1851) PW II: 205.
68 Wagner *Jesus of Nazareth* (1995) 302–3.
69 Letters: 25/26 January 1854.
70 Nietzsche (1911) 10.
71 Nietzsche (1887) First Essay section 13.
72 Nietzsche (1874). Web PDF.
73 *Religion and Art* (1881) PW VI: 246.
74 Ibid., 235.
75 *Jewishness in Music* (1869 edition) PW III: 113.
76 Barenboim (1998).
77 CD: 23 January 1879.
78 *A Communication to My Friends* (1851) PW I: 307–8.
79 Wagner (1911–14) Vol 11: 404–5.
80 Borchmeyer (1991) 407.
81 Quoted in Rose (1992) 71.
82 Grey (2008) 215.
83 Adorno (2005) 13–4.
84 *Jewishness in Music* (1850) PW III: 90.
85 CD: 9 February 1883.
86 *Know Thyself* (1881) PW VI: 268.
87 Rosenberg (1934) 456.
88 See Millington (1996).
89 Borchmeyer (2002) 13.
90 Ibid., 262.
91 Vaget (1995).
92 Tanner (2010) 243.
93 Ibid., 244.
94 Viereck (2003) lviii.
95 Mann (1979) 114.
96 Magee (2000) 357.
97 CD: 28 November 1878.
98 *Jewishness in Music* (1850) PW III: 85.
99 Ibid., 85.
100 CD: 7 April 1873.
101 *Know Thyself* (1881) PW VI: 271.
102 Ibid., 264.
103 CD: 19 January 1881.
104 CD: 13 July 1876.
105 Nietzsche (1911) 7.
106 CD: 4 November 1872.
107 Letters: 23 October 1872.
108 See Seymour (2004) 164.
109 Carpenter (1992) 194.
110 See Seymour (2004) 19.
111 See Brett (1983) 191.
112 Elliott (2006) 31.
113 Ibid., 30.
114 Seymour (2004) 16.
115 Kildea (2013) 462–3.
116 Letters: 5 October 1858.
117 Nietzsche of 23 October 1872.
118 See Brett (2006) 214.
119 LfL 3: 88.
120 Powell (2013) 17.
121 Keller (1987) 130.
122 LfL 6: 234–5.
123 LfL 5: xlii.
124 Seymour (2004) 275.

Four: Religion and Philosophy

1 Elliott (2006) 28.
2 Mitchell (1987) 160–1.
3 Ibid., 161.
4 Schopenhauer (1958) I: 278.
5 Kildea (2013) 457.
6 LfL 5: 408.
7 *On the Womanly in the Human Race* (1883) PW VI: 335–7.
8 Letters: 30 May 1859.
9 Ibid.
10 *Religion and Art* (1881) PW VI: 213.
11 *The Wibelungen* (1848/49) PW VII: 293.
12 Kant (1952) [§ 8].
13 Ibid., [§ 29].
14 *Religion and Art* (1881) PW VI: 218.
15 Ibid., 232.
16 Ibid., 233–4.
17 Wagner *Jesus of Nazareth* (1995) 297.
18 *Religion and Art* (1881) PW VI: 233.
19 CD: 11 June 1878.
20 *Public and Popularity* (1878) PW VI: 77f.
21 *Opera and Drama* (1851) PW II: 181.
22 Ibid., 182.
23 Masson (1985) 270–3.
24 *Opera and Drama* (1851) PW II: 182.
25 Ibid.
26 Schopenhauer (1958) I: 566.
27 *Opera and Drama* (1851) PW II: 184.
28 Ibid., 189.
29 See Ibid., 189–90.
30 Goethe (1985) vol. 19: 542.
31 Brown (1988) 16.
32 Xenophon *Symposium* (1897) chapter XIII.
33 Ibid.
34 In Cohen (1991) 200. Original: Xenophon *The Memorabilia* (updated 2013) Book One.

35 See Hubbard (2003) 172–4.
36 Xenophon *Symposium* (1897) chapter VIII.
37 Plato *Symposium* (updated 2014).
38 Xenophon *Symposium* (1897) chapter VIII.
39 Plato *Phaedrus* (360 BCE) PDF 48.
40 Ibid., 64.
41 Ibid., 62.
42 Mann PDF (2001) 40.
43 Ibid., 25.
44 Plato *Phaedrus* (360 BCE) PDF 65.
45 Plato *Charmides* (updated 2013).
46 Plato *Symposium* (updated 2014).
47 Ibid.
48 Mann PDF (2001) 14.
49 Plato *Phaedrus* (360 BCE) PDF 65.
50 Ibid., 62.
51 Ibid.
52 Ibid., 49.
53 Ibid., 57.
54 Ibid., 55.
55 Nietzsche (1886) section 2.
56 Mann PDF (2001) 22.
57 Ibid., 38.
58 Seymour (2004) 312.
59 Mann PDF (2001) 19.
60 Carpenter (1992) 546.
61 See Powell (2013) 451.
62 Wills (2002).
63 Xenophon *Symposium* (1897) chapter VIII.
64 Mann PDF (2001) 14.
65 Ibid., 25.
66 Ibid., 26 (my emphasis).
67 LfL 6: 555–6.
68 Ibid., 3: 34.
69 Evans (1996) 415.
70 Mitchell (1987) 21.
71 Siegel (1978) 4.
72 Weiss (2008) 6.
73 Ibid., 23 & 29.
74 Ibid., 46.
75 Kirsch (2005) 172–3.
76 Ibid., 173.
77 Ibid.
78 Ibid., 173.
79 CD: 1 April 1881.
80 See Borchmeyer (1991) 46.
81 See Mitchell (1987) 21.
82 Schopenhauer (1958) I: 266.
83 Ibid., I: 257 & *passim*.
84 Ibid., I: 184 (my emphasis).
85 Ibid., II: 137.

Five: Redemption

1 Emslie (2012).
2 Kirsch (2005) 111.
3 Carpenter (1992) 248.
4 LfL 6: 584.
5 Powell (2013) 314.
6 Kennedy (1981) 199.
7 Seymour (2004) 150–1.
8 Howard (1969) 98.
9 Evans (1996) 167.
10 Mitchell and Keller (1952) 208–9 (my emphasis).
11 See Kildea (2013) 353 footnote.
12 Letters: 5 October 1858.
13 Schopenhauer (2014).
14 Wagner (1983) 511. The letter is not in the Spencer/Millington collection.
15 *Opera and Drama* (1851) PW II: 285–6.
16 CD: 23 January 1883.
17 Wagner (1911–14) Vol 14: 186 & see Borchmeyer (1991) 240–1.
18 CD: 4 September 1879.
19 Barenboim (2006) Lecture 5: 'The Power of Music.'
20 Vaget (1993).
21 Kant (1952) [§ 6].
22 Ibid., [§ 2].
23 Ibid., [§ 29].
24 Plato *Philebus* (updated 2014) 64d & 65a.
25 Hughes (2016) 7.
26 Ibid.
27 CD: 18 December 1881.
28 CD: 18 August 1870.
29 Letters: 22 November 1881.
30 Should the reader wish to pursue this matter, my more detailed criticisms of Hughes' position can be found in Emslie (2017). Meanwhile Hughes' reply is in Hughes (2018). All the relevant pieces are in *The Wagner Journal*.
31 LfL 2: 1015–16.
32 See Mitchell (1987) 22.
33 Ibid 21.
34 Mann PDF (2001) 4.

Bibliography

Abel, S., *Opera in the Flesh: Sexuality in Operatic Performance* (Colorado 1996).

Adorno, T., *In Search of Wagner* (London 2005).

Banville, J., 'Learning a Lot About Isaiah Berlin' *New York Review of Books* (December 19 2013).

Barenboim, D., 'Wagner and Ideology' A discussion with Edward Said *Raritan* (Spring 1998). http://danielbarenboim.com/wagner-and-ideology/

Barenboim, D., *Reith Lectures 2006* http://www.bbc.co.uk/radio4/reith2006/

Borchmeyer, D., *Richard Wagner: Theory and Theatre* (Oxford 1991).

Borchmeyer, D., *Richard Wagner: Ahasvers Wandlungen* (Frankfurt am Main 2002).

Brett, P., *Benjamin Britten: Peter Grimes* (Cambridge 1983).

Brett, P., *Music and Sexuality in Britten. Selected Essays* ed. G. E. Haggerty (California 2006).

Bridcut, J., *Britten's Children* (London 2006).

Britten, B., *Letters from a Life: Selected Letters and Diaries of Benjamin Britten* eds. D. Mitchell and P. Reed Volume One 1923–39 (London 1998).

Britten, B., *Letters from a Life: Selected Letters and Diaries of Benjamin Britten* eds. D. Mitchell and P. Reed Volume Two 1939–45 (London 1998).

Britten, B., *Letters from a Life: Selected Letters and Diaries of Benjamin Britten* eds. D. Mitchell, P. Reed and M. Cooke Volume Three 1946–51 (London 2004).

Britten B., *Letters from a Life: The Selected Letters and Diaries of Benjamin Britten (1913–1976)* eds. P. Reed, M. Cooke and D. Mitchell Volume Four 1952–57 (Suffolk 2008).

Britten, B., *Letters from a Life: The Selected Letters and Diaries of Benjamin Britten (1913–1976)* eds. P. Reed and M. Cooke Volume Five 1958–65 (Suffolk 2010).

Britten, B., *Letters from a Life: The Selected Letters and Diaries of Benjamin Britten (1913–1976)* eds. P. Reed and M. Cooke Volume Six 1966–76 (Suffolk 2012).

Brown, P., *The Body and Society. Men, Women, and Sexual Renunciation in Early Christianity* (New York 1988).

Carpenter, H., *Benjamin Britten: A Biography* (London 1992).

Cohen, D., *Law Sexuality, and Society. The enforcement of morals in classical Athens* (New York 1991).

Elliott, G., *Benjamin Britten. The Spiritual Dimension* (Oxford 2006).

Emslie, B., *Narrative and Truth: An Ethical and Dynamic Paradigm for the Humanities* (New York 2012).

Emslie, B., 'The *Volk* That Wagner Loved to Hate: A Reply to Derek Hughes' *The Wagner Journal* (Volume 11, Number 3, 2017).

Evans, P., *The Music of Benjamin Britten* (London 1979; Oxford 1996).

Fichte, J. G., *Addresses to the German Nation* trans. R. F. Jones and G. H. Turnbull (Chicago 1922). http://archive.org/stream/addressestogerma00fich#page/54/mode/2up

Freud, S., *On the Universal Tendency to Debasement in the Sphere of Love* (in *Contributions to the Psychology of Love*) (1912). Standard Edition Volume 2, 179–190 http://math.msgsu.edu.tr/~dpierce/Texts/Freud/freud_debasement.pdf

Freud, S., *Civilization and its Discontents* trans. J. Riviere, revised and newly edited by J. Strachey (London 1930, 1973).

Goethe, J. W., *Sämtliche Werke nach Epochen seines Schaffens* ed. K. Richter with H. G. Göpfert, N. Miller and G. Sauder (Munich 1986).

Grey, T. S. (ed.), *The Cambridge Companion to Wagner* (Cambridge 2008).

Harper, K., *From Shame to Sin. The Christian Transformation of Sexual Morality in Late besides or beside the point? Antiquity* (Massachusetts 2013).

Herder, J. G., *Briefe zur Beförderung der Humanität* ed. H. Stolpe with H-J Kruse and D. Simon (Berlin & Weimar 1971).

Howard, P., *The Operas of Benjamin Britten* (New York 1969).

Hubbard, T. K. (ed.), *Homosexuality in Greece and Rome. A Sourcebook of Basic Documents* (California 2003).

Hughes, D., 'Wagner: The Pogrom and the Critics' *The Wagner Journal* (Volume 10, Number 1, March 2016).

Hughes, D., 'Wagner: Race, Nationalism and Other Distractions' *The Wagner Journal* (Volume 11, Number 1, March 2017).

Hughes, D., 'Wagner and the Boryspil Pogrom: A Reply to Barry Emslie. *The Wagner Journal* (Volume 12, Number 1, March 2018).

Kant, I., *The Critique of Judgement* in *Great Books of the Western World* trans. James Creed Meredith (Volume 12, Chicago 1952) (section number is given in square brackets) https://ebooks.adelaide.edu.au/k/kant/immanuel/k16j/complete.html

Keller, H., *Criticism by Hans Keller* ed. J. Hogg (London 1987).

Kennedy, M., *Britten* (London 1981).

Kildea, P., *Benjamin Britten: A Life in the Twentieth Century* (London 2013).

Kirsch, A., *Auden and Christianity* (New Haven 2005).

Koestenbaum, W., *The Queen's Throat: Opera, Homosexuality and the Mystery of Desire* (New York 1994).

Köhler, J., *Wagner's Hitler: Der Prophet und sein Vollstrecker* (Munich 1997).

Köhler, J., *Friedrich Nietzsche and Cosima Wagner: Die Schule der Unterwerfung* (Hamburg 2000).

Magee. B., *Wagner and Philosophy* (Harmondsworth 2000).

Mann, T., *Briefe III: 1948–1955* ed. E. Mann (Frankfurt am Main 1979).

Mann, T., *Death in Venice* [translation Neider, C., *Short Novels of the Masters* (New York 2001)] http://www.24grammata.com/wp-content/uploads/2011/11/Mann-death-in-venice-24grammata.com_.pdf

Mann, T., *Pro and Contra Wagner* (Faber and Faber 1985).

Mann, W., 'Solti, champion of Strauss' *Opera* (December 1984).

Masson, M., (ed. and trans.) *The Complete Letters of Sigmund Freud to Wilhelm Fliess 1887–1907* (Massachusetts 1985).

Millington, B., 'Nuremberg Trial: Is there Anti-Semitism in *Die Meistersinger*?' *Cambridge Opera Journal* 3 (1991).

Millington, B., 'Wagner Washes Whiter' *The Musical Times* (Volume 137, Number 1846, December 1996).

Millington, B., *The New Grove Guide to Wagner and His Operas* (Oxford 2006).

Millington, B., *Richard Wagner: The Sorcerer of Bayreuth* (London 2012).

Mitchell, D., (ed. and compiled by), *Benjamin Britten: Death in Venice* (Cambridge 1987).

Mitchell, D. and Keller, H., (eds), *Benjamin Britten: a Commentary on his works from a group of specialists* (Connecticut 1972).

Moffat, W., *E M Forster: A New Life* (London 2010).

Nietzsche, F., *Werke* (Frankfurt am Main 1999).

Nietzsche, F., *On the Use and Abuse of History for Life* trans. I. Johnston (1874). http://la.utexas.edu/users/hcleaver/330T/350kPEENietzscheAbuseTableAll.pdf

Nietzsche, F., *The Genealogy of Morals* trans. I. Johnston (1887). http://home.sandiego.edu/~janderso/360/genealogytofc.htm

Nietzsche, F., *Birth of Tragedy* (3rd ed. 1886) 'Attempt at a Self-Criticism' added and a new title *The Birth of Tragedy Or: Hellenism And Pessimism* (from the Nietzsche Channel) Compiled from translations by Francis Golffing and Walter Kaufmann http://nietzsche.holtof.com/Nietzsche_the_birth_of_tragedy/index.htm (last update January 1 2002).

Nietzsche, F., 'The Case of Wagner' and 'Nietzsche Contra Wagner' in *Selected Aphorisms* (trans. Anthony M. Ludovici) (Edinburgh 1911).

Plato, *Charmides* in *The Dialogues of Plato* trans. B. Jowett http://www.gutenberg.org/files/1580/1580-h/1580-h.htm (updated online 2013).

Plato, *Phaedrus* (*BCE 360*) trans. B. Jowett http://sparks.eserver.org/books/plato-phaedrus.pdf

Plato, Philebus trans. B. Jowett (The University of Adelaide Library) https://ebooks.adelaide.edu.au/p/plato/p71phi/introduction.html#philebus (last updated December 17 2014).

Plato, *Symposium* trans. B. Jowett (The University of Adelaide Library) http://ebooks.adelaide.edu.au/p/plato/p71sy/symposium.html#symposium (updated online March 2014).

Powell, N., *Benjamin Britten. A Life for Music* (New York 2013).

Rieger, E., *Richard Wagner's Women* trans. C. Walton (Suffolk 2011).

Robinson, P., *Opera, Sex, and Other Vital Matters* (Chicago 2002).

Rose, P. L., *Wagner, Race and Revolution* (New Haven 1992).

Rosenberg, A., *Der Mythus des 20. Jahrhunderts. Eine Wertung der seelisch-geistigen Gestaltenkämpfe unserer Zeit* 33.–34. (München 1934). http://www.thule-italia.net/Storia/LibriTedesco/Rosenberg

Rupprecht, P., (ed.), *Rethinking Britten* (Oxford 2013).

Schopenhauer, A., *The World as Will and Representation* trans. E. F. J. Payne (New York 1958).

Schopenhauer, A., 'On Women' in *Essays of Schopenhauer* https://ebooks.adelaide.edu.au/s/schopenhauer/arthur/essays/chapter5.html (2014).

Seymour, C., *The Operas of Benjamin Britten Expression and Evasion* (Suffolk 2004).

Siegel, Lee., *Sacred and Profane. Dimensions of Love in Indian Traditions as exemplified in the Gitagovinda of Jayadeva* (Delhi 1978).

Spencer, S., *'Wagner and Gaetano Ghezzi' The Wagner Journal* (Volume 1, Number 1, March 2007).

Sutcliffe, T., *Benjamin Britten 'A Failure'* https://www.youtube.com/watch?v=_NvhhZG4IBA (television documentary uploaded 31 January 2012).

Tanner, M., *Wagner* (London 1996).

Tanner, M., *The Faber Pocket Guide to Wagner* (London 2010).

Vaget, H. R., 'Wagner, Anti-Semitism, and Mr Rose: *Merkwürd'ger Fall!*', *German Quarterly* 66/2 (1993).

Vaget, H. R., 'Sixtus Beckmesser: a 'Jew in the brambles'?', *Opera Quarterly*, (Volume 12, Number 1, Autumn 1995).

Viereck, P. R. E., *Metapolitics: From Wagner and the German Romantics to Hitler* Transaction Publishers, Auflage expanded (December 2003).

Wagner, C., *Cosima Wagner's Diaries* ed. and trans. M. Gregor-Dellin and D. Mack; trans. G. Skelton (London 1978–80).

Wagner, R., *Das Braune Buch. Tagebuchaufzeichnungen 1865–1882* Vorgelegt und kommentiert von Joachim Bergfeld, (Zürich 1975).

Wagner, R., *My Life* ed. M. Whittall and trans. A. Gray (Cambridge 1983).

Wagner, R., *Richard Wagner's Prose Works* ed. and trans. W. Ashton Ellis (London, 1892–99). http://users.belgacom.net/wagnerlibrary/prose/index.htm

Wagner, R., *Sämtliche Schriften und Dichtungen* 16 vols. (Leipzig 1911–14).

Wagner, R., *Selected Letters of Richard Wagner* trans. S. Spencer and B. Millington (London 1987).

Wagner, R., *Jesus of Nazareth and Other Writings* trans. W. Ashton Ellis (Nebraska 1995).

Weiss, A., *In the Shadow of the Magic Mountain: The Erika and Klaus Mann Story* (Chicago 2008).

Whittall, A., 'From Wagner to Boulez: a Modernist Trajectory' in *The Wagner Journal* Volume 9, Number 3 (November 2015).

Wille, E., *Erinnerungen an Richard Wagner* (Zurich 1982).

Williams, J., *Jon Vickers: A Hero's Life* (New Hampshire 1999).

Wills, G., *Priests and Boys* (*New York Review of Books* June 13, 2002).

Xenophon, *Oeconomicus* [*The Economist*] *A Treatise on the Science of the Household in the form of a Dialogue* trans. H. G. Dakyns (1897) (The University of Adelaide Library) http://ebooks.adelaide.edu.au/x/xenophon/x5oe/

Xenophon, *Symposium Or The Banquet* trans. H. G. Dakyns (1897) (The University of Adelaide Library) http://ebooks.adelaide.edu.au/x/xenophon/x5sy/

Xenophon, *The Memorabilia. Recollections of Socrates* trans. H. G. Dakyns (online: http://www.gutenberg.org/files/1177/1177-h/1177-h.htm#link2H_4_0003) (last updated 2013).

Index

Index